Economics and the Historian

Economics and
the Historian

Thomas G. Rawski
Susan B. Carter
Jon S. Cohen
Stephen Cullenberg
Peter H. Lindert
Donald N. McCloskey
Hugh Rockoff
Richard Sutch

UNIVERSITY OF CALIFORNIA PRESS
Berkeley · Los Angeles · London

University of California Press
Berkeley and Los Angeles, California

University of California Press, Ltd.
London, England

© 1996 by
The Regents of the University of California

Library of Congress Cataloging-in-Publication Data

Economics and the historian / Thomas G. Rawski
. . . [et al.].
        p.   cm.
    Includes bibliographical references and index.
    ISBN 0-520-07268-5;—ISBN 0-520-07269-3
(pbk.)
    1. Economics—Methodology.   2. Historiogra-
phy.   I. Rawski, Thomas G., 1943–   .
HB131.E258 1995
330—dc20 94-24931
CIP

Printed in the United States of America
9 8 7 6 5 4 3 2 1
The paper used in this publication meets the minimum requirements of American National Standard
for Information Sciences—Permanence of Paper for
Printed Library Materials, ANSI Z39.48–1984.

Contents

Tables and Figures

Contributors

SUSAN B. CARTER is Professor of Economics at the University of California, Riverside. Her specialty is the development of the American labor market in the nineteenth and twentieth centuries. She is the author of articles on women's education and work, gender-based occupational segregation, unemployment, retirement, and long term change in labor market institutions and outcomes. Together with Roger Ransom and Richard Sutch she founded the University of California's Historical Labor Statistics project, which collected, coded, and distributed microlevel data on working conditions, living standards, family demography, and household economy from the turn of the century.

JON S. COHEN is Professor of Economics and Dean of the School of Graduate Studies at the University of Toronto. He specializes in the economic history of modern Europe, with particular emphasis on Italy. His current research focuses on small credit institutions, especially rural credit cooperatives in early twentieth-century Italy. In addition to his work on Italian economic history, his publications include studies of English enclosures, Marxian perspectives on economic history, and Canadian public policy issues.

STEPHEN CULLENBERG is Associate Professor of Economics, University of California, Riverside. His research areas are economic methodology, international political economy, and Marxian economics. He is the author of *The Falling Rate of Profit: Recasting the Marxian Debate* (1994), and coeditor of *Marxism in the Postmodern Age* (1994) and *Whither Marxism? Global Crises in International Perspective* (1994). He is an editor of *Rethinking Marxism*.

PETER H. LINDERT is Professor of Economics and Director of the Agricultural History Center, University of California, Davis. His books and articles range broadly over modern economic history and international economics. Recent publications have dealt with the comparative history of social spending, the international debt crisis, America's foreign trade position, and trends in the quality and price of agricultural land. His textbook *International Economics* (9th ed., 1991) has been translated into seven foreign languages. He served as coeditor of the *Journal of Economic History* from 1990 to 1994.

DONALD N. MCCLOSKEY is John F. Murray Professor of Economics, Professor of History, and director of the Project on Rhetoric of Inquiry at the University of Iowa. Educated as an economist, he has worked on economic history and more recently on language and economic development. He is a past president of the Social Science History Association and the Economic History Association and has written on British industrial and agricultural history. His recent books include *Knowledge and Persuasion in Economics* (1994), *If You're So Smart: The Narrative of Economic Expertise* (1990), *Second Thoughts: Myths and Morals of U.S. Economic History* (edited; 1992), and *The Economic History of Britain since 1700* (edited with Roderick Floud; 1994).

THOMAS G. RAWSKI is Professor of Economics and History at the University of Pittsburgh. His research focuses on the economy of China, including studies of contemporary as well as historical issues. His investigation of China's modern economic history, which resulted in a book on *Economic Growth in Prewar China* (1989), revealed the need to create opportunities for expanded dialogue between economists and historians. He organized and directed the project on economic methods for Chinese historical research that created this book and a companion volume, *Chinese History in Economic Perspective* (coedited with Lillian M. Li; 1992). He is a past president of the Association for Comparative Economic Studies.

HUGH ROCKOFF is Professor of Economics at Rutgers University and a research associate of the National Bureau of Economic Research. His specialties are monetary and banking history, and price controls. He is the author of *The Free Banking Era: A Re-examination* (1975), *Drastic*

Measures: A History of Wage and Price Controls in the United States (1984), and numerous papers in professional journals. Together with Claudia Goldin, he edited *Strategic Factors in Nineteenth-Century American Economic History: A Volume to Honor Robert W. Fogel* (1992).

RICHARD SUTCH is Professor of Economics and History at the University of California, Berkeley, and a past president of the Economic History Association. He currently serves on the executive committee of the International Economic History Association. Sutch has worked extensively on the economic history of slavery and emancipation and is coauthor, with Roger Ransom, of *One Kind of Freedom: The Economic Consequences of Emancipation* (1977). He is now working on the histories of saving and retirement in nineteenth- and twentieth-century North America.

Preface

This volume evolved from papers and discussion at a workshop and conference, Economic Methods for Chinese Historical Research, sponsored by the Henry Luce Foundation, the American Council of Learned Societies, and the National Science Foundation and held in Honolulu, Hawaii in January 1987 and Oracle, Arizona in January 1988. In the 1987 workshop, a number of economists who specialize in economic history presented seminars on broad subjects: choice, long-term trends, macroeconomics, international issues, and economic institutions, for which the historian-participants had prepared by completing a series of readings. These materials formed the basis for the present volume.

The same group of historians and economists met again in 1988, with the historians presenting papers developed using the guidelines and suggestions of the first session, and the economists serving as discussants. Their papers were collected in a separate volume, *Chinese History in Economic Perspective* edited by Thomas G. Rawski and Lillian M. Li and published by the University of California Press.

The completion of a revised and expanded version of the initial economics presentations has benefited immensely from the contribution of many people whose names do not appear in the table of contents. They include Lynda S. Bell, Claudia Goldin, Van Beck Hall, Lillian M. Li, Susan Mann, Margaret Maurer-Fazio, Jack Ochs, Evelyn S. Rawski, Samantha Roberts, Julius Rubin, Werner Troesken, Jerome C. Wells, and two anonymous reviewers who combined fierce critiques with enough praise to persuade the press to support our project.

In producing this volume, we have relied on the elegant editorial work of Edith Gladstone, on the constant support of Sheila Levine, Scott Norton, Monica McCormick, and Laura Driussi at the University of California Press, and on the endless ingenuity of Della Sinclair, Hillary Sinclair, Pam Trbovich, and Penny Weiss at the University of Pittsburgh. Paul Spragens prepared the index.

We are deeply grateful to the Henry Luce Foundation, the American Council of Learned Societies, the National Science Foundation, and the East-West Center for encouraging and supporting our vision of using economic theory to enrich the study of Chinese history and our belief that the initial results might benefit the broader community of historians.

Above all, we have benefited from the opportunity to exchange ideas with the historians and economists who participated in the economic methods project: Lynda S. Bell, Loren Brandt, Cameron Campbell, I-chun Fan, Emily Honig, James Z. Lee, Bozhong Li, Lillian M. Li, Susan Mann, Peter Perdue, Kenneth Pomeranz, Barbara Sands, Guofu Tan, Yeh-chien Wang, R. Bin Wong, and Guangyuan Zhou.

Economics and the Historian

THOMAS G. RAWSKI

We aim to broaden and deepen the exchange of ideas between economists and historians. Our specific purpose is to show how to apply the core ideas and methods of economics to a wide range of historical issues.

Historians who neglect economics can lose sight of factors that affect every historical situation. Saints and sinners, elites and masses, rich and poor—all require food, clothing, and shelter. Even if man does not live by bread alone, economics lurks beneath the surface of any historical inquiry. The economist who hesitates to peek outside the confines of his models can overlook cultural influences on markets. Likewise the historian of labor, of agriculture, of trade policy, of elite politics, of the church, of international conflict, of the arts, of migration, ideas, industrialization, universities, technology, demography, or crime ignores the economic approach at the risk of losing important lines of explanation.

Historians often shy away from economics because of its reliance on models apparently devoid of institutions. But the model of *homo economicus,* the hyperrational actor, deserves a place in the scholar's analytic repertoire. This model implies, and statisticians confirm, for instance, that female children receive better nutrition (relative to their male siblings) in regions of India where the wages of female adults (relative to male adults) are high, and that wealthy parents receive more attention from their offspring than poor parents, but only if they have more than one child.[1]

---

1. On Indian child-rearing, see Rosenzweig and Schultz 1982. The results reflecting competition among children of wealthy parents are from Kotlikoff 1988.

Although these and other examples demonstrate the power of models, economics is not a discipline wholly preoccupied with their construction. The development of economics is itself a historical process tied to the evolution of the economy. Take the example of economic thinking about corporations. In 1776 Adam Smith, thinking of conflicts of interest among owners and managers, opined that "negligence and confusion . . . must always prevail, more or less, in the management of" joint stock companies. He predicted that corporations could not succeed without special monopoly rights: "They have . . . very seldom succeeded without an exclusive privilege; and frequently have not succeeded with one. Without an exclusive privilege they have commonly mismanaged the trade. With an exclusive privilege they have both mismanaged and confined it" (Smith 1937 [1776], 700). Events of the two centuries following showed the breadth of Smith's misjudgment. Alfred Chandler (1962, 1977) has chronicled the triumph of corporate organization over individual and family enterprise.

In this case as in others, changes in the economy have influenced economic theory. The traditional idea of a market economy based on exchange among autonomous and independent agents begins to crumble if the "individual agents" include complex organizations like General Motors, Hitachi, or the Department of Defense. Thinking about organizations raises issues that cut to the core of economics. To ask Smith's question: how can the corporation function effectively if the interests of its members (workers, middle managers, executives, shareholders) pull in different directions?

Efforts to answer the question (Simon 1991; Williamson and Winter 1993) focus on internal mechanisms of bargaining, contracting, monitoring, enforcement, and governance—matters that play no part in standard economic thinking. Theorists cannot penetrate these mechanisms without drawing on law, psychology, and sociology. They must adopt a comparative approach, and study the consequences of different structures (the multidivisional firm; the Japanese firm), the effects of specific market mechanisms (e.g., for the hiring of medical interns), and the implications of information flows and blockages for the rate of technical change (Aoki 1990; Roth 1990; Milgrom and Roberts 1992).

This sort of theorizing, known as the "new institutional economics," involves modeling, but it builds on the information treasured by historians: detailed appreciation of actual business practice. It moves away from the abstraction of *homo economicus* to "study man as he is, acting within restraints imposed by real institutions" (Coase 1984, 231).

New institutional economics is not an isolated instance of linkage between changes in the economy and changes in economic theory. The observation that poor farmers often reject "improved" seed varieties sparked a revolution in the economic analysis of risk (Schultz 1964; Calabresi and Bobbitt 1978; Lipton 1989). Systematic exploration of the idea that information is scarce and costly rather than freely available has spawned a rich and varied literature (Stigler 1968, 171–190; Akerlof 1984, chap. 2; Stiglitz 1986). Growing discomfort with the incongruity between traditional analysis of international trade, which assumes small producers and pure competition, and the reality of huge volumes of exchange involving related products and powerful multinational firms has sparked the development of new trade theories based on economies of scale and departures from atomistic competition (Krugman 1987, 1990b, 1991). Observation of large expenditures on research and development led to a new vision of technical change as a commodity capable of being produced rather than an external phenomenon like "manna from heaven" (Nelson 1987; "Symposium" 1994). The rapid growth of Japan and other East Asian nations whose governments reject laissez-faire principles has forced proponents of free-market orthodoxy to rethink their analysis of long-term growth (Wade 1990; World Bank 1993). The recent and often painful experience of economic transition in the former communist states of Europe and Asia, a market birthing that fascinates even the purest of laissez-faire theorists, demonstrates how economic analysis can fall short if it overlooks the cultural forces in history.

Our book is rooted in the conviction that historians will find it useful to acquaint themselves with economics. The chapters that follow provide repeated examples of how standard items in the economist's intellectual arsenal extend the reach of historical source materials by revealing unexpected connections between different elements of market systems.

Historians who do incorporate economic analysis into their working vocabulary can expect to find an enthusiastic response from economists. Rising interest in history is visible at every level of the economics profession. Robert Fogel and Douglass North, two economic historians, shared the 1993 Nobel prize. The work of other Nobel recipients, such as James Buchanan, Ronald Coase, Simon Kuznets, W. Arthur Lewis, T. W. Schultz, and Herbert Simon, reflects a commitment to historical and institutional studies. Robert Solow, another Nobel laureate, advises colleagues to seek inspiration for theories of technological change and long-term growth from "case studies, business histories, interviews, expert testimony" (1994, 53).

Richard Sutch, a coauthor of this volume, notes in his presidential address to the Economic History Association that economists now recognize "the central importance of institutional innovation and path dependencies to the dynamics of economic change." He emphasizes that "the rhetorical importance of arguments from history, the need for historical consistency, and the value of historical perspective are now, as never before, appreciated by young economists" (1991, 276–277). These new realities are visible in graduate schools. A survey of Ph.D. students in top-ranked economics programs places history second only to mathematics as a cognate field: 92 percent of the respondents regard a knowledge of history as "important to their development as an economist" (Klamer and Colander 1990, 16).

If economists have much to learn from history, it is equally true that historians can benefit from integrating economic methods into their research. To do so, the historians must acquire a *working* knowledge of *relevant* aspects of economic theory. It's not easy. Introductory texts tend to ignore historical issues; advanced treatments are preoccupied with mathematical techniques.[2] Economists have a well-deserved reputation for infelicitous writing.[3] The fundamentals of economics remain inaccessible to historians.

This volume seeks to bridge the gap that separates historical researchers from the insights of economics. Our plan is to introduce fundamental concepts and to provide sufficient vocabulary, bibliography, and analytic depth to enable readers to begin exploring. We began with a group of China historians who, after working with the initial draft chapters of the present volume and a set of related readings (see the Suggestions for Readings), produced a collection of essays, *Chinese History in Economic Perspective* (Rawski and Li 1992). The success of this experiment persuaded us to write this book.

We do not insist that all is well in economics. The authors sympathize with insiders like Nobel laureate Wassily Leontief (1971), who criticizes contemporary economics for its narrow assumptions and elaboration of technique at the expense of relevance. Just as drug companies maximize profit rather than human welfare by focusing their research on the hairlines and waistlines of affluent populations, economists often pursue trendy research that yields job offers rather than deeper knowledge

---

2. Texts by McCloskey (1985a), a coauthor of this volume, and by Milgrom and Roberts (1992) are exceptions; both link theory with specific historical issues.
3. Blinder 1974 offers a deft parody of conventional economic writing.

(Colander 1989). Yet despite its limitations, economic theory provides a base line against which the historian (or the economist) can compare actual outcomes. This base line (statisticians call it a "null hypothesis") builds on the assumption that

> people's choices are based on informed, autonomous decisions made under the conditions of a competitive market. You might believe this extremely simple null hypothesis is wrong 98 percent of the time in the real world. I'd be sympathetic. But as an analytic device, a standardized and widely accepted null hypothesis is a wonderful thing to have. (Blank 1993, 139)

If you are investigating a historical situation in which markets are not competitive, or women cannot own property, or large groups of people feel "dominated, oppressed, passive, stuck, ill, unsure . . . or unaware of alternatives," standard models still provide a valuable point of departure in the search for "more realistic variations" (Blank 1993, 139, 141).

Furthermore, the economics that concerns us here bypasses the intricacies of Nash equilibrium or dynamic programming and concentrates on what is best described as the logic of self-interest. Such theory is neither mysterious nor especially complex; basic economic thinking is perhaps best described as refined common sense. But it is "refined," as one might expect from the product of generations of concentrated intellectual effort (McCloskey 1987, 20). Many propositions of economics are not apparent to the untrained eye. This capacity to expose causal ties between seemingly unconnected phenomena offers opportunities to the historian.

ECONOMICS AND SOCIETY

Economic theory is built around the logical analysis of profit-seeking behavior by large numbers of well-informed, independent individuals in competitive markets governed by legal systems that enforce contracts and ensure the rights of private owners. Jon Cohen's essay on institutions and Susan Carter and Stephen Cullenberg's dialogue on labor economics explain how economists expand the basic model to encompass situations involving departures from the core assumptions about personal objectives, individual behavior, information structures, market organization, and property rights.

A SINGLE MARKET IN ISOLATION

Imagine the market for grain as a single entity in which price and sales volume emerge from the interaction of supply and demand. Bad weather, for example, will curtail supply and raise prices. The effect of rising prices on consumers is obvious, but the impact on farmers is uncertain—if food prices rise more than harvests decline, which is often the case, the total amount of farm income will increase even though some farmers will suffer losses. The argument immediately highlights the conflict inherent in the dual role of the market price in "determining food consumption levels, especially among poor people, and the adequacy of food supplies through incentives to farmers" (Timmer, Falcon, and Pearson 1983, 11).

The same framework, which treats the marketplace as a venue for organized, regulated strife between sellers seeking high prices and bargain-hunting buyers, can serve as a vehicle for analyzing the impact of new crops, new markets, new credit arrangements, or transport innovation. It reveals, for example, the brutal choice arising from a famine. Prompt relief may save lives, but at the cost of undercutting the profitability of traditional behavior (planting quick-growing tubers in response to higher grain prices) without which the severity of *future* famines may increase.

Although many implications of market forces are widely understood, others are not. A governmental initiative that establishes stockpiles of grain to reduce seasonal price fluctuations and guard against shortage, such as the policies of imperial China analyzed in Will and Wong (1991), may have no lasting impact on price. Price variation provides the rationale for grain storage by private agents seeking to profit from anticipating a price rise, and so a policy aimed at limiting price fluctuations is likely to reduce the amount of privately held grain. Private storage will drop as public storage expands, quite possibly on a one-for-one basis. Conversely, policies that exclude speculators from the market are likely to enlarge the magnitude of price fluctuations. This is because such policies curtail the activity of people who make it their business to buy grain when prices are low (thus counteracting falling prices) and try to sell grain at the peak of the price cycle (which pushes prices downward).

NETWORKS OF MARKETS

Visualizing the food economy as a network of interrelated markets expands the range of possibilities. If an urban uprising leads to "the enforced sale of provisions at the customary or popular price" (Thompson 1964, 65), there is an initial transfer of resources from merchants to "the masses." But this transfer must affect rural markets as well. Any reduction in the price obtainable for selling grain in the city will push down the prices that merchants offer to their rural suppliers. If political forces maintain urban grain prices at their new low levels, we would anticipate lower prices in rural grain markets. This in turn may affect the direction of trade, the mix of crops, the rents charged by owners of land suitable for grain cultivation, the incomes of farmers, the wages of laborers who grow and transport grain, and the earnings of traders and craftsmen who serve the grain growers. The result, in E. P. Thompson's words, is "something in the nature of a war between the countryside and the towns" (1964, 66).

Since there is a conflict of interest between food producers and consumers of food, it makes little sense to speak of "the people" or "the masses" as a homogeneous group.[4] If the initial incomes of urban grain-eaters exceed those of rural wheat-growers, a political uprising directed at prosperous urban merchants may end up transferring income to poor city-dwellers at the expense of poorer villagers. In essence the enforced reduction of urban prices is equivalent to a tax on grain arriving in urban marketplaces, reducing the merchant's expected revenue from selling in city markets. The consequences for rural grain producers are analogous to the impact of higher cigarette taxes on the incomes of tobacco farmers.

We expect market forces to eliminate interregional differences in wheat prices that exceed the cost of moving wheat from one location to another. As long as excessive price differences persist, traders can profit by moving wheat from low-price to high-price sales points. The same quest for profit will compress differences in the financial returns available from alternative uses of funds. Grain prices follow well-known seasonal patterns. Prices are low at harvest time, rise during the winter months, and reach peak levels prior to the new harvest. After the harvest merchants, farmers, or anyone with cash balances can buy grain at low prices for storage in anticipation of selling at higher prices several months in the future. Alternatively, the same funds can be loaned to borrowers, again in anticipation of the future receipt of larger sums. Faced with the choice of buying grain or buying IOUs, most people look for high returns (taking into account the cost of storing grain and the risk that borrowers may default). With large numbers of people involved in

4. "The final years of the 18th century saw a last desperate effort by the people to reimpose the older moral economy as against the economy of the free market" (Thompson 1964, 67).

the markets for grain and loans, the financial returns to these two opportunities should be approximately equal over a period of many years. This application of the economist's "law of one price," which works to equalize the financial returns to similar resources in different markets as well as compressing price differentials across space, implies that the seasonal changes in grain prices can be used to trace changes in the rate of interest, a fundamental parameter that influences decisions about consumption, saving, and investment at every level of society (McCloskey and Nash, 1984).

MACROECONOMICS: VIEWING THE ECONOMY AS A SINGLE ENTITY

The fate of individuals depends in part on changes in the level of aggregate output, a quantity that workers and firms cannot predict. The 1929 stock market crash and the ensuing depression turned capable workers into vagrants and shrewd entrepreneurs into paupers. Pity the small Japanese manufacturer whose carefully nurtured business collapses not because he manages badly but because a political joust between Tokyo and Washington leads traders to drive up the international value of the yen.

Inflation, which measures changes in the value of money relative to commodities and services, affects many issues of concern to historians. The benefits that inflation bestows on borrowers and its cost to lenders are well understood. If rapid monetary expansion causes prices of many goods to rise simultaneously, the researcher must guard against the danger of exaggerating the significance of common price trends as measures of interregional integration in large economies like China (Rawski and Li 1992, part 1), India (McAlpin 1983, chap. 5), or Russia (Metzer 1974). Inflation is one of many areas in which government policy is a crucial determinant of outcomes. Consider the oil price shocks of the 1970s, in which the industrial nations were stunned by huge increases in the price of Middle Eastern crude oil. The 1973 shock brought sharp price increases everywhere. But after 1978, the inflationary impact of higher oil prices was much smaller in Japan than in the United States even though Japan imports nearly all of its energy supplies. The reason: firm credit restraint by Japan's central bank swiftly extinguished pressures for successive rounds of price increases to "pass along" higher costs (Ito 1992, chap. 3).

Economists have recently devoted much effort to showing how expectations can affect outcomes in many markets. The basic idea of "rational expectations" (Scheffrin 1983) is simple and appealing. Individuals and businesses react to economic change. They also seek to position themselves advantageously *in anticipation* of new developments. Property owners who expect an upsurge of inflation will seek large fixed-rate mortgages. These new directions in economic theory reflect undeniable realities of human behavior. "Rational expectations" also involve a political and philosophical reaction against the Keynesian idea that governments can use policy to manipulate the economy. Theorists of rational expectations extend the notion of individual choice by arguing that only *unforeseen* government actions in the monetary and fiscal sphere can affect macroeconomic outcomes. A *systematic* policy will fall victim to the rational responses of alert individuals.

Historians familiar with studies of crowds and mob behavior will recognize that the importance of expectations undercuts the economist's assumption of independent individual choice. Expectations can be contagious, and widely shared beliefs can drive events. If enough people believe that the dollar or the stock market will rise, the result may be a self-fulfilling prophecy. The psychology of the crowd surely contributes to the emergence of booms and panics in contemporary or historical equity markets (Kindleberger 1978; Galbraith 1993). Nor is the herd instinct limited to ordinary folk: witness the losses by bankers who raced one another to increase loans to Latin America in the 1970s and to Eastern Europe in the 1980s.

MARKETS AS PART OF SOCIETY

Market activity does not occur in isolation but depends on institutions. The disposition of household labor resources, the intensity of cultivation, and the level of crop yield will vary with the nature of landholding arrangements (owner-cultivation, tenancy with fixed or share rents, cultivation by hired workers, collective farming).

The consequences of alternative arrangements are far from obvious. If tenants pay fixed cash rents and enjoy security of tenure, the theory predicts that crop selection, cultivation methods, and farm output will be the same on farms tilled by tenants and by owner-operators. Economics focuses on *marginal* or incremental decisions. At the margin, the financial consequences of adding an extra hour of labor or an extra ton of fertilizer are identical for owner-farmers and for secure tenants paying fixed rents; with identical costs and benefits, theory anticipates identical decisions.[5]

As a result, and contrary to widespread belief, land reform need not improve farm productivity. Proponents easily forget that land reform transfers resources from upwardly mobile, efficient cultivators to idlers and wastrels at the same time that it shifts ownership from the incompetent rich to the deserving poor. The losses from the first type of transfer may cancel the gains from the second, as in Japan, where Dore (1959, 217) finds no association between the amount of land redistributed and postreform gains in productivity, or in China, where land redistribution in the 1950s produced nothing comparable to the output spurt that followed the abolition of collectives three decades later. Collective production suffers from serious incentive problems but contributed substantially to Israel's development (Aharoni 1991, chap. 4). Even where collectives sapped productive efficiency, as in China, the reinstatement of household farming has crippled collective systems that effectively promoted health care and transport development (Perkins and Yusuf 1984).

The influence of ownership rights extends beyond the household. The issue of whether cultivators can obtain exclusive access to the land appears again and again in the annals of agrarian history, ranging from the English enclosures, the American West, and Latin America (Thiesenhusen 1989) to the Sahel region of Africa, where the spread of commercial cropping has pushed nomadic herdsmen toward starvation (Sen 1981, chap. 8) and to southern Spain, where the continued right of herders to move their sheep through farming regions held back agrarian development for centuries (North 1981, chap. 11). North and Thomas view the emergence of the property rights that undergird the modern capitalist system as a central element in the political evolution of modern Europe, during which rulers systematically strengthened private ownership rights in return for the loyalty and tax payments of their propertied subjects (1973, chap. 8).

The study of property rights does not begin to exhaust the external forces that condition market behavior. Noting the flagrant asymmetry of the rich nations' efforts to expand international capital flows while

---

5. Things are different for the sharecropper, who must share the fruits of adding extra labor or fertilizer with the landlord rather than retaining 100 percent of the extra output. If output is split between tenant and landlord on a 50:50 basis, the calculating tenant will refrain from applying extra fertilizer unless the cost of doing so is no more than half of the incremental return. The theorist thus expects share tenants to devote less labor, fertilizer, etc. to their plots than owner-farmers or tenants paying fixed rents.

tightly restricting migration into their own territories, Carlos Diaz-Alejandro observes that "market rules . . . and the determination of which markets are allowed to operate, are essentially political decisions" (1975, 218).

Market behavior also reflects ideas and values. If Japanese feel that prestigious corporations should never dismiss long-term employees, while Americans believe that it is fair for hard-pressed businesses to dismiss employees but not to reduce wages for the remaining workers, these contrasting visions of equity and property surely leave their mark on employment arrangements in Japanese and American companies. The economic consequences of beliefs are evident in the "immense resources expended . . . to convince participants that particular forms of political or economic organization are fair" (North 1984, 257). The current explosion of discussion and confrontation over affirmative action, empowerment, and comparable worth exemplifies the cost of accommodating new ideas about fairness and justice.

Amartya Sen's (1981) investigation of famines in Asia and Africa illustrates the extent to which the market activities that dominate the concern of economists are constrained by institutions that, in their widest dimensions, encompass the entirety of culture. Although we think of famine as arising from a sudden decline in the availability of food, Sen's case studies show that hunger can appear in the midst of plenty. To Sen, famine represents a failure of *entitlement* to food. Reduced food output is only one possible cause of famine. Sen's analysis "places food production within a network of relationships" that encompasses law, politics, social security, kinship, and ecology, as well as markets and market-linked economic institutions. He finds that "shifts in some of these relations can precipitate gigantic famines even without receiving any impulse from food production" (1981, 158).

If the market system, including the whole penumbra of legal, financial, and other enabling institutions, operates within a broader sociocultural matrix that helps to determine the course of economic evolution, then the study of any economy, past or present, must involve a range of knowledge that reaches far beyond the focal points of conventional economic theory. The Nobel laureate James Buchanan asks economists to investigate the processes that lead to the emergence of market structures and market activity (1979, 19). This formulation is sufficiently broad to encompass the Marxian notion that economic outcomes arise from an interaction between physical and human resources and "structures of social power . . . that determine the influence exercised by different classes of people over how goods are produced and how the resultant income is distributed" (Lazonick 1987, 258). It resonates with Nancy Folbre's view that economic factors "constrain and influence," but cannot fully determine human behavior (1986a, 7).

HOW ECONOMICS CAN CONTRIBUTE
TO HISTORICAL RESEARCH

Consider the problem of America's relative economic and political decline during the past half century. The history of this transition must encompass such factors as political objectives, ideology, and national aspirations in the United States and in other nations. But purely economic explanations deserve careful scrutiny, for they may provide the core of a satisfactory analysis. Gavin Wright (1990) argues that American industrial dominance, like Britain's, was a predictably transient phenomenon based on superior access to resources that gradually declined in cost outside the U.S. and also lost their central position in the industrial economy.

The competitive strength of Japanese manufacturers arose partly because extensive corporate borrowing, the prevalence of long-term employment, and seniority-based wage systems forced managers to focus on sales growth and output volume (to spread high fixed costs including interest and wages) rather than on current profit. This enabled them to continue production even when competition drove price below average cost, an inference that arises from pure textbook economics (e.g., Samuelson and Nordhaus 1985, 479). If selling price falls below average total cost of production, a profit-maximizing firm will temporarily continue to produce as long as sales revenues exceed all variable costs. This allows the firm to cover some of its fixed costs (which must be paid even if output ceases) from sales income. If a price war breaks out between firms that differ only in that the share of fixed costs in (identical) total outlays is higher for Japanese than for American rivals, the Japanese will continue to operate at prices so low that the Americans cease production and lay off their work force.

Textbook analysis, of course, does not tell everything we want to know. Why did Japanese firms borrow more than their American rivals? How did Japan's banks cope with the risks of lending to firms with high ratios of debt to equity? Should we expect recent increases in the debt load of U.S. corporations and concurrent reductions in the ratio of debt to equity among Japan's blue-chip companies to reverse long-standing patterns of corporate strategy on either side of the Pacific? When and how did the Japanese develop a tenure system for a substantial segment of their labor force? Is this system beginning to crack under the pressure of accelerated technical change and intensified global competition? If long-term employment offers important competitive advantages, why have American managers failed to adjust employment arrangements in this direction?

Although it cannot answer such questions, textbook theory offers a plausible interpretation of market competition between American and Japanese manufacturers in many industries. It even explains the mutual incomprehension displayed by both sides, with American managers complaining that the Japanese must receive huge government subsidies (they don't) because no rational manager could operate at the low prices offered by the Japanese (true, but only under American rather than Japanese cost structures), while the Japanese ridicule the Americans' inability to compete.

Here, as elsewhere, economics gives partial answers to our historical inquiries. The economic perspective often establishes unexpected connections and reveals new vantage points that enable historians to expand the range of their studies and enlarge the value of source materials. For the historian who finds that available materials do not bear directly on the desired research objective, economics may open new vistas by connecting land prices and benefits from transport improvements (Ransom 1970) or nonfarm wages and agrarian productivity (Bairoch 1989; Rawski 1989, chap. 6).

Even in the absence of statistical materials, economic theory provides a fruitful means of organizing a historical analysis. Studies of discrimination in labor markets can draw on theories of market segmentation, which portray employers (or landlords, or bank managers) as resorting to rules of thumb based on race, religion, education, ethnicity, or language as inexpensive substitutes for costly information about individuals (Doeringer and Piore 1985; Honig 1992). Research on ties between business and government can benefit from the theory of rent-seeking, which depicts people as dividing their resources between competing in the marketplace and in Congress (Krueger 1974; Buchanan, Tollison, and Tullock 1980).

A PROSPECT

This book reviews seven aspects of economics. The authors are economists with long experience of studying historical problems and working collaboratively with historians. Each chapter illuminates a particular subdivision of economics in a lucid and nontechnical fashion. The chapters are complementary but can be read in various orders.

We begin with trends, institutions, and labor, subjects that historians study from noneconomic perspectives. The chapter on trends describes the economist's method of organizing data and leads the reader through a number of practical examples that illustrate simple procedures for validating quantitative information and constructing effective arguments based on statistical information. The chapter on institutions focuses on three examples: the household, the farm, and the firm, showing how economists analyze the institutional arrangements that condition and mediate links between individuals and markets for commodities and services. The chapter on labor uses the device of a dialogue between a historian and an economist to examine the ways in which economic methods contribute to the study of labor markets.

The next two chapters concern the heart of the discipline. The chapter on microeconomics illustrates the myriad variations on the economist's central vision of economic life as the outcome of a vast array of self-interested choices by individuals. The chapter on macroeconomics pursues a series of examples that show how system-wide thinking avoids pitfalls and leads to fresh conclusions.

The final chapters highlight monetary economics and international trade. The chapter on money develops a historical parable to lay out the principles of money and banking, a subject that often confuses economists as much as historians. The chapter on trade offers a guide to the study of international economics, in particular the interactions between growing trade and the domestic distribution of income. At the end is a list of suggested readings, with advice on how to approach them.

Issues in the Study of Economic Trends

THOMAS G. RAWSKI

Investigation of economic trends occupies an important position in historical research. Did prices or output of particular commodities or services or broad aggregates rise, fall, or remain constant over various periods? Can we detect substantial change in levels of economic welfare, distribution of income and wealth, degree of commercialization, patterns of cropping, organization of economic activity, or significance and functioning of various economic institutions? Answers to these questions and many others involve systematic study of economic trends. Attempts to ascertain the presence and determine the direction and magnitude of economic trends call for certain procedures and encounter characteristic difficulties that display strong similarities regardless of the trends being studied. The objective of this essay is to discuss the methods and problems that can properly be regarded as typical ingredients in the study of economic trends.

THE MEANING OF ECONOMIC TRENDS

What do we mean by economic trends? Nobel laureate Simon Kuznets, whose work shaped the way that all economists think about long-term economic change, emphasized that any effort to define economic trends requires a suitably *homogeneous* economy and time period within which we seek to identify *unidirectional* changes that are sufficiently *persistent* and *sustained* to allow us to identify them as long-term trends, as opposed to short-term fluctuations or cycles (1961, chap. 2).

Several essential points emerge immediately. The study of economic trends is an art or craft rather than an exact science. While technical procedures unfamiliar to most historians may play a role, for instance in determining whether long-term changes "produce movements that dwarf the short-term variations" in some particular context (Kuznets 1961, 45), there are crucial issues of judgment and evidence that every historian is trained to comprehend. What is the appropriate period of analysis? How do we determine if a change is "unidirectional" or "persistent"? How can we satisfy ourselves that we have sorted out the causes of long-term change and short-term fluctuations?

Kuznets's criteria also help to explain why we can rarely expect finality in controversies about economic trends. If one's view of certain trends is shaped by judgments concerning the scope of inquiry; if it is possible to reinterpret trend X as the outcome of forces A, B, E, and F twenty years after another scholar has received general acclaim for an explanation focusing on forces A, B, C, and D, we can imagine successive rounds of inquiry into broad issues such as the British industrial revolution or American slavery even in the absence of new sources, flawed data, or disagreement about the validity or interpretation of certain evidence, all of which are, of course, commonplace.

Of particular importance here is the passage of time. Access to long series of quantitative or qualitative evidence enormously simplifies the determination of trends. When the data span is short, ambiguity is unavoidable. Scholars concerned with measuring the growth rate of China's post-1949 economy engaged in sharp controversy during the 1960s and early 1970s. While political viewpoints no doubt contributed to these disputes, the main problem was insufficient evidence. At a 1972 conference, Simon Kuznets attacked China specialists for their inability to determine whether output per head had risen or fallen since 1949.[1] Five years later, these disputes ceased, not because of any change in the sympathies of the combatants or in Peking's publication policies, but simply because the passage of time and accumulation of (scattered and fragmentary) evidence left no room for doubt that substantial increases in per capita output had occurred in the People's Republic.

Unfortunately, historians cannot always rely on the passage of time to generate new raw material; only diligent search for unused evidence or for new ways of using well-known sources can add to our stock of data. When we focus on a short period, it can never be easy to separate

1. Kuznets's comments were initially directed at the draft version of Perkins 1975a.

trend and cycle. For example, we find one scholar of early twentieth-century China who predicts that "as we undertake more studies of local conditions . . . brief moments of prosperity will continue to reveal themselves, to be sure. . . . But the long-term pattern" will be quite different (Bell 1985, 26). There are others who acknowledge instances and periods of decline but see an overall pattern of economic growth and rising average incomes in the same times and places (Rawski 1989, chap. 6). Such disagreements can stimulate fresh research and invigorate the field, or degenerate into fruitless debate among inflexible adversaries.

HOW ECONOMISTS ORGANIZE DATA
FOR STUDYING ECONOMIC TRENDS

Once you decide that certain data are reasonably accurate and germane to your research (a process discussed later in this essay), the matter of presentation demands attention. The object is to clarify the significance of the materials, first for your own benefit, and later, for the benefit of an audience. Rather than enter into detail about construction of tables and graphs,[2] it is important to emphasize the need to display data in the relevant economic context and not, as happens all too often, in splendid isolation. You have figures, but are they typical or unusual? You have a growth rate, but is it large or small? The reader requires your guidance in these matters.

Suppose you discover that Smith paid $12 in taxes in 1925. Was Smith heavily taxed? It depends on whether his income was $100 or $10,000. What do we mean by heavy taxation anyway? In part, the meaning depends on the ratio of taxes to income elsewhere—for other taxpayers in Smith's community, for Smith's community fifty years earlier or later, for taxpayers in other economies. Did Smith's taxes, which amounted to only $6 in 1915, rise rapidly? Again, a sensible answer requires additional information. What happened to related costs in Smith's economic world between 1915 and 1925? What change occurred in Smith's income? In the value of land (especially if land is taxed)? In the prices of basic necessities? Doubling the money value of taxes means one thing in a world of stable prices and money incomes, and something quite different in a period of inflation.

The historian will often find it advantageous to arrange data according to categories established by economic statisticians. The economist's

2. See Floud 1973 and Tufte 1983.

conception of national product and of business cycles, to cite two prominent examples of special methods used by economists to organize time series data, is the product of previous studies of economic trends, and is therefore designed to focus attention on aspects that scholars have found to be of significance in the analysis of economic change. To follow the canons of economic statistics brings researchers the added advantage of easy comparison with relevant data sets compiled by students of other times and places.[3]

NATIONAL INCOME AND PRODUCT ACCOUNTS

National-income accounting in its modern form dates from the 1920s, when Simon Kuznets and others devised systematic and standardized methods for measuring the level and growth of overall economic activity in nation-states. Like any effort to reduce a complex process to a single linear measure, national-income accounting is far from perfect. We can briefly review three (of many) problem areas: household production, the hidden or underground economy, and unrecorded costs.

Household production.   The basic strategy of national-income statisticians is to count all activities that are *productive* (i.e., drug smuggling and other criminal enterprises are omitted) and *result in marketed products.* The focus on markets is practical—markets generate prices that are essential to the valuation of disparate outputs according to a common monetary standard. Practicality also dictates the convention of including specific nonmarket items such as the estimated value of owner-occupied housing and of homegrown foodstuffs consumed by farm households.

The exclusion of most household production considerably reduces the coverage of conventional measures of total output. The most obvious omission involves housewives' unremunerated production of meals, clothes, and household services (child care, financial management, marketing, cleaning, nursing, etc.). The volume of these activities is large. Working with antebellum U.S. data, Folbre and Wagman (1993) estimate that nonmarket production by women may have amounted to more than half the total of marketed output. Despite women's increased participation in paid employment outside the home, household production remains large even today: Bonke finds that unrecorded household pro-

---

3. For example, Mitchell 1982, 1988, 1992, 1993; U.S. Bureau of the Census 1975; Summers and Heston 1988.

duction "amounts to 40–50% of the GNP in most West European countries and in the U.S." (1992, 281).

The implications of excluding household production extend far beyond the possible mismeasurement of economic growth. American society is built around the expectation that parents will equip their children with the intellectual and emotional faculties needed to benefit from attending school. If this traditional process of household "production" fails, children become first uneducable and later unemployable, unless they are rescued by programs like Head Start. This specific variety of household production, although widely regarded as crucial to the nation's social stability, completely escapes the economist's effort to measure total output.[4]

Underground economy.   Even if there is no disagreement over which activities should be measured, the efforts of citizens to escape taxation and regulation cause important segments of economic activity to escape the statistician's net. Changes in tax rates and in the balance of forces between evaders and enforcers can produce large swings in the share of hidden output. Several estimating methods suggest a large jump in the share of underground production in the U.S. economy between 1950 and 1980 (Porter and Bayer 1989); for China, one researcher finds that the share of hidden activity rose from near zero to about 30 percent of total output between 1978 and 1989 (Lu 1993).

Unrecorded costs.   The whole idea of national-income accounting is surrounded by philosophical issues. It is not easy to determine what is a final product and what is a cost of production. Do urban transit systems represent a cost of modern industrial society rather than a welfare-enhancing output? To what extent should expenditures on education and health care count as investment (well trained, healthy workers have high productivity) rather than, as is now the case, as consumption? Should the cost of emissions and congestion resulting from the operation of automobiles be deducted from the auto industry's contribution of total output? What of the consequences of rapid exploitation of fisheries, forests,

---

4. Strassmann criticizes the tendency of work on "human capital" (a subfield of economics that portrays education and training as investments that increase the recipients' future productivity) to neglect household activity. "Because economic theory examines adult behavior, parents' gifts of time, love, and money to infants and children are reconceptualized as 'natural endowments.' . . . These lost gifts, forgotten or ignored by economic theory, are yet another manifestation of the invisibility of women's work" (1993, 58).

or mineral deposits, which raise current production but lessen the economic prospects for future generations? Nordhaus and Tobin (1972) considered these possibilities in computing a "measure of economic welfare" for the United States over the period 1929–1965. Their results show a considerably slower advance for per capita material welfare than the conventional national accounts. Official U.S. statistics have begun to include calculations that reflect "the impact of economic growth on the environment" (Harper 1994).

These examples make it abundantly clear that national-income accounting is beset with gaps and flaws involving both concepts and measurement. This does not mean that the statistics of national income are without value, particularly if our purpose is to look at broad trends rather than to focus on specific areas (like the transition from household autarchy to specialized production for the market) where standard accounting procedures conceal large defects. We cannot doubt the broad parallel between trends in national-income statistics and in the real phenomena of material well-being that they seek to measure. An interlude of economic stagnation, as measured by the national-income accounts, squelched a brief flurry of interest in the idea of "zero economic growth" precisely because the correlation between growth in national income per person and in people's well-being is no figment of the economist's imagination. Furthermore, a generation of experience with national-income statistics has produced a wealth of empirical lore that economists constantly use to assess the significance of new sets of national accounting data. This treasure house of comparative insights awaits the historian who begins to think within the framework of national income accounting.

How do economists set out to measure the total annual value of commodities and services produced by a national economy? An attempt to record the value of every transaction will vastly overestimate annual output because the same commodity may change hands several times, as when wheat is sold by farmers to millers, then to bakers, wholesalers, and retailers before being consumed in the household. Economists have devised three separate procedures for measuring the totality of economic activity without this multiple counting; in principle, each should produce the same result. In practice, alternative calculations help to identify sources of error in the national accounts and also provide a means of estimating categories for which there is no direct measurement.

First, we may restrict our observation to *final transactions* in which a product or service is sold to its ultimate user. Wine purchased by consumers (but not grapes purchased by vintners or beer sold to restaurants), machines installed in factories (but not autos purchased by auto dealers), or domestic goods sold to foreign buyers represent typical transactions that are included in this conception of aggregate economic activity. Calculations based on this concept lead to measures of gross national expenditure (GNE), which is the sum of several components: private consumption spending, investment (encompassing increased inventories as well as new buildings and equipment), current government consumption (including salaries of public employees as well as paper clips, gasoline, and other supplies purchased for current use), and net exports (defined as the difference, positive or negative, between exports and imports of commodities and services).[5] The composition of total output measured in this fashion provides shorthand descriptions of important features of economic activity: the ratio (or long-term trends in the ratio) of government spending, investment, consumption or foreign trade to national aggregates are often cited in discussions of contemporary as well as historical economic circumstances.

Alternatively, we can measure the contribution of each producer to total output by using the concept of "value added" to eliminate multiple counting. Instead of combining the sales of each producer, we restrict our attention to the difference between sales and purchases from other enterprises. For the baker, "value added" is the difference between total sales and purchases (of flour, yeast, electricity, health insurance) from other enterprises; it measures the value that the baker's business operations add to these interenterprise purchases by the application of land, labor, and capital. This arithmetic, applied to all producers, circumvents the problem of multiple counting and produces a total figure for gross national product (GNP) that, in theory, corresponds exactly to the sum of final outputs known as GNE. Results based on the value-added approach are often arranged by economic sector, allowing us to decompose total output to observe the shares (of value added) contributed by three major sectors: primary (agriculture, forestry, fishing, extractive industries), secondary (manufacturing, utilities, construction, transport and communication) and tertiary (government, commerce, finance, services) and their components.

This form of national accounting reveals important regularities in

5. Imports are already included in consumption (French wine), investment (Japanese machine tools), and government spending (foreign arms purchases) and must therefore be subtracted to derive a composite measure of national economic activity.

long-term patterns of development. The most notable of these, the declining share of agricultural production and the rising share of industry in total output, is illustrated in Figure 1. The relative decline of farming and rise of industry during the process of economic growth is common to large and small nations, to early and late industrializers, to capitalist and socialist systems, to exporters and importers of food, and to rich and poor nations.

The regularities elucidated from systematic comparison of national accounts for various nations deserve careful attention. Students of agricultural history, for example, must recognize that the share of agriculture in the national labor force invariably declines even in early phases of industrialization. Later phases typically bring rapid reductions in the absolute number as well as the share of farm workers. In Japan, for example, the number of workers occupied in agriculture, forestry, and fishing dropped by 42 percent between 1950 and 1970 (Ohkawa and Rosovsky 1973, 311).

Donald McCloskey's essay explains how economists visualize the economy as a giant circular flow of products and services between businesses and households (see Figure 11). Businesses sell products to households in return for flows of money. The same businesses hire the services of productive resources (land, buildings, labor, borrowed funds) in return for financial payments delivered to households whose members own these resources. We have described how one can measure the level of economic activity by studying expenditure on current output (to generate estimates of GNE) or by focusing on production operations in the business sector (using the value-added approach to calculate GNP). Alternatively, we can study the income flows paid by businesses to owners of productive resources. After deducting payments for interenterprise purchases from the sales revenue generated within the business sector, the remaining amount (which is exactly the same as value added discussed above) is distributed among owners of productive resources in the form of payments: wages, interest, rent, and profit. Since profit is a residual category that absorbs whatever income (positive or negative) remains after all other resources receive their compensation, the total of compensation paid to owners of productive resources provides a third tabulation of overall economic activity that, in principle, coincides exactly with the GNP and GNE totals calculated from information on expenditure and production. This form of accounting produces information on the distribution of national income between owners of labor, capital, and land.

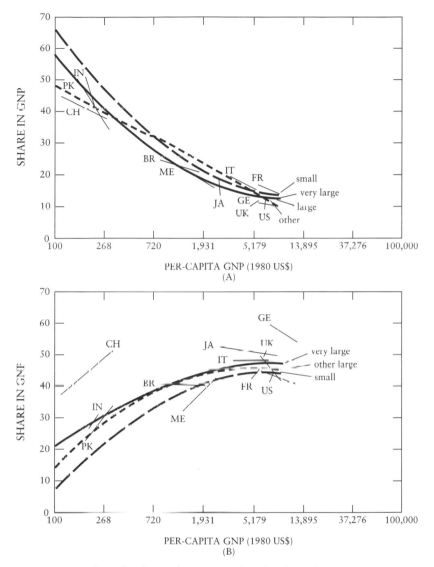

FIGURE 1. Trends in the share of agricultural and industrial output in gross national product. Cross-country comparisons show changes in the share of agriculture (part A) and industry (part B) in gross national product (GNP) for very large countries (over 50 million people), large countries (15–50 million people), and small countries (under 15 million people). Note individual trends for very large countries: Brazil (BR), China (CH), France (FR), India (IN), Italy (IT), Japan (JA), Mexico (ME), Pakistan (PK), United Kingdom (UK), United States (US), and West Germany (GE). (Gillis et al. 1992, 52; based on Perkins and Syrquin 1989, 2:1726; reprinted by permission of the publisher.)

The possibility of multiple approaches to estimates of national income allows statisticians to estimate the magnitude of error involved in their unavoidably imperfect efforts to measure the various components of total output or expenditure. The theoretical identity between the results of different calculations can also be used to fill lacunae in existing figures. In the case of China, for example, one can use estimates of GNP growth based on estimated output growth for various sectors (agriculture, manufacturing, etc.) and separate figures for investment, government spending, and net exports to calculate the level of consumption spending during 1914–18 and 1931–36. Even though we have no data that would permit a direct estimate of private consumption spending in either period, the accounting identity:[6]

$$\text{GNP} = \text{GNE} = \text{Private Consumption} + \text{Investment} +$$
$$\text{Government Spending} + \text{Net Exports}$$

makes it possible to derive figures for private consumption as a residual from the following equation:

$$\text{Private Consumption} = \text{GNP} - \text{Investment} - \text{Government}$$
$$\text{Spending} - \text{Net Exports}$$

ECONOMIC CYCLES

Economic trends rarely unfold in a unilinear fashion. An expanding economy need not grow each and every year; even if it does, we do not expect identical annual growth rates. Accumulation of information regarding variations in economic performance has led to theories of economic cycles of which historians should be aware. When economists speak of cycles, they refer not merely to variations in economic performance, but to cyclical phenomena driven by self-contained internal dynamics. It is not merely that the level or growth rate of output, employment, profits, or prices first rises and then falls. The idea of economic cycles—as opposed to fluctuations stemming from random occurrences—is that the characteristics of the upward phase themselves give birth to forces that reverse the direction of movement; similarly, downward cyclical movement is first slowed and then reversed by forces contained within the cyclical process.

---

6. This formulation assumes (realistically, for China during the relevant years) that government spending included little or no investment; otherwise it would be necessary to split public spending into consumption and investment components to avoid duplication of public investment.

Theories of economic cycles range from Karl Marx's grand overview of capitalism, in which declining profit rates bring about eventual social collapse, to mundane analyses of particular industries. The "corn-hog cycle" provides a classic example of the latter. If corn is cheap, hog farmers will take advantage of low feed prices by raising more pigs. A rising hog population exerts upward pressure on corn prices (demand for feed increases) and forces pork prices down (increased meat supply). Rising feed costs and falling product prices cause hog raisers to increase the rate of slaughter and encourage grain growers to plant more corn. Declining pig herds and rising corn output restore the profitability of pork production and the cycle renews itself.

There is no general theory of economic cycles. Most cycle theories originate in empirical observation rather than logical deduction. Researchers detect regularities in historical data and search for possible causes of repetitive cyclical patterns. We expect technology and institutions to affect the nature of cyclical behavior. New methods that shorten the growing season for corn, hasten the fattening of hogs, open new markets to the products of Midwestern farms, or offer new credit arrangements to hog producers will almost certainly affect the timing and perhaps the basic nature of the corn-hog cycle.

It is therefore not surprising to discover that a particular type of cyclical movement may be confined to a specific time and place. In his analysis of the Kuznets cycle, for instance, Moses Abramovitz argues that the "15 to 20-year waves in the growth rates of smoothed series" of industrial output or GNP that Kuznets observed for the United States economy between 1840 and 1914 cannot help us to understand recent changes because "the economy's underlying structure and institutions have so changed as to render the old model defunct" (1968, 351, 359).[7] Furthermore, we cannot expect mechanical replication of cyclical patterns even if institutional change is absent:[8]

> depending on circumstances, this and that cycle may either fade out or become prominent. Economic conditions do not automatically arrange cycles in such a way that two or three Kitchin cycles make a Juglar; two Juglars a

---

7. A "smoothed" series of GNP (or industrial output, unemployment, etc.) is a moving average of annual data (e.g., the entry for 1881 is the arithmetic average of annual figures for 3 or 5 or 7 years centered on 1881) intended to remove the influence of short-term business fluctuations. See Floud (1973, 112–116).

8. Braudel and Spooner (1967, 431); their essay offers an excellent introduction (430–442) to various types of economic cycle theories. See also Abramovitz 1989 and Solomou 1988.

hypercycle; and two hypercycles a Kondatrieff. . . . The interplay of cycles amongst themselves and within the secular trend determines a series of actions and reactions, which upset individual movements completely, often changing their duration. . . . But, however irregular they may be, these cycles combine to form a rhythm which is *broadly* periodic or recurrent.

The historical researcher is well advised to investigate the literature of those economic cycles that may relate to a specific research project: Kuznets on nineteenth-century America; Braudel and Spooner on preindustrial Europe; W. Arthur Lewis (1976) on the international economy of the late nineteenth century, and so on. Even without a universally applicable theory of cycles, there are important regularities of which historians should be aware. Economic fluctuations do not affect all segments of the economy in a uniform fashion. Some components of the national economic aggregates—for example, investment and profits—are far more volatile than others. Between 1952 and 1986, for example, annual percentage changes in United States GNP at constant prices (i.e., excluding the effect of inflation) ranged from −1.1 to +5.8 percent. Annual changes in gross private domestic investment, also in constant prices, were much larger: for the five years beginning in 1972–73, for instance, the figures were +11.9, −7.6, −20.4, +18.3 and +15.0 percent. Agricultural prices, reflecting the inelasticity of both supply and demand typical of farm products, tend to experience wider fluctuations than prices generally.[9]

Our perception of economic trends necessarily reflects the time frame of our analysis. We can illustrate this point with reference to long-term indexes of real wages and living costs presented by Braudel and Spooner and reproduced in Figure 2. The index of real wages for building craftsmen in Vienna indicates a long-term decline in real wages from 1521–30 to the mid-eighteenth century. The line marked 2 in the figure represents a rough linear expression of this falling trend that might usefully summarize the experience of 230 years. But suppose we wish to study the Viennese working class in the first half of the seventeenth century. Then the rising trend summarized by line 1 in Figure 2 rather than the longer-

---

9. Inelastic demand or supply describes situations in which quantity shifts relatively slowly in response to changes in price; i.e., quantity transacted is inflexible or "inelastic" when confronted with a price change. More precisely, inelastic demand means that if price changes by 1 percent, quantity purchased will move in the opposite direction, but by less than 1 percent. If quantity shifts by more than 1 percent, we speak of demand or supply as being "elastic." Inelastic supply occurs when a 1 percent price change affects quantity supplied by less than 1 percent, with price and quantity moving in the same direction. Demand elasticity for basic commodities or "necessities" tends to be lower than for inessentials or "luxuries."

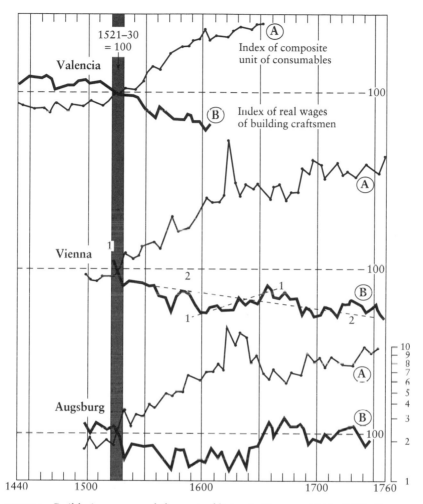

FIGURE 2. Builder's wages and the cost of living in Europe, 1440–1760: five-yearly averages. (Based on Braudel and Spooner 1967, 482; reprinted by permission of Cambridge University Press.)

term decline would appropriately reflect the life experience of workers born, say, in 1590.

The same graphs illustrate the danger of using extreme points as a baseline for quantitative analysis. The long-term trend of living costs shown by the series marked A is clearly upward in Valencia, Vienna, and Augsburg. Living costs rose to a peak in the decade of the 1620s in Vienna and Augsburg before falling to levels that remained substantially above sixteenth-century figures. The unusual figures of the 1620s do not provide a suitable baseline for studying trends. A price index for the period 1600–1620 or 1550–1620 is likely to exaggerate the long-term impact of inflation, while an index covering the period 1620–1650 or 1620–1700 may understate the long-term impact of inflation.

Here again, there is no clear guide to demarcating trends. In seeking to identify long-term trends, we must avoid measurements from "trough to peak"—exaggerating rates of growth—or from "peak to trough"— exaggerating rates of decline. This advice is difficult to follow when we do not know the timing of cyclical peaks and troughs, but it is still worth remembering. What we need to avoid is a statement like the following (Liang 1982, 52–53):

> The ascendancy of Tientsin as the trade and commercial capital of North China owed much to an expanded trade hinterland provided by five trunk railway lines. Between 1900 and 1912, the real value of Tientsin's export trade jumped more than eightfold and its share in the national total of export-import trade rose from 1.3% to over 6%.

While railways surely stimulated the development of Tientsin, the selection of 1900, a year in which the current value of the city's import-export trade plunged by 80 percent on account of the Boxer Uprising and subsequent international military expedition into North China, could hardly be more inappropriate. If the base of comparison is shifted to 1899, we find that Tientsin's share in China's export-import trade did indeed rise, but only from 5.45 percent (1899) to "over 6" percent thirteen years later (Hsiao 1974, 23, 175)—a much different outcome from that implied by Liang's thoroughly misleading comparison.

When we present statistical comparisons over a period of time, we are essentially assuming that the time span involved is in some sense "homogeneous," to use Kuznets's term. If not, the comparison implied by the data may lose its meaning. Even though chronology may be dictated by availability of data, it behooves us to think carefully about the suitability of time spans covered in statistical comparisons—especially those offered in our own work. In short-term comparisons, seasonal variation requires attention. Even a modern industrial economy experiences regular and predictable seasonal variations: in the United States, unusually large numbers of job seekers appear when the school year ends in June, and demand for part-time workers peaks before Christmas. Published data on employment, unemployment, and inventories are often "seasonally adjusted" to reflect these patterns (see Floud 1973, 89–90, 108–110). Historians studying economies dominated by agriculture must not overlook the far larger seasonal variations of prices, wages, labor supply and demand typical of any agrarian economy. And since weather fluctuations regularly produce large changes in annual harvests and—given the inelasticity of both demand and supply typical of markets for farm products—even bigger fluctuations in prices of farm goods, most societies that we study experience sharp fluctuations in prices, incomes, food supply, and many other variables. It is all too easy for the modern researcher, accustomed to the nonseasonal life typified by the American supermarket, to misread the wide cyclical fluctuations embodied in any unregulated farm economy as indicative of long-term trends.

ECONOMIC DATA FOR HISTORICAL RESEARCH

Suppose now that you have some quantitative data and also some idea about how to organize them to support a nascent research hypothesis. What next? Comparison of the requirements of establishing and verifying economic trends—homogeneity, consistency, persistence, unidirectional change, and so on—with the reality of limited, fragmented, error-ridden, unreliable, and distorted source materials may encourage the feeling that "the data just aren't there."

But wait! Generations of historians have not hesitated to write about economic trends without careful and systematic attention to economic data. A group of "new economic historians," focusing their attention on the economies of North America and Great Britain, has demonstrated that better, fuller results and sounder interpretations are often available when we combine research using traditional sources with diligent mining of available data, which are *always* deficient.

Before succumbing to the defeatist view that your data are uniquely defective, consider the implication of Nicholas Crafts's study (1985) claiming that average annual growth of British per capita income between 1801 and 1831 should be reduced from the earlier result of 1.6 percent obtained by Phyllis Deane and W. A. Cole (1967) to a much lower figure of 0.5 percent, implying that per capita incomes rose by 16 rather than 61 percent during 1801–31.[10] If British historians cannot yet determine whether industry and commerce grew slower (Deane and Cole) or faster (Crafts) or whether agriculture grew much faster (Deane and Cole) or much slower (Crafts) during 1760–80 than during 1700–60, perhaps

10. Note how the passage of time translates small differences in rates of change into very significant disparities.

their data, which have supported hundreds of studies in what McCloskey calls "econometric history," are no better than yours.

Indeed, we should abandon the notion, dispensed by glib doctors of economics on the evening news, that precise and accurate economic data exist even for advanced economies that employ veritable armies of specialized economic statisticians. Consider relatively simple concepts, neglecting the thorny complexities of "national product" or "capital stock." What is the rate of unemployment? The answer is based on questions asked of a (presumably representative) sample of respondents. Some respondents work part-time but desire full-time jobs; some are satisfied with part-time work; some claim to be unemployed but work part- or full-time in the underground or "black" economy. Which of these people is fully employed? With these and other uncertainties, it makes little sense to attach much significance to small monthly variations in reported rates of unemployment. Yet even though reported unemployment of 6 percent need not mean that 6 percent of the labor force (another tricky concept) is unemployed, it undoubtedly signifies that joblessness is less prevalent than when the same survey methods yield an unemployment rate of 10 or 12 percent.

If short-term variations can be problematic, long-term changes are even more difficult to pin down because institutions take on other forms. In the 1930s unemployed workers with no savings could find work, find charity, or go hungry. In the 1990s unemployed workers are sometimes prevented from finding work by laws designed to protect them (minimum wage, social security, workmen's compensation, etc.); they also have access to unemployment compensation and welfare programs that hardly existed sixty years ago. What rate of unemployment would result from the surveys carried out by our economic statisticians if social legislation and "safety net" programs did not exist? Christina Romer (1986a, 1986b) uses evidence about measurement practices to challenge the outcome of the "Keynesian revolution" in U.S. macroeconomic policy, arguing that "the stabilization of the unemployment rate between the pre-1930 and post-1948 eras is an artifact of improvements in data collection procedures" (1986b, 1).

Even if we ignore obstacles arising from inadequate data or institutional change, precise measurement is often impossible because of what economists call the "index-number problem." The difficulty quickly becomes evident when we seek to determine the rate of British industrial growth during the industrial revolution. Since some industries (cotton textiles) grew much faster than others (leather goods), computation of an overall growth rate requires some form of arithmetic weighting with which to combine the growth rates of different industries into a single overall total. One sensible approach is to construct weights on the basis of the relative importance of different industries as measured by their shares in total output. But these shares change substantially over time. In Britain, the share of cotton textiles rose from 3 to 22 percent of industrial output between 1770 and 1831, while the share of leather declined from 22 to 9 percent during the same period (Crafts 1985, 17). Using 1770 output shares will give a much lower weight to the dynamic textile sector and a higher weight to the slow-growing leather industry than if we employ 1831 output shares to construct our weights. Since cotton textiles grew faster than leather goods, it is easy to see that weights based on 1770 shares will produce a much lower growth rate for industrial production than weights drawn from 1831 shares. Neither growth rate is "correct." We must accept the reality that sensible measures of a single quantity will produce not a single figure, but a range of equally significant results. Here is the essence of the index-number problem.

Measurement of price change encounters the same difficulty. Unless all prices rise or fall together, with no change in the relative price of different commodities, we cannot construct an index to measure the extent of inflation or deflation without a system of weights to reflect the relative importance of food, fuel, clothing, and other categories of expenditure. To calculate an index of consumer prices, we sensibly look to the structure of household budgets for the required weights: if consumers spend 1.5 percent of their incomes on beef and 13.3 percent on clothing, let .015 and .133 serve as the weights attached to the price of beef and clothing in our calculation of overall price change. Here again, ambiguity reigns. Do we use budgets for urban or rural households? for rich or poor? for the beginning of our period or the end? There is no correct answer and, as before, no exact measurement.

These examples lead to the uncomfortable conclusion that precise measurement of economic magnitudes is often unattainable even with the best possible data. The index-number problem arises whenever we seek to measure the extent of output growth or price change over time. It also pops up when we compare living standards between nations or regions: do we use Brazilian or American prices to compare the quantity of goods and services consumed by residents of Rio and New York?

Economists have discovered regularities in the ranges of results arising from index-number calculations. If we seek to measure the long-term

growth of industrializing economies, we expect growth rates to be higher
if we use prices drawn from the early years of our time period to calculate the growth of output value. This phenomenon, known as the Gerschenkron effect, arises because the relative prices of goods whose production grows rapidly tend to decline.[11] Early prices give high weights
to fast-growing segments of the economy (e.g., cotton textiles in Britain
during 1770–1831), thus generating high growth rates. Since the relative price of cotton goods declined sharply during Britain's industrial revolution (a typical illustration of the Gerschenkron effect), we expect output indexes based on 1831 prices to grow more slowly than indexes based
on eighteenth-century prices, because the use of late prices lowers the statistical weight attached to cotton textiles and other fast-growing segments
of the economy. A comparison of output levels in advanced and underdeveloped economies that uses rich-country prices normally reduces the
international output gap by applying the high (often subsidized) agricultural prices typical of developed economies to the large farm sector
of the poorer nations.

Realization that economic data routinely used by historians and by
policymakers in governments or international agencies may contain errors and distortions and that, in any case, calculations based on these
data often encounter index-number problems, should convince us that
perfection, or anything close to it, is not a prerequisite of quantitative
historical research. This knowledge, however, cannot relieve us of the
obligation to identify and respond to the shortcomings of our own materials. We desire to collect and apply data that are free of bias, that bear
on the problems and hypotheses with which we are engaged, and that
incorporate margins of error that are small relative to our proposed conclusions. Once again, note that these requirements are not purely technical. To decide whether, and if so, how, certain data can be useful and
relevant to the issues at hand is a matter that calls above all for sound
judgment.

The issue of "bias" itself in its statistical sense has a much broader
meaning than the normal usage. To begin with, we must question the
judgment, whether couched in generalities or embodied in quantitative
indications, of observers who have a vested interest in one side of an argument. We cannot easily accept the testimony of revolutionaries who
insist that the people are worse off, of government supporters who claim

---

11. Named after Alexander Gerschenkron, who described this phenomenon in a study
of Soviet machinery prices (1951).

that the same people are better off, of taxpayers who insist that taxes are too high, of buyers (or sellers) who complain that prices have risen (or fallen) precipitously, and so on. A properly skeptical investigator will have little difficulty in identifying and discounting self-interested testimony of this type.

Matters become more complicated as witnesses become more sophisticated. Consider Han-seng Chen's study of prewar tobacco cultivation in China, which concludes that (1939, 85):

> whatever uncompensated surplus labor is spent on American seed tobacco only goes as profit to foreign financial capital or widens the opportunity for exploitation by the Chinese landlords, merchants and usurers. Often the tobacco cultivators have lost more than they can possibly gain. The introduction of this new crop has certainly reduced the standard of living among the peasantry of the tobacco regions in China.

Much of Chen's analysis is based on a sample of "two representative villages in each of the three tobacco regions" (1939, 17). But given Chen's strong views, can we accept the "representativeness" of the chosen villages? If a proposed research site had produced unexpected evidence of rising household income, might the investigators have selected a more "representative" site? In fact, data samples are often loaded with observations that, by design or accident, push the outcome in some specific direction. The lesson here is simple: DON'T ASSUME YOUR VIEW IS CORRECT. Be prepared for defeat at the hands of the data. Think twice and thrice before you discard inconvenient scraps of evidence as mistaken or irrelevant. Beware the thought "atypical," which assumes knowledge of what is typical.

Sample bias need not result from intentional action on the investigator's part. Selection of convenient research sites (near transport centers, for example) may be enough to push results askew. Or, as is common with fiscally related data, the original compiler may have faced severe problems of deceptive reporting from would-be tax avoiders. Consider the following illustration from my own work (Rawski 1989, 287):

> Between 1929 and 1933, John L. Buck, an American economist teaching at the University of Nanking, collected large quantities of data on China's farm economy by sending his students to study the local economies of their native areas. The result was a large sample of economic conditions that covered substantial regions of rural China. One of the questions asked by Buck's interviewers concerned recent changes in living standards. . . . Only one area, the winter wheat and millet region of northern Shensi, produced negative reports. . . . Even with Shensi included, more than 80 percent of reporting localities noted rising standards of living.

But Barry Naughton observes that the farms whose owners responded to this query were nearly twice as large as the average for all farms surveyed by Buck. What I present as a (presumably random) survey of a "large" number of farms is thus, for Naughton, a biased investigation showing that a data sample taken from "the top quarter of Chinese farmers [by farm size] reported rising standards of living." Possible explanations of this outcome include rising living standards (my suggestion), a deteriorating income distribution (i.e., income concentration in the hands of the same large farms that dominate the sample) with average incomes moving in either direction, or what Naughton sees as most likely, a statistical quirk "in which it is specifically the changes that the upper section has experienced to raise their [farm size, presumably associated positively with their] incomes that places them in the sample group covered."[12]

Do not make the mistake of discarding data simply because they appear biased. If your hypotheses generate implications that run counter to the inherent sample bias, flawed data may be particularly valuable. The Buck survey, for example, showing that even large farms (no doubt including a good share of successful operators enjoying upward socioeconomic mobility) reported falling living standards in Shensi, points strongly toward declining economic welfare as a general phenomenon there. Where sample bias slants the results in the direction of desired inferences, the value of the biased results is weakened, but not entirely destroyed. Note that rising living standards are (one of several outcomes) consistent with the results of the (biased) Buck sample. Our goal is to search out data that can be shown to be consistent with only one of two or more competing hypotheses. Our evaluation of implications drawn from the data depends significantly upon the direction and extent of bias that we perceive. It is therefore essential to scrutinize data for indication of bias and, when possible, to use alternate sources that may help us identify deviations from the "typical" or "representative" samples that we seek.

What is meant by "scrutinizing data"? We find a source containing quantitative information about variables that seem relevant to our re-

---

12. Quotation from unpublished material provided by Naughton; data on farm size from Buck (1937a, 437). To elaborate Naughton's point: suppose there are 300 identical farms and that random changes raise income and farm size for 100 households, lower income and farm size for 100, and leave income and farm size unchanged for the final group of 100. A subsequent survey dominated by larger farms will produce a sample in which most respondents report rising income even though the average has not changed.

search. What do we do next? One essential step is to look very carefully at the new source. Do the data seem reasonable? Are there internal contradictions? Do changes from month to month or from year to year fit with what we know of such things? Do simple manipulations (that divide crop output by area and compare it with reported yield) produce glaring inconsistencies? Do successive editions or issues of the same source repeat the same figures, or do the tables contain unexplained changes? The main methodological ingredients at this stage are no more than attention to detail and, above all, experience, which gives the researcher a "feel" for whether data seem to have been prepared by a careful analyst (a fellow connoisseur of statistics) or thrown together willy-nilly.[13]

Consider the data for grain crops in China's Shansi province from 1914 to 1918 (see Table 1). Can we give credence to huge percentage changes in rice acreage between 1914–15 and 1915–16? Is there reason to anticipate a near doubling of rice yields between 1914 and 1918? Was 1914 a particularly poor year for Shansi rice, or 1918 an especially good one (note our immediate desire for qualitative information to check the data)? Rice is a minor crop in Shansi, and weak data here may not be important. But the data for wheat, the staple food crop, are equally dubious. Unless 1918 is a famine year (again, qualitative data needed), can we credit the possibility of a decline of more than two-thirds in wheat output between 1916 and 1918 with no major shift in acreage? What do these output figures imply for per capita wheat supplies? No change of this magnitude could have passed without extensive comment from Chinese and foreign observers.

In addition to checking qualitative information for corroboration, we can learn much by breaking statistics into their component parts and by comparing alternative sources of data. Estimates by several authors place the cumulative growth of Chinese foodgrain output between 1914–18 and 1931–36 within a relatively narrow range of 7–18 percent, indicating annual growth of about 0.5–1.0 percent (Perkins 1969, 289; Yeh 1979, 127; Hsü 1983, 339). With population expanding at about the same rate, are we justified in concluding that per capita output of foodgrains showed no substantial change during the decades between the two world wars? This inference could be dangerous.

If we examine provincial estimates of rice output presented by two

---

13. Butler, Heckman, and Payner 1989 provide an extended example of this process.

TABLE I
GRAIN CROPS IN SHANSI PROVINCE, 1914–18

	Ordinary Rice			Glutinous Rice			Wheat		
	Area[a]	Output[b]	Yield[c]	Area	Output	Yield	Area	Output	Yield
1914	4,642	2,225	48	826	370	41	12,611	15,117	110
1915	2,164	1,520	65	246	164	61	...[d]	...	...
1916	4,626	3,389	68	723	495	63	13,450	36,570	251
1918	3,928	3,387	80	650	538	76	11,853	11,571	90

SOURCE: Hsü 1983, 13.
[a]Units of sown area are in 1,000 *shih mou*; [b]output is in thousand *shih tan*; [c]yield is in *shih chin* per *shih mou*; [d] . . . indicates missing data.

TABLE 2   ESTIMATES OF CHINESE PROVINCIAL
RICE OUTPUT, 1914–18 AND 1931–37

Province	1914–18 Output		1931–37 Output			
	Kiangsu = 100		Kiangsu = 100		1914–18 = 100	
	Perkins	Hsü	Perkins	Hsü	Perkins	Hsü
Kiangsu	100.0	100.0	100.0	100.0	98.8	267.4
Chekiang	152.7	115.5	123.0	84.6	79.6	196.1
Anhwei	104.4	85.5	93.5	38.9	88.4	121.7
Hupeh	119.5	170.2	120.9	65.6	100.0	103.1
Hunan	165.3	140.4	154.3	98.0	92.3	186.8
Kiangsi	119.2	239.0	87.0	69.4	72.2	77.7
Kwangtung	179.3	n.a.	181.4	154.4	100.0	n.a.
Szechwan	215.6	n.a.	218.1	134.0		100.0

SOURCES: Perkins 1969, 276; Hsü 1983, 23–54, 339.
   Rice output from the Hsü compendium is the sum of separate figures for ordinary and glutinous rice. In calculating average output from Hsü's data, I omit all years for which production figures for either or both varieties are missing, or for which Hsü identifies the data as incomplete or dubious.
   Growth of average annual rice output in the first six provinces from 1914–18 to 1931–37 was –12%, according to Perkins, and +22%, according to Hsü. Output from the first six provinces as share of estimated national total for 1914–18 was 54% according to Perkins and 34% according to Hsü. That for 1931–37 was 50% according to Perkins and 49% according to Hsü.

authors, Dwight Perkins and Hsü Tao-fu, and summarized in Table 2, we encounter a morass of contradictions. Was Szechwan's average rice harvest during 1931–37 more than double (Perkins) or only one-third larger (Hsü) than Kiangsu's? Was Anhwei's harvest similar to (Perkins) or only a small fraction (Hsü) of Kiangsu's? Did Kiangsu's rice crop zoom upward between 1914–18 and 1931–37 with an increase of 167 percent (Hsü) or drift marginally downward (Perkins)? Did Chekiang nearly double its harvest over the same period (Hsü) or experience a substantial decline (Perkins)? Perkins finds that rice output in six major producing provinces slipped by 12 percent between 1914–18 and 1931–37. Hsü's data indicate an increase of 22 percent in average rice production for the same provinces. Perkins's data indicate that the share of the six provinces in national rice production fell from 54 to 50 percent between 1914–18 and 1931–37; Hsü's show the share of the same provinces jumping from 34 to 49 percent of the national total in the same period. Without further research to sort out the provincial figures (and possibly even with such an effort), these data simply cannot tell us whether the output of rice (or any other major crop) was higher, lower, or about the same in 1931–36 as in 1914–18.

If your source passes the "taste test" of close scrutiny, the next essential task is what economists call "cleaning up" the data. Any collection of data is beset with minor problems. The figure for this year or that month is missing. The series starts out in *taels* but continues in dollars. The measure of weight changes from pounds to kilograms. The entry for March 1924 is an obvious misprint. There are two figures given for February 1921. And so on. To bring the data recorded in your source to a form suitable for graphing or statistical analysis requires what amounts to a series of *assumptions,* which may be large or small, important or trivial. Two key points to remember here are first, keep careful note of all assumptions from the start; and second, beware of inadvertently building conclusions in the form of assumptions.

Careful record-keeping is absolutely essential to any quantitative work. Any researcher with a quantitative bent can regale listeners with tales of feckless Dr. X or Professor Y whose results *cannot be recalculated* because of unspecified assumptions or shoddy procedures (the reader cannot easily distinguish between the two). To avoid identification as the X or Y of future generations, be thorough and precise. Numbers without attribution are like quotations without sources. As any practitioner who has spent long nights reconstructing forgotten calculations must know, you will be the first and foremost victim of your own sloppy practice.

Accurate information about assumptions large and small is crucial because of the logic of quantitative research. Since the evidence is always defective, the argument must run as follows:

> If I assume A, B, C, D, all seemingly reasonable and unlikely to bias the data toward supporting my hypothesis, then my data can be applied to the question at hand. Since they then are consistent with my view and not with the competing approach, I conclude that these particular data support my view.

The test of this logic comes when you (or someone else) bends the assumptions to see whether this maneuver changes the conclusions, as follows:

> Rawski has assumed A, B, C, D and used the resulting data to support his case for proposition P. Now A, B, C, D are not unreasonable assumptions, but he could have assumed instead E, F, G, and H, which are no less reasonable than A, B, C, D. Do the data, shaped with these assumptions, fit proposition P as well?

If the argument passes the test of revised assumptions, we say it is "robust," meaning that its sense is intact despite a reasonable magnitude of error. "Sensitivity analysis" is another term used to describe this type of query, which occupies a deservedly important position in quantitative research of all types. If you fail to specify assumptions, you or anyone else may find it difficult or impossible to determine whether or not the analysis is highly sensitive to certain errors or, what amounts to the same thing, whether small changes in assumptions will produce big changes in results. Every quantitative researcher has embarked on promising lines of argument that were destroyed by this type of testing. A friend is someone who detects the vulnerable segment of the argument before your research is delivered to the wolves in the employ of editors and publishers.

Historians unfamiliar with quantitative research complain that this type of scholarship is no more than a tissue of assumptions, with results predetermined before pencil meets paper. Nothing could be further from the truth. Assumptions there are, all laid out for the reader's scrutiny and critical evaluation, and precisely to show that they do *not* control the conclusions. The quantitative researcher invites critics to show that replacement of an assumption that is crucial to producing the advertised results by an equally reasonable variant generates different conclusions. If this can be done, the analysis is shown to lack "robustness" and the conclusions lose their force.

There are many famous examples of close ties between assumptions and conclusions. Malthusians feared that population would outrun resources. And if population is assumed to grow *geometrically* (i.e., increasing by a constant *percentage* each year) and resources *arithmetically* (i.e., by a fixed *amount* each year), disaster is inevitable, BY ASSUMPTION. More recently, the authors of *The Limits to Growth* (Meadows et al. 1972) produced comparable results from intricate computer simulations. In both cases, assumptions guaranteed that population would outrun production before the race commenced.

Let us consider a more complex illustration of the power of assumption, this one concerning the evolution of cotton textile handicrafts in nineteenth- and early twentieth-century China. Handicraft output was dispersed in millions of farm households; obviously, no comprehensive output data exist. Even so, we know how much cotton is required to produce a bale of factory or handicraft yarn and how much yarn is needed to produce a bolt of factory or handicraft cloth. Armed with these "input-output coefficients" (i.e., figures telling how much cotton, labor, electricity, machine time, etc., is required to produce one bale of yarn or one unit of any other product), we can use data on the size of China's cotton harvest, factory output of yarn and cloth, and international trade in cotton and yarn to calculate approximately what output of handicraft yarn and cloth *must have been*. The arithmetic is complex, but the idea is simple. Domestic cotton production minus cotton exports plus cotton imports gives the domestic supply of cotton. Subtract the amount needed to produce factory yarn, make allowance for wastage and other uses of cotton (for padded clothing), and you have an estimate of the cotton available for handicraft spinning. Apply the relevant input-output coefficient, and you have an estimate of handicraft yarn output. A similar calculation of domestic yarn supply less yarn consumed in producing factory cloth yields yarn supply for handloom weaving, which is easily converted to an estimate of handicraft cloth output. The results of such calculations appear in part B of Table 3.

Bruce Reynolds studied the history of cotton textile handicrafts from another perspective. He began by *assuming* that annual per capita consumption of cotton cloth held steady at 5.8 square yards between 1875 and 1931 (1975, 58). Starting from this fixed point, he used input-output data, production estimates for factory yarn and cloth, and figures for China's international trade in yarn and cloth to derive his own estimates of handicraft production of yarn and cloth. The results of his calculations appear in part A of Table 3. Both sets of estimates are presented in terms of value added, or contribution to national product.

Comparison of parts A and B shows that the history of handicraft activity implicit in the two sets of calculations is very different. Both calculations show that the growth of manufacturing (and of imports of manufactured textiles from abroad) affected handicraft spinning more than weaving. But version B indicates an important revival of handicraft spinning in the 1910–20 decade; Reynolds finds no evidence of this. Reynolds depicts a steep decline for handicraft yarn, which ends up at about 25 percent of its initial output level; the alternate figures place the overall decline at less than 50 percent of the initial output level. Reynolds finds the terminal output total for handicrafts about 20 percent less than the 1875 figure; the alternate data show an increase of about 30 percent over the same fifty-year period.

Just as readers wish to scrutinize sources and references when literary historians clash over, say, the role of Germany's business elite in Hitler's rise to power, careful review of assumptions and methods is essential when quantitative research produces differences of the sort visible in Table 3. We need to know what "drives" the calculations to their

TABLE 3   ALTERNATIVE ESTIMATES OF VALUE
ADDED IN CHINESE COTTON TEXTILES,
1870S–1930S (MILLION 1933 YUAN)

	Cotton Yarn		Cotton Cloth		Totals		
	F[a]	H	F	H	F	H	Sum
A. Reynolds							
1875	0	39.74	0	65.48	0	105.22	105.22
1905	9.13	24.84	1.24	79.24	10.37	104.08	114.45
1919	28.71	20.70	7.27	71.92	35.98	92.62	128.60
1931	95.26	10.76	38.50	72.60	133.76	83.36	217.12
B. Alternative							
1871–80	0	40.57	0	64.48	0	105.05	105.05
1901–10	13.05	19.87	1.10	74.00	14.15	93.87	108.02
1921–23	61.33	52.16	14.26	116.96	75.59	169.12	244.71
1931–33	113.54	22.36	44.16	115.60	157.70	137.96	295.66

SOURCES: Part A—physical output figures from Reynolds 1974, 6. Part B—alternative figures compiled (with some modifications and interpolations) from physical output and trade data reported in Feuerwerker 1978; Kraus 1980; and Hsiao 1974. Physical output totals are converted to value added using 1933 prices and rates of value added from Liu and Yeh 1965, 448, 449, 480, 522 and Chao 1977, 234.
[a]F and H represent Factory and Handicraft production.

different conclusions. In other words, what are the key assumptions? Essentially, we must "take apart" each set of calculations.

Reynolds's results are "driven" or "determined" by the key assumption that per capita consumption of cotton textiles did not change between 1875 and 1931. Since production of factory yarn and cloth is taken from the relatively reliable (everyone agrees on this) figures available from other sources, any error in the assumption of constant per capita consumption will translate into a comparable error in the results for craft output. If per capita consumption actually rose, Reynolds's estimates will understate actual trends in production of handicraft yarn or cloth; if per capita consumption fell, Reynolds's method will exaggerate handicraft performance. But without reliable independent estimates of handicraft yarn or cloth output (otherwise we could abandon indirect methods), how can we check Reynolds's assumption?

One possibility is to consider the implications of his results for cotton requirements. Using the input-output figures mentioned above, we can calculate cotton requirements for Reynolds's menu of factory and craft output in each year. Adjust for China's international trade in cotton and for cotton wadding, and we obtain figures for what China's cotton harvest "must have been"—the cotton gospel according to Reynolds. We then compare the cotton harvest implicit in Reynolds's analysis with other estimates (Rawski 1989, 100—all in piculs, each 133.3 lbs.):

AUTHOR (date of estimate)	(millions of piculs)
Reynolds (1931)	7.9
Kraus (1931)	12.9
Perkins (1931–37)	15.6
Liu and Yeh (1933)	15.7
Feuerwerker (1931–36)	13.4
Hsü (1933)	11.4–15.9
Chao (1923–36)	11.0–19.9

We see from this comparison that Reynolds's results imply a supply of cotton far lower than what emerges from any of several available estimates of the cotton harvest during the 1930s. This suggests that Reynolds's calculations may understate the volume of craft textile production during the 1930s, and that his assumption of constant per capita cloth consumption may be seriously mistaken. Further support for this view comes from the observation of H. D. Fong, a well informed Chinese economist writing during the 1930s, that available figures generally underestimated China's total cotton harvest (1932, 1:chap. 2).

The alternative figures indicate a large increase in per capita consumption of cotton cloth, suggesting that Reynolds's whole procedure is gravely flawed and supporting an alternate hypothesis of rising per capita output in prewar China (see below on this). But the calculated increase in per capita cloth consumption—50 percent—is suspiciously large, and its timing is also odd (the increase occurs between 1901–10 and 1921–23). These results, too, deserve careful scrutiny. They are obviously "driven" by estimates of the cotton harvest. Even for the 1930s, when many government and private agencies, foreign as well as Chinese, made great efforts to produce accurate estimates of cotton output, the figures are by no means exact. A glance at the estimates for 1933, shown above, suggests a range of 13.6 million piculs plus or minus 2.2 million, an error margin of nearly 20 percent on either side of the output estimate. For 1901–1910 and especially for 1871–1880, the error margin must be far larger, perhaps 40 percent on either side of a point estimate. If our flimsy estimates of cotton output for 1871–80 and 1901–10 happen to *understate* the cotton harvest, then the distinctive conclusions of the figures in part B, including the implication of sharply rising per capita consumption of cotton cloth, may collapse.

METHODOLOGICAL ILLUSTRATIONS: ECONOMIC TRENDS IN EARLY TWENTIETH-CENTURY CHINA

I conclude this chapter by discussing three topics that have arisen in my own study of China's economy in the early twentieth century. I present these matters not as arguments intended to convince but as illustrations of applying economic methods to the study of historical trends.

THE FATE OF TRADITIONAL JUNK TRANSPORT

Information about trends in traffic by traditional sailing vessels (junks) is an important ingredient in any overall evaluation of China's prewar economy.[14] We have reasonably accurate information about trends in the development of modern transport modes, but without comparable figures for junk transport (by far the largest segment of traditional transport activity) we cannot tell whether rapidly growing freight carriage by railways and steamships represents *trade creation*—an important sign of commercialization and/or economic expansion—or *trade diversion*—mere replacement of old technology with new in transportation, and entirely consistent with economic stagnation or decline. We have some information about changes in the volume of junk traffic (omitted here: the figures show the volume of junk traffic into and out of several major ports increasing at modest, and occasionally not so modest, rates during the 1910s and 1920s), but not a great deal. The question is, how can we ascertain, at least in a general sense, what happened to junk traffic during the prewar decades in the absence of detailed port records or ship registry information?

What can we learn from simple theory? We attempt to exploit the systematic link between changes in the level of production (in this case, of junk-borne transport services) and the level of capital formation (construction of new junks). Wooden sailing vessels have long service lives. A 1941 survey noted that many older vessels remained in use even though their cargo capacity declined unless periodic repairs were made; the survey vessels included four craft over forty-five years old, of which one was

14. This section is based on Rawski (1989, chap. 4).

reportedly built sixty years earlier (*Chûshi* 1943, 25–27). Under these circumstances, a decline in the volume of junk traffic should create a surplus of equipment. Since idle junks can be kept in readiness while stored in or alongside local waterways, we should expect a backlog of idle vessels to sharply erode the demand for new ships. With stagnant or declining traffic, trade should be dominated by old equipment. This is exactly what occurred on the Liao River in Manchuria, where diversion of riverine traffic to the railways prompted observers to note that "there are no new ships built for the river and [the] majority of the ships now being used are those constructed more than ten years ago" (*Manchuria* 1932, 284).

Information about boat building in the Yangtze delta (including Shanghai), however, shows that the industry continued to thrive throughout the prewar period. The persistence of demand for new junks supports the view that junk traffic expanded despite unrestricted competition from new carriers. The 1941 survey data for Soochow reveal an average age of nineteen and a median of sixteen years for the ships studied; fourteen of thirty-six ships were less than ten years old. Furthermore, the 1941 report indicates that the junks enumerated in the survey were built at shipyards throughout the delta area, including Shanghai and other centers of motorized water traffic (*Chûshi* 1943, 4, 26–27). Another study lists over twenty places near Shanghai and along both banks of the Yangtze in the delta region where junkyards continued to operate after 1940 despite a precipitous decline in junk traffic after Japan's occupation of the lower Yangtze region ("Survey" 1941; *Shina* 1944).

Evidence of the continued vigor of the junk construction industry, which prompted comment on the "never-ceasing demand of the native shipwrights" for the products of Kiangsi's timber industry, confirms the view that transport activity by traditional sailing craft did not decline prior to the Pacific War even in the Yangtze delta area where junk transport faced unlimited competition from every form of mechanized vehicle (Wright 1980 [1920], 32). The argument here rests on an obvious link between production and investment that hardly deserves the sobriquet of "theory," and on the usual assumption that participants in the shipping sector are motivated by self-interest (shippers do not abandon useful vessels in the absence of significant technological change; shipyards do not continue to operate if sales volume and price plummet). There is a possibly tricky implicit assumption about structure: if the impact of steamship competition forces junks into new types of operations for which older craft were ill-suited, it might make sense to build many new boats even with falling business and a surplus of old-style equipment (consider the contemporary U.S. textile industry as an example of on-going new investment cum declining business). However, the main technological change in the prewar junk industry involved substitution of cloth sails for sails made of reed matting—an innovation that did not require new boats.

If evidence from boat building convinces us that junk traffic *did not decline* prior to 1937, how can we test the stronger proposition that junk shipping *actually increased* despite competition on many routes from steamships, motor launches, railways, and trucks? Fortunately, we have some data showing that the junk trade fared well in competition with rail, steamship, and cart traffic in delivering cotton to the major textile center of Tientsin. This helpful information may be supplemented by estimates of trends in the volume of wheat arriving at Shanghai by junk. We proceed as follows:

Wheat arriving by junk=[1] Wheat required by Shanghai flour mills
  −[2] Import of wheat into Shanghai from abroad
  −[3] Maritime customs inflow of domestic wheat carried by steamships into Shanghai
  +[4] Maritime customs exports of wheat from Shanghai (to foreign or Chinese ports)
  −[5] Inflow of domestic wheat into Shanghai by rail

Other than any defects in data for items [1] through [5], the main weakness of this approach is the possibility of understating the volume of wheat carried by junk (but not necessarily its rate of growth) through omission of possible junk-borne shipments out of Shanghai and through the assumption that all wheat arrivals were destined for the city's modern flour mills. We ignore possible arrivals by cart or pack animal, which are surely trivial.

The results of our calculation, presented in Table 4 (note the careful enumeration of assumptions), show that estimated arrival of wheat by junk increased from a maximum (assuming no rail shipment of wheat into Shanghai) of 139,000 tons in 1914 to 233,000 tons in 1932, 163,000 tons in 1933, and 337,000 tons in 1934. These results surely understate the growth of junk shipments, perhaps by a large margin, because we have no figure for railway shipments of wheat in 1914.

We conclude that sailing craft delivered much larger quantities of wheat to Shanghai in the 1930s than two decades earlier. The average of 244,000 tons for 1932–34 derived from Table 4 is *75 percent* above the (excessive) figure of 139,000 tons obtained for 1914. Any rail ship-

TABLE 4   SOURCES OF WHEAT SUPPLY FOR
SHANGHAI FLOUR MILLS, 1914–34

	1914	1932	1933	1934
Shanghai flour output (10,000 bags)	496	2,896	3,368	3,067
[1] Wheat required by mills (1,000 metric tons)	161	938	1,091	994
[2] Net import from abroad (1,000 metric tons)	0	666	858	465
[3] Customs inflow from Chinese ports (1,000 metric tons)	23	3	19	59
[4] Maritime customs exports to all ports (1,000 metric tons)	1	16	25	0
[5] Wheat arrival by railway (1,000 metric tons)	?	52	76	133
Residual: junk shipments (1,000 metric tons) [1]–[2]–[3]+[4]–[5]	139–?	233	163	337

SOURCES: [1] Wheat requirements are based on reported flour sales (assumed identical with flour production) by Shanghai mills. Annual data for 1914–36 appear in *Chiu Chung-kuo* 1966, 52. The missing figure for 1934 is filled in by linear interpolation. These data are in bags of 49–50 pounds (May 1924 switched from 50 to 49). Each bag of flour requires 53.57 catties of wheat (137). With this information, we can convert flour sales (assumed to equal output) to wheat requirements as shown in line [1] (ignoring differences in the conversion rate of Chinese and foreign wheat). We ignore possible differences between wheat requirements and wheat arrivals caused by changes in Shanghai wheat inventories.

[2] Shanghai imports of wheat from abroad are reported in *Chiu Chung-kuo*, 116–117, but with major unexplained differences from the maritime customs figures from 1933 on; I assume these are errors—if not, our argument will be strengthened. There are no imports in 1914. For 1932–34 I use the largest import figures available to me (larger imports produce smaller residual estimates of junk traffic): for 1932 and 1933, China 1933, 3:229; for 1934, Ch'en 1936, tb. 7 (note that in this table Ch'en also gives a smaller import total of 408,000 tons).

[3] Wheat inflow by steam or motor vessel: maritime customs imports from domestic ports reported for 1914 in China 1914, 3:752; for 1932–34 see *Shang-hai* 1935, 14.

[4] Original exports to Chinese or foreign ports as reported by the maritime customs: for 1914, China 1914, 3:772; for 1932–34 see *Shang-hai* 1935, 14.

[5] Wheat arriving by rail: for 1932–34, based on *Shang-hai* 1935, 19. The figure for 1932 excludes the four months of February through April; I therefore multiply the amount given in the source by 4/3; figure for 1934 is double the amount shown in the source, which covers only the first six months of the year.

ments of wheat to Shanghai in 1914 would increase this difference. Indeed, if we accept the Chinese Native Customs figures for 1914, which report junk-borne wheat imports into the city of only 24,000 tons (implying a residual inflow by rail of 115,000 tons—surely not implausible), then our figures show that average junk-borne wheat imports into Shanghai during 1932–34 were *exactly ten times* the amount observed in 1914 (China 1914, 3:768).

Whether the volume of wheat shipped by junk into Shanghai increased by 75 percent or by 900 percent between 1914 and 1932–34 is not clear. What is clear is that even with assumptions (no wheat shipped into Shanghai by rail in 1914; using the highest available figure for wheat imports in 1932–34) that produce high junk-trade figures for an early year and low figures for later years, our calculations show an increasing volume of junk traffic into the port of Shanghai during the prewar decades.[15]

The tactic of demonstrating one's assertion to be valid even under assumptions that "stack the deck" against the proposed conclusion is commonly used in economics. In a world of imperfect data, we can never make a convincing case for arguments that require fine quantitative distinctions that may be obliterated by measurement error. If, however, our conclusion is so striking that it emerges even from data that are skewed in ways that suppress the very trend we seek to establish, even a skeptical audience will be impressed. The art of manipulating assumptions involves delicate balance: we must convince critical readers that any bias in the data will act to impede, rather than enhance our assertions, but avoid swamping genuine historical trends in a tide of hostile assumptions.

TOBACCO CULTIVATION IN NORTH CHINA

The study by Han-seng Chen, cited above, is a weak one from the technical point of view. the story told in the text is often somewhat different from the story as read from the tables (economists tend to read the tables first to discover what happened, then check the text to see what the author has to say). Never mind. Chen's efforts to calculate costs and profits make me yearn for the sweet harmony of fingernails across black boards.[16] Never mind. Chen concludes that introducing a new crop, tobacco, "has certainly reduced the standard of living among the peasantry of the tobacco regions" (85). He is saying something more than that living standards fell, which may have stemmed from other factors he cited: population pressure against fixed land resources, cessation of opportu-

15. This type of calculation, although always time consuming, often fails to produce useful results. A parallel effort to elicit estimates of junk-borne cotton shipments into Shanghai yielded negative quantities. Conclusion: the implicit assumption that most or all the cotton arriving in the city was destined for modern textile factories (for which we have detailed output figures) was far off the mark, with a large share of total cotton arrivals destined for handicraft textile producers in and around Shanghai (supporting the alternate version of textile history discussed above) or a large amount of cotton arriving by steamship or train being destined for outward-bound shipment via junk.

16. Chen's table 38, for example, is said to show that landlords earn higher returns than tenants but ignores the cost to the landlord of buying and holding land!

nity to migrate to Manchuria, the destruction of handicraft industries by competition from factory products (this last is exaggerated and probably wrong). Chen insists that growing tobacco actually reduced people's incomes in the sense that costs exceeded revenues.

This statement is not easy to accept. Just as we give little credence to surveys of the taxi industry in our major cities, which invariably show that incomes of operators are low and falling (the owners need a fare increase) even though the price of a taxi medallion (a document giving its owner the right to earn this low and falling income by deploying one taxi) is high and rising, it is difficult to believe that impoverished farm households will buy or rent expensive land (or refrain from selling or renting out their own valuable land), build expensive capital equipment (for drying tobacco leaves—see Chen 1939, 58), and incur various other expenses, all for the privilege of undertaking a labor-intensive crop that will fail to repay expenses. Anyone can make a mistake, but how do we explain persistent income-reducing errors not just by farmers who foolishly pay peak rents for tobacco land that will give them lower income than growing sorghum on cheaper land (83–85), but also by landlords and merchants, who pay top prices for the same land (Swen 1928, 645)? The picture of diverse actors bidding up the capital value and annual rental of an asset that produces a steady stream of losses defies the economist's faith in the capacity of farmers, landowners, and merchants to avoid activities that undercut their own economic self-interest. What is happening here?

The road to clarity in this case begins with consideration of seasonal variations in the *opportunity cost* and hence the value of labor. When Han-seng Chen states that farmers make losses from growing tobacco, what he really means is that their residual income, when divided by the number of days of family labor embodied in the tobacco harvest, is less than the average wage rate, so that "the peasants cannot receive the wage that is due them" (61). But the "wage that is due" to self-employed farmers depends on earnings available in the marketplace; with huge fluctuations in seasonal labor demand, these amounts in turn vary widely from month to month. Thus our analysis of the labor income of tobacco growers must consider the seasonal pattern of labor requirements for this most labor-intensive of Chinese farm crops. In Wei county, Shantung (one of the principal tobacco regions), the seasonal distribution of labor requirements for tobacco had the effect of extending the demand for farm labor without significantly increasing peak labor requirements.

A 1924 survey of twenty-four farms in this locality showed that tobacco, which accounted for 5.2 percent of cultivated area, contributed no less than 79 percent of the total demand for labor from October 15 to November 30. Eliminating all labor requirements for tobacco would reduce peak labor requirements (in late June) by only 3.8 percent (Swen 1928, 657). Even without considering the possible labor requirements of drying, bundling, carrying, and processing locally grown tobacco leaves, these survey data show that addition of tobacco to the local crop- ping pattern significantly reduced the agricultural slack season, which, without tobacco, would extend from mid-October to late March. Since peak labor requirements were increased only slightly, we conclude that the opportunity cost attached to the labor absorbed in tobacco growing was small. Whether or not the hourly or daily earnings from tobacco cul- tivation fell below the year-round average, as Chen reports it did, the re sulting extra income probably represented a significant gain to local farmers, whose best alternative might have involved unremunerative idleness.[17]

Without questioning Chen's calculations or his description of the market for tobacco as characterized by extensive monopsonistic (lit- erally a market with only one buyer) control by mercantile representa- tives of the British-American Tobacco Company, our introduction of seasonal considerations leads us to a revised interpretation. We see to- bacco as an opportunity for farmers to make productive (i.e., income- enhancing) use of otherwise idle time in the agricultural slack season. The central point is not Chen's (possibly correct) observation that income earned per hour of labor devoted to tobacco growing was less than pro- ceeds per hour of effort for other crops but rather that income earned per hour of tobacco growing was higher than income available from the next-best opportunity (often leisure). Furthermore, extra income from growing tobacco was "worth the effort" in the sense that farmers demon- strably preferred the more-work more-income combination offered by tobacco growing to the less-work less-income alternative associated with slack-season leisure.

This presentation improves on Chen's analysis because it encompasses significant phenomena that Chen cannot explain: the willingness of farm- ers to continue growing tobacco, the high prices and rents attached to

---

17. Chen (*Industrial Capital and Chinese Peasants,* chap. 7) and other authors argue that average returns to labor supplied by owner-cultivators fell below the implicit wages associated with other crops. These authors do not consider the implications of seasonal variations in demand for, and hence opportunity for, cost or value of farm labor.

tobacco land, and the rising real wages of farm laborers in Wei county.[18]
An economist's enthusiasm for this alternative explanation arises essentially from theoretical considerations. Economic logic teaches that the
demands for labor, land, and equipment (in this case drying houses for
processing tobacco leaves) are *derived demands* that arise from the anticipated sale value of the outputs that these "factors of production" can
be combined to produce. If the value of the output is less than or no
greater than the cost of purchased resources—leaving no compensation
for the labor, managerial effort, and funds invested by the entrepreneur-
farmer—we expect entrepreneurs to abandon the loss-making output,
which in turn suggests reduced demand for specialized land, equipment,
and other materials and falling output for crop-specific resources associated with the profitless activity. If farmers act in a self-interested way
and are given sufficient time to learn that tobacco is a losing proposition, the combination of steady losses, rising production, and higher sales
and rental prices for tobacco land implicit in Chen's analysis can never
be observed. In addition to factual information, the argument is based
on several *assumptions:* that economic logic linking conditions in product markets (tobacco sales, prices, costs) and factor markets (land rents,
land prices, wage rates) is valid; that Chinese farmers were strongly motivated to act in ways that increased family income; and that they were
reasonably skillful in doing so. The China-specific assumptions draw support from other accounts of farm household behavior in the 1930s and
from the dynamic response of Chinese farm households to recent rural
reforms that essentially recreate market economy conditions reminiscent
of prewar days.

RISING PER CAPITA OUTPUT/INCOME
FOR PREWAR CHINESE FARMERS?

Here I propose to review some of the arguments advanced in my own
study of economic growth in prewar China (1989, chap. 6) from a
methodological viewpoint, with particular emphasis on labor markets.
I focus on labor market issues—already touched upon in the discussion

---

18. Swen (1928, 652) shows average pay for laborers on yearly contract of 25 Chinese
yuan (cash) or 55 *yuan* (cash plus board, etc.) in 1924. Buck (1937b, 328) gives figures of
38.3 *yuan* (cash) or 85.3 *yuan* (cash plus board, etc.) for the early 1930s, suggesting increases of more than 50 percent. During the same period, the Nankai index of Tientsin
wholesale prices rose only 31 percent, from 93.6 in 1924 to a peak of 122.6 in 1932 (*Nan-
k'ai* 1958, 11).

of tobacco growing—because many current controversies in modern Chinese economic history unexpectedly (to me at least) cluster around widely differing views about the functioning of prewar labor markets (Rawski 1992).

The poor quality of available data on agricultural production (Table 2) and the flawed nature of the Buck surveys (above) eliminate the possibility of resolving disputes over prewar trends in rural per capita output by appealing to direct evidence. Data on wages paid to hired laborers are consistent with the notion of rising per capita output, but both the number of citations and the share of hired workers in the farm labor force (about 15 percent) are too small for this type of evidence to be convincing. So we must appeal to indirect evidence. Figures for cotton textile consumption (based on part B of Table 3) implying large increases in per capita consumption of cotton cloth are potentially conclusive, but the present data are quite literally "too good to be true," and therefore not convincing.[19]

The indirect connection between farm incomes and wages for unskilled female textile workers in Shanghai and for unskilled male coal miners in the northern provinces of Hopeh and Shantung thus emerges as an important building block in my thesis of rising per capita output and income in the prewar farm sector. We should note that the argument concerns *output* rather than *distribution*. The central issue concerns the quotient of farm output and rural populace, however distributed.

The argument based on coal miners' wages in North China poses the essential questions. Since most observers agree that per capita output and income rose faster in the rapidly modernizing Yangtze delta area near Shanghai than anywhere else in China except the northeast, a demonstration of rising rural income levels for this region may have no national significance. A demonstration of rising rural output/income for North China, however, is a different matter.

The basic conception underlying the analysis is that local village mar-

---

19. The *logic* of the textile argument (as opposed to the data in Table 3) is very clear. Studies of consumer behavior in many societies show that the "income elasticity of demand" for textiles clusters between 1.0 and 1.5, meaning that a 1 percent increase (or decrease) in household income is usually associated with an increase (or decrease) of 1.0–1.5 percent in household expenditure on textiles (see Houthakker 1957, Tables 2–3). For very poor people to suddenly consume more textiles without obtaining higher incomes is extremely improbable unless there is a large drop in the relative cost of cloth (not observed in prewar China). Unless a sudden change in mass psychology converted the Chinese farming populace into anorexic dandies, a significant increase in per capita textile consumption (say, 10–15 percent) with no major decline in relative price, is almost impossible unless accompanied by significantly higher average incomes.

kets for labor across large areas of China's landscape were linked together into systems that can be viewed as integrated markets for labor
services. The idea is simple. Each locality has its labor market. Figure 3
shows such markets in two localities, A and B. In each market, the supply curve shows the quantity of labor offered at various wage rates, while
the demand curve indicates the quantities of labor that employers wish
to hire at various rates. Higher wage rates draw larger supplies of labor
into the marketplace because local residents, including owner-farmers,
will respond to higher wages by offering more labor (if I get $1 per day
for hauling goods I prefer to devote my efforts to extra weeding of my
cotton field; for $2 per day I let the weeds grow), and because news of
rising wages will attract outsiders from nearby places. As we have seen,
the demand for labor is *derived* from the value of output that extra workers can produce. If I have to pay $2 for hired labor, it makes sense for
me to hire less labor than if I can get similar services at a daily rate of
$1 (consider my response under alternative wage rates to the suggestion
that I hire a certain Lin, whose labor will permit me to increase daily sales
by $1.50).

If the equilibrium wage rates in markets A and B are different, as in
Figure 3, and the two markets are linked, then workers will begin to move
from the low-wage market (A) to the high-wage market (B). The resulting increase in labor supply in B and contraction of supply in A will begin
to compress the wage differential between the two markets. Employers
may accelerate this tendency by recruiting workers from A for jobs in B;
or they may move their businesses from B to A. As long as migration from
A to B (for workers, or from B to A for employers) is costly (in time,
money, or risk of not finding employment at the destination), we cannot expect this wage differential to disappear. But if the two markets are
linked in the sense that information, workers, and perhaps even work
can travel between them, then we expect a tendency toward compression of wage differentials. The "speed of adjustment" in the direction of
the ideal (and unattainable) state of wage equalization may be slow, but
the existence of wage convergence and the presence of labor flows from
low- to high-wage markets demonstrate the existence of links between
A and B.

Readers should note the key role of a presumed tendency toward
wage equalization. This explains an economist's dissatisfaction with
Philip Huang's conclusion that incomes earned by agricultural wage laborers were (a) larger than incomes earned by owner-farmers in the
same localities and (b) equal to about one-fourth or one-third of the value

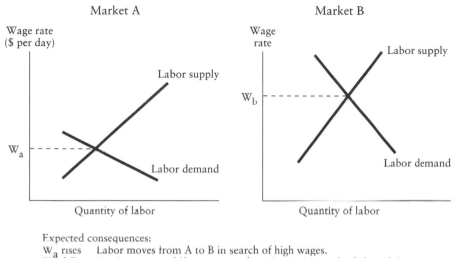

Market A   Market B

Expected consequences:
W_a rises   Labor moves from A to B in search of high wages.
W_b falls   Employers may shift operations from B to A in search of cheap labor.

FIGURE 3. Labor markets in two localities.

of the output they provided for their employers (1985, 254, chaps. 9, 11).
Readers should by now be prepared to anticipate the economist's automatic (Pavlovian?) response to such findings and the accompanying assertion that "many poor peasants earned less from their farms than they
could earn by working the land of others" (196).

Why didn't farmers facing a return of only $1 a day for tilling their
own fields saunter across the path and offer their services to managerial
landlords for $1.25 (if incumbent laborers were being paid the equiva-
lent of $1.30)? If managerial landlords could get $3 worth of revenue
from hiring a laborer at a daily wage of $1.30, why didn't they raise their
profits by hiring more workers? Here we have a series of findings that
violates the economist's basic *assumption* that economic agents (in this
case, owner-farmers and managerial landlords) pursue self-interest on the
basis of well-informed calculation. Note that this instinctive reaction
arises not because all economists dispute the general thrust of Huang's
arguments and is entirely separate from the possibility raised by Brandt
(1987) that Huang's conclusions are not sustained if his analysis is repeated for a broader range of data than are used in his original study.

What of "surplus labor"? As we have seen in discussing tobacco,
farmers in North China experienced long periods each year during which
agricultural labor requirements were extremely low. Although some of

the unused labor power was redirected toward handicrafts, transport work, and migration to seasonal jobs in the cities or in Manchuria, millions of workers wasted millions of man-days doing no productive work. How can economists prattle about "well-functioning" or "well-integrated" labor markets under these conditions of surplus labor?

While nobody denies the reality of widespread seasonal idleness, economists usually reserve the term "surplus labor" for a situation in which workers can be removed *permanently* from the workplace without causing production to drop. During the 1950s, Ragnar Nurkse (1953) and others viewed this kind of labor surplus as a widespread phenomenon that presented significant developmental opportunities for many poor nations. The idea was to remove surplus workers from the farms (without reducing farm output), tax away the food that they normally ate at home, use the tax receipts to pay the formerly surplus laborers for working to enlarge society's capital stock (by building roads, waterworks, etc.), and watch the economy expand following the nearly costless increase in productive assets. These ideas stimulated extensive study of rural labor conditions in many economies. The results of this research gradually convinced most economists that "surplus labor" is very difficult to find, even in the most densely populated economies. China offers no exception to this generalization, for we know that labor supplies were stretched to the limit during the peak farming season, with many localities unable to implement technically feasible intensification of cropping systems because of peak-season labor bottlenecks.

From this viewpoint, there is no intrinsic contradiction between the claim that labor markets "functioned effectively" and the existence of large-scale seasonal (but not year-round) unemployment. Seasonal idleness is costly to its victims, but with limited access to cheap and convenient transportation (able to whisk workers or products of their home handicraft workshops to short-term jobs or distant commodity markets), cheap funds (available to obtain materials and equipment for off-season productive activity), or wealthy communities (willing to buy outputs of off-season productive activity), a seasonal mismatch between labor supply and labor demand may produce regular bouts of idleness even in the presence of reasonably well integrated labor markets. Although idle farmers will work for very low wages in December and January (remember the tobacco discussion), it will not be profitable for urban employers to dismiss their regular workers and replace them with inexperienced farmers (or cut the wages of regular workers in half), then rehire the regular workforce (or restore normal wages) when the farming season commences in April. Nor can we expect merchants or any-one else to tie up scarce funds in projects designed to employ seasonally idle farmers. Even though off-season wages fall to bargain-basement lev-els, high interest rates (both in the marketplace and from society's view-point) mean that seasonally idle equipment (farm labor disappears into the fields in summertime) is no improvement over seasonally idle labor. An integrated labor market can (gradually) remove differences between wage levels in different trades or different regions, but it cannot rectify gross imbalance between labor supply and demand either seasonally or, if suitable technology is lacking, in the longer term.

Now abandon the textbook world of A and B for the reality of North China. We have not two or even two hundred, but literally thousands of local labor markets, each corresponding, perhaps, to the standard mar-keting districts studied by G. W. Skinner (1964). To identify the totality encompassing these many venues in which labor services are exchanged for money as an integrated labor market is to assert that changes in wage rates in one trade or locality will reverberate through the entire system, causing labor to migrate away from low-wage centers or trades toward high-wage localities or occupations. As in the simpler case of A and B, we look for compression of wage differentials, not wage equalization, and expect gradual adjustment via labor flows in directions that we pre-dict from wage differentials, but whose actual pace depends on a vari-ety of factors including the magnitude of the wage gap, but also the cost (time, money, risk) of migration.[20]

This statement conceals a number of complications. First, the degree of linkage between labor market conditions in markets A and B, A and C, or A and D will not be identical but must vary with distance, ease of communication, presence or absence of regular migration between the two localities, and so on. When wages begin to rise in Manchuria, not all villages in North China respond at the same time or at the same rate. We anticipate the quickest response in communities that have convenient transport links as well as a history of migration to the high-wage region. But as workers from these centers take advantage of their close ties and abandon their current activities for more promising opportunities in Manchuria, local labor shortages may appear in the migrants' home vil-

20. Here we should note that, after two centuries of economic integration, average per-sonal income in Connecticut is 34 percent above the U.S. average for 1986 and 102 per-cent above the figure for Mississippi (*New York Times*, 23 August 1987, 10). Evidently interregional inequalities can persist for long intervals despite labor market integration and the resulting tendency toward wage convergence.

lages, creating secondary ripples of migration that will widen the scope of employment and wage adjustment to encompass a growing number of communities.

Another complication arises on the institutional side. Our discussion of labor markets has assumed that bargains are struck between employers and workers. But nonfarm workers in prewar China often had no direct relation with the management of the enterprise where they worked. Instead, they were recruited by a labor contractor who received a lump sum for supplying an agreed number of workers to the enterprise manager, pocketed a portion of this payment as his own compensation for assembling and supervising the workforce, and used the remainder to pay the workers. This system was common in both textiles and mining. Even in the absence of labor contractors, employment arrangements often involved the services of guarantors or other intermediaries.

The significance of these complications depends upon the objective of our research. If we are interested in recruitment patterns or in social relations among workers, the difference between employment arrangements built on individual bargaining between worker and manager and arrangements concluded through the intermediation of labor contractors may become a central feature of the research. But from the perspective of achieving a broad overview of labor market conditions, these complexities do not significantly affect our analysis. The supply curve of labor is based on workers' response to alternative wage offers. They presumably concern themselves with what they actually receive. If I am initially unaware that the labor contractor will not transfer the full amount of "my" wages to me at the end of the week or month, this error will quickly come to my attention; I can change my behavior accordingly and alert my neighbors to the true wage package. Instead of one demand curve for labor, we have two: the employer's demand for workmen supplied by the labor contractor and the contractor's demand curve for recruits. This situation produces two equilibrium wages: one paid to the contractor and a smaller figure paid to the workers.[21] If some workers contract directly with an employer who hires other personnel through labor

21. Diana Lary points out that labor contractors often made lump-sum payments to the parents of new recruits before the young people went off to work. This arrangement can also be incorporated into our analysis. At any wage rate, we assume the quantity of labor offered increases (i.c., supply curve shifts outward) as the "signing bonus" increases. If the bonus is high enough, parents might allow their children to be put to work at extremely low wages.

contractors (this was common in Chinese mining enterprises), there may be yet another wage level.

But the addition of labor contractors makes little difference to our analysis of the consequences of rising wages at point A. If wages rise at A, both contractors and individual workers will hasten to increase the local labor supply. If contractor X customarily recruits workers only from village C where he has long-standing ties with the headman, he may experience difficulty in obtaining more volunteers. This may lead him to offer higher wages and/or to seek connections in villages D, E, and F where more workers may be available. If X's fees for supplying workers at A rise excessively, China's "abundance of small-time entrepreneurs" ensures that other contractors Y and Z will rush to offer their services (Wright 1981, 325), and their efforts will begin to raise wages in the communities G, H, and K from which their recruits are chosen. The existence of labor contractors affects the channels through which the consequences of changing labor market conditions are transmitted, but it does not change the nature of the process or the end result, namely the tendency toward wage compression and the movement of labor toward high-wage localities and trades.

Does the idea of an integrated labor market provide a reasonable description (or model) of conditions in prewar North China? I claim that it does. The development of transport and communications (railway, steamship, telegraph, even telephone) vastly accelerated the circulation of information about wages, job opportunities, and working conditions in nearby and distant places. A rising volume of trade meant that rising numbers of buyers, sellers, traders, and porters moved to, from, and between various markets spreading information as well as commodities. Improved monetary and fiscal arrangements made it easier for even poor laborers to remit funds across long distances.

We know that large numbers of laborers and farmers left their North China villages to seek better opportunities in the mines, in the cities, and in the frontier regions of Manchuria. The recorded two-way flow of migrants between North China and Manchuria at times surpassed one million persons per year. Thomas Gottschang's (1987) study of these labor flows reveals a high degree of labor market integration between North China and Manchuria. His calculations show that the volume of migration increased when wage differentials between North China and Manchuria expanded (and contracted with wage differences declined), increased during periods of natural or man-made disaster in North China (and declined during years of disaster in Manchuria), increased with the expansion of Manchuria's rail network (which allowed migrants easier access to job opportunities), and declined with the expansion of railway lines in North China.

This last result is particularly noteworthy. We might expect railway expansion in the migrants' home regions, by reducing travel costs and transit time, to stimulate the exodus of labor to the Northeast. But Gottschang finds that the beneficial consequences of local railway construction on economic opportunities for inhabitants of nearby villages were so strong that local railway development is negatively associated with migration despite its tendency to stimulate migration by making it easier and cheaper to travel to distant places.

With this strong evidence of integration between labor markets hundreds of miles away, can we doubt the presence of similar links between wages offered by North China mining companies and employment opportunities in North China farming communities, including those not immediately adjacent to the mining districts? Does it not seem reasonable to suppose that the mine owners, operating in labor markets in which total labor supplies amounted to a huge multiple of their own requirements, could obtain the desired mine workforce without substantially increasing the level of real wages unless the supply price of mine labor (farm income plus migration costs plus a premium for dangerous work) was being forced up by rising rural living standards? I therefore conclude that rising real wages among unskilled coal miners reflect increasing real incomes in the village economy from which miners were recruited.

There is considerable information showing that miners' wages in the 1920s were lower than both miners' wages *and agricultural wages* of the 1930s (all in real terms). If we reject the argument that agricultural wages rose (and also the implication that agricultural labor productivity, and hence incomes of self-employed farmers as well as hired workers all increased) during the late 1920s and early 1930s, how can we explain the ability of mines to attract strong young men into their workforce in the 1920s?

While I regard these arguments as powerful stuff, there are, as always, various impurities in the mixture. The possibility that trade union pressure or a general fear of pro-labor intervention by the Nanking government contributed more to rising textile and mine wages than rising supply price cannot be lightly dismissed. A more fundamental problem concerns timing. If the combined impact of new demands (from foreign trade) and improved transport, communication and monetary facilities stimulated a deepening of rural specialization and consequent increase in individual labor productivity and per capita output and income, we expect these increases to be *gradual* and spread out. If rising wages for unskilled workers outside agriculture are tied to farm labor productivity by way of the labor market links described above, should we not see *gradual* upward adjustments of wages rather than the abrupt jumps more characteristic of the wage series in textiles and coal mining? Even if we accept the idea of labor market linkage between farming and non-agricultural occupations, are these wage shifts during 1910–36 (cotton textiles) and 1920–36 (coal mining) sufficiently *persistent* to qualify as indicators of long-term shifts in underlying patterns of farm labor productivity?

These questions return us to our initial objective of encouraging historians to take maximum advantage of the insights offered by economic theory and empirical methods into the study of economic trends. The preceding survey shows that research based on economic sources and methods must stand or fall by the same canons of historical judgment that we apply to archival scholarship or studies built on archaeological evidence. But this unity of method does not diminish the benefit to historians of understanding how economists use theoretical concepts, national income accounting, techniques of data analysis, and comparative economic experience to motivate and structure their studies of economic trends. Even for historians whose research plans do not include the use of quantitative materials, an appreciation of these matters will enhance their capacity to evaluate the success of scholarship based on economic models and methods in satisfying the fundamental requirements of any historical endeavor. Are the proposed conclusions plausible? Does the evidence support the putative findings? Can the same evidence be construed to support alternative viewpoints? Do we have significant bodies of evidence excluded by the author that point in other directions? On balance, what viewpoint makes the most sense?

Institutions and
Economic Analysis

JON S. COHEN

To the economist, institutions represent efficient ways of organizing human activity where markets alone will not suffice. To understand why institutions are often required to supplement or even replace markets, it is necessary to begin with a brief sketch of two abstract models of how a decentralized market economy works, one the general competitive equilibrium, the other Marxian. The sketches are not intended to provide complete representations of the two but merely to highlight those features of each that relate to institutions. For the purposes of this analysis, institutions are broadly defined as those commonplace organizations such as households, farms, and firms where much of society's economic activity takes place.

At its most formal level, the competitive equilibrium approach has no place for institutions. Its world is highly abstract and exists only under very restrictive assumptions. Since these assumptions are crucial for what follows, they must be made explicit. It is assumed that each good or service in the economy is identical with all others in its class but distinct from those in a different class. Thus, steel is steel, wheat, wheat—or, as Gertrude Stein put it, a rose is a rose is a rose but not, as it were, a tulip. Goods and services, in other words, are homogeneous. Technology is such that the cost of producing one unit of a good or service is identical to the cost per unit of producing one million; that is, there are no economies of scale. Each individual begins with a set of independent preferences (independent from the preferences of other individuals) and endowments, both of which are established outside the context of the model. Or, as the economist would say, preferences and endowments are determined exogenously. On the basis of these preferences and endowments each individual, as an individual (not as a group or a class), decides what and how much to consume, and what type and how much work to perform. A market (in which the costs of executing transactions are zero) exists for every economic good, where "economic" means scarce, that is, the good has a price. Individuals behave rationally and have all the information and knowledge they need to make rational decisions about present and future consumption and production.

The great attraction of the general competitive model is that when the economy, defined by all these assumptions, comes to rest (in equilibrium), allocation and distribution are perfectly efficient. To interpret this result, it is important to understand exactly what the economist means by "efficiency." An equilibrium is economically efficient when no reallocation of inputs can increase the output of one good without reducing the output of another or, in terms of consumption, when it is not possible to redistribute goods among consumers in a way that will make everyone better off. An economically efficient equilibrium then is one that maximizes the output from resources and best satisfies consumers' preferences and endowments. Such a result can also be described as "doing the most with the least" and that of course is its appeal.

It must be emphasized that this kind of equilibrium is achieved in the model by rational individuals pursuing their own self-interest through a series of unregulated market transactions without any help from the government, regulatory agencies, families, friends, firms, unions, clubs, and so on—that is, without institutions!

Anyone familiar with Marxian economics knows that institutions are central to the Marxian model. Unlike the general competitive equilibrium approach, the Marxian model is neither static (timeless) nor preoccupied with equilibrium. In fact, Marx explicitly tried to lay bare the laws of motion of the capitalist system. And, in his analysis, institutions play a crucial role: enclosures create the initial conditions for a "free" wage labor force; the family provides the context for reproduction of labor power; the factory facilitates control of the production process, raises the rate of exploitation, and speeds up accumulation; the reserve army of labor enhances the rate of accumulation and provides the institutional setting for growing class consciousness. In spite of the importance of institutions in Marx's own analysis, until recently (the last twenty-five to thirty years) Marxists made relatively little effort to develop the institutional features of Marx's thought. This was a most unfortunate omission, since many of Marx's arguments fared poorly in the light of subsequent research and were thus badly in need of revision. Marxian economists were, therefore, only marginally better equipped to deal with institutions than were their orthodox counterparts.

The problem for the orthodox economist was clear. Her elegant and in many ways compelling model excluded institutions, a major feature of the real world. The model had to be changed—the question was how? The obvious procedure, and the one followed, was to ease the restrictive assumptions of the model and see what happened. A simple example illustrates this approach. Ronald Coase (1937) in a seminal article (perhaps the progenitor of the new institutional economics) asks why, if markets are so efficient (as the competitive equilibrium approach leads us to believe), firms exist? In a firm, he points out, labor is allocated to jobs not by a series of individual transactions as in a market but by command, much as a master orders a servant. In effect, a firm circumvents the market. Coase reasons that since both methods of allocation exist in most economies, choice between the two must reduce to a question of costs. If, contrary to competitive equilibrium analysis, market transactions (negotiating and writing contracts, monitoring performance, and so on) are costly, the market-firm trade-off depends on the relative cost of the two.

Two features of this example must be emphasized since they form the foundation of the new institutional economics. First, as Coase indicates, markets and institutions (as defined here) are substitutes—they perform essentially the same job in different ways. Second, the choice between the two is determined largely by the costs and benefits associated with them. Institutions, like markets, are susceptible to economic analysis.

Moreover, on these two points most Marxian and neoclassical economists are in complete agreement. They just disagree on the implications. The neoclassical economist is preoccupied with the efficiency implications of institutions, but the Marxist is more concerned with their impact on distribution and accumulation.

This chapter focuses on three institutions, the household, the farm, and the firm, and sets out to explore the answers given by economists to three questions: why do institutions exist? what tasks do they perform? and what impact, if any, do they have on economic activity and economic well-being? I preface the discussion of these institutions with a brief review of property rights and contract theory, which together form the theoretical underpinnings of most modern analyses of the economics of institutions.

PROPERTY RIGHTS AND CONTRACTS

Institutions exist because they perform the tasks of allocation and/or distribution more effectively than markets do. Why? For one of two general reasons, most economists would respond—either because property rights are incomplete or ill defined or because contracting costs (the costs of using the market) are positive. Let us consider each in turn.

Property rights in a resource or commodity give the owner the power to sell it and/or the prerogative to exclude others from using it. It is a relatively short (if complex) step from this observation to the more heroic claim favored by some property-rights theorists that if every economic resource or commodity had an owner, the economy would be able to achieve full economic efficiency (Libecap 1986). While most economists contend that such an ideal is, like nirvana, unattainable (any property owner knows that the mere act of assigning and monitoring property rights is costly), they agree that the more complete and well-defined property rights are, the better for everyone (Matthews 1986). In fact, it is precisely in those instances where ownership is muddled that trouble starts (Demsetz 1967).

An example will clarify the point. Imagine that there is a fishing pond that no one owns. Local fishermen earn their livelihood by selling the fish they catch in the pond. Each fisherman owns the fish he catches; each, in effect, has property rights in caught fish. The problem is that no one owns the uncaught fish, those still in the pond. It is easy enough to see that the average fisherman has an incentive to catch as many fish as he can as quickly as possible. After all, the only cost to him is his time and he knows that what he does not catch his neighbor will, so he works fast and furiously. The unfortunate result of this is that too much labor goes into fishing, too many fish come to market at the same time, and future customers will, in all probability, have fewer fish to eat than good management would provide because the pond will be overfished and stocks severely depleted. One way to avoid these undesirable consequences (the one favored by many economists) is to allow someone or some group to own the pond. As a profit maximizer, she, he, or the group will raise the price of fishing privileges to reflect the true cost of fish, fewer fishermen will work the pond and at a more modest pace, and the stock of fish will be maintained for future generations (Libecap 1986).

This is known among economists as the common-pool problem and applies to all cases where property rights in a resource or the equivalent are absent or ill defined. Many examples of common pools exist, including cod fisheries (Innis 1954), fur trapping (Innis 1962), open-field farming (Cohen and Weitzman 1975), crude oil production (Libecap and Wiggins 1984, 1985), western land settlement, and the Canadian-Spanish turbot war. It is particularly important for the historian to note that because the assignment of property rights usually has important distributional implications (some people will be excluded), common-pool problems persist in spite of strong efforts (and often good economic reasons) to eliminate them. For example, the Tudors and the Stuarts may have resisted pressures from the aristocracy and gentry to take a more liberal line on enclosures not because these monarchs were ignorant of the economic benefits promised by enclosing land but because they feared the political unrest that the assignment of property rights would provoke among those who were denied them. To pursue this hypothesis, it is possible to argue that when the balance of political power shifted after the English Civil War, the threat of political unrest diminished and, not surprisingly, the pace and scope of enclosures picked up dramatically (Cohen and Weitzman 1975).

Explicit ownership rights resolve some economic problems, yet others remain. Take, for example, the lucky farmer who, following enclosure, obtains clear title to her share of the commons, wastes, and woods. She now has a large estate and must decide how to work the land. Does she sign a long-term lease with one or more tenants, does she hire workers and run the estate herself, or does she perhaps enter into some type of share tenancy agreement? The point is that each of these options entails transaction (contract) costs that property rights do nothing to eliminate. The question is how these costs affect the market-institution trade-off.

When economists talk about costs of contracting, they have in mind both the *ex ante* costs of negotiating and drawing up the contract and the *ex post* cost of monitoring it to make sure that the terms are honored. In most cases, these costs exist because the interests of the two parties to the contract differ. To pursue the above example, assume that the farmer decides to run the farm herself with wage labor. If output per worker depends on the effort of each worker (a reasonable assumption), the farmer will do everything she can, short of paying them more, to get her workers to work hard each hour of the day. But the workers have different perceptions of work, leisure, and pay. They prefer to minimize effort, enjoy a little on-the-job leisure, and, of course, end up with the same take-home pay. The interests of the farmer and her workers obviously differ. The farmer may try, with a package of rewards, penalties, monitoring devices, and other institutional arrangements to encourage the workers not to loaf, and the workers may, at times, try to ease the fears of the farmer by putting up bonds or the equivalent, but all these arrangements are costly. And even with an elaborate set of checks and balances, the workers may end up working less diligently than the farmer would like but it may be too expensive for her to do anything about this undesirable outcome.

Another problem exists. Some workers may be more prone to loaf than others but it is the workers, not the farmer, who know which ones do so. Economists call this the problem of asymmetric information. The farmer may rely on signals or screening devices such as educational background or letters of reference to gather information about prospective workers but these methods are at best imperfect and always costly. Insurance against malfeasance is another possibility that has its own set of problems. The farmer, in this case, has a strong incentive to exaggerate her labor troubles and the insurer may find it expensive to check her story. Insurance, if it exists at all, will be very costly. The difficulty here is one of imperfect or incomplete markets. A third option for the hard-pressed farmer is to rely on implicit contracts in which each worker is hired at a wage below his or her actual worth with the understanding that compensation will be forthcoming at some later date when reliability has been established. Both parties to such contracts have an incentive to stick around, the worker to obtain payoff, the farmer to keep reliable workers once she has identified them. The two may even set up an internal job ladder or sign some sort of seniority agreement (Williamson 1975; Gintis 1976; Huberman 1986). Institutions may step in where markets fail to produce efficient outcomes, but all institutional arrangements consume scarce resources.

The point of these examples is simple but very important. In a world where transactions are costly and where it may be difficult, if not impossible, to establish property rights to all assets, it is no longer possible to argue that a decentralized market economy will do the most with the least. Markets fail to live up to their billing and complete economic efficiency cannot be achieved.

The process that adds realism to orthodox models also nudges them closer to Marxian ones. Unemployment, in the form of the reserve army of jobless workers, has always been viewed by Marxists as a mechanism to discipline labor. Orthodox economists now view it in much the same way. Property always confers, in Marxian analyses, privilege; the same is now true in many neoclassical studies. Class matters to both Marxists and orthodox economists. At the same time, modern Marxians have adopted the theoretical insights about costly information, risk, and imperfect markets discovered by neoclassical economics. The best way to appreciate the similarities and differences in the two approaches (and their usefulness for historical research) is to see them in action.

INSTITUTIONS

Households, farms, and firms—the three institutions that anchor this discussion—are neither the only economic institutions nor, in many societies, the most important ones, but the literature on them is extensive and accessible, and it illustrates the techniques economists use to analyze institutions. The underlying theme is that transaction costs and/or ill-defined property rights give rise to specific institutional arrangements. The task of the economist is to find out why and to identify the consequences.

HOUSEHOLDS

Households did not arise simply to resolve economic problems that markets could not. Even the most materialistic of economists would be reluctant to make such a claim. Yet even the least materialistic of historians would agree that households have taken on two major tasks, producing and raising children (which gives them a major role in determining population size) and regulating the supply of labor (Folbre 1986), both of which have important economic implications.

Economists assume that households make rational decisions about how to allocate their resources among alternative activities in order to maximize family welfare, rather than simply carry out economic calculations. Economists also assume, if only implicitly, that households take on certain tasks and not others because they can accomplish them more efficiently than markets or other institutions. As economic conditions change, so do relative costs and, as a result, the tasks that households take on. It is just a question of identifying the resources, the alternatives, and the preferences of the household. For the time being, we are viewing households as if they were a single individual. While this may contrast with reality, such an assumption permits us to focus sharply on particular features of household behavior. Problems of intrahousehold allocation and distribution are taken up later.

Families have children, according to economists, for one of two reasons: either because they like them (in this case children become consumption goods); or because they need them to work today and to serve tomorrow as a kind of old age pension program (here, investment goods). Childbirth and child care take time and resources, so that a trade-off exists between the return from children (as either consumption or investment goods) and their cost. Since the ultimate goal of the economist, when concerned with the family as a unit, is to gain some insight into population size, what he or she wants to know is how a family decides whether to have more children, whether to devote extra resources to enrich those already born, or simply to use the available resources for other purposes. These decisions, summed across all families in a community, determine population size, population growth, and the quality of child care. The method, simple in theory but complicated in practice, is to estimate the cost of and return from having another child.

Any factor that affects the return to labor, especially female labor if women are the ones responsible for child care, influences the cost of raising children. If a textile factory comes to town, hires women workers, and pushes up the potential income of village women, the real cost (the wage foregone by not working in the factory) of child care rises, and, if nothing else changes, the optimum average family size may decline. Education may influence the cost of child care. If women with more schooling have greater earning power, the cost to them and their families of child care is higher and, *ceteris paribus*, they will opt for smaller families.[1]

Family structure may matter. Nuclear families must, in most cases, rely on their own resources for child care while extended families frequently have older people on hand to help with such tasks. If the textile factory in the above example appears in a village where extended instead of nuclear families are the norm, the impact on family size may be insignificant.

Influences on expected returns, and thus on family size, include considerations that affect the pleasure of nurturing offspring, laws that regulate child labor and thus the potential earning power of young children, and alternative forms of old-age pensions. Consider the dramatic decline that took place in the size of American families during the nineteenth century, the so-called demographic transition. Sutch (1991) sees this change

1. *Ceteris paribus*, which means "other things equal," invokes the economist's tactic of freezing all aspects of a situation other than the specific issue under examination. For further discussion of this logical tactic see Carter and Cullenberg, 88–89.

in family size and in attitudes toward children as the direct result of new opportunities to settle in the territories west of the Appalachian mountains. Young people in the eastern states left home in response to the lure of cheap and fertile western farmland (Sutch 1991, 285). Parents could no longer rely on their numerous children to provide them with security in their old age and found themselves compelled to seek alternatives. They began to save during their productive years and chose to have fewer, better educated children.

These changes transformed the economy and society of the United States. Higher saving rates created a pool of investible funds. Smaller families reduced self-sufficiency and stimulated the demand for manufactured goods. Towns expanded, schools developed, banks and other financial institutions matured, and industry flourished. This process of modernizing an agrarian society demonstrates the transformative power of a change in the economic role of children within the family.

Most economists subscribe to the notion that households make rational economic decisions about how many children to have (Folbre 1986a). There is less unanimity when it comes to household behavior and the supply of labor.

To clarify the connection between households and the labor supply, we need an analytical framework. Look first at the employment options open to household members. Family members can limit their work strictly to noncommodity production within the household, from simple housework and child care to the production of clothing and the growing and processing of food. Much of this work often fell to women but, of course, such need not be the case. Still within the physical confines of the household, householders can engage in commodity production, that is, they can produce goods for the market. In eighteenth-century England boots and shoes, nails and other small metalwares, thread and cloth were all products of cottage industry. Finally, some or all family members can work outside of the household. Conventional estimates of the labor supply include only these last two activities.

Consider now the choice between work and leisure. It is commonly assumed that each family member tries to maximize her or his satisfaction (utility), which depends on income and leisure. The trade-off is obvious—less work, less income, but more leisure. As an example of the potential usefulness of this way to conceptualize the issue, attempts to boost the labor supply in seventeenth- and early eighteenth-century England by increasing wages induced the able bodied to work less not more (Landes 1969; Marglin 1974). A worker had a target income: the increase in wages permitted him or her to reach the target with fewer hours of labor and thus to substitute leisure for work as wages rose.

The final feature of our framework deals with alternative schemes of intrafamily allocation of work, leisure, and income. Allocation among family members may be based on a consensus of those concerned, in which case the household as a unit maximizes utility and distributes the spoils according to a principle that all consider fair. This is the communal solution. In an alternative model, which might be called the hierarchy solution, some family members (say male heads) have more bargaining strength than others (females) and use it to redistribute some of the available income and leisure to themselves. The behavioral implications of the two models are, as one can imagine, different.[2]

An example will illustrate the usefulness of this framework. To return to the case of the textile factory, the millowner sets up shop in a rural area, fully expecting to exploit the pool of cheap female labor hidden in the local farm households only to discover, to his consternation, that the wages he has to pay to attract these women are not so low after all. Where did he go wrong in his calculations? He estimated the implicit wage that women earned from the sale of yarn spun at home and figured that, if he offered a wage slightly above it, he would attract all the workers he needed. He failed to realize that spinning at home allowed the women to carry out at the same time a variety of household chores such as child care, cooking, and cleaning that they would be unable to accomplish if they went full-time into the factories. Although these services did not go through the market, they used scarce resources and thus had a price. The real wage for these women was therefore not simply what they earned from selling homespun yarn but included what they would have to pay to get someone else to do their household jobs.

The millowner made another mistake. He forgot about the contribution the women made to the family farm, especially at times of peak labor demand. The men worked the farms on their own for most of the year but at harvest time, the entire family worked full tilt to bring in the crops before frost or rain destroyed everything. Full-time factory work for the women meant that hired hands, at very high wages, would have to be brought in for the harvest—if they were available at all. The opportunity wage of the farm women was thus a good deal higher than that calculated by our disillusioned millowner.

2. Kahne and Kohen 1975 and Folbre 1986a, 1986b review these differences. Moore 1993 and Collier 1993 review studies of household economics in African nations.

We can use this same example to explore intrahousehold distribution. Why did the millowner focus his search for cheap labor on the women and not the men? Obviously because his estimates led him to believe that the opportunity wage of the men, measured by income earned from the family farm, was much higher. We now know that he underestimated the women's real wage but even if he did his sums correctly he may have found that the women's labor was cheaper than the men's. Why? The conventional explanation is that women are less productive than men and are thus paid less. There is another possibility. Assume that households are hierarchical, not communal, and that men have relatively more clout in the family than women. Men may undervalue the leisure of women and thus push down the wage for which the women are willing to work. In such a case, even if family income were divided equally between men and women, the latter would be underpaid, the former overcompensated. And, of course, income may not be divided equally. The men, not surprisingly, may find this alternative very attractive.

There are a number of behavioral implications of the hierarchical model. In one scenario, our poor millowner sets up in another village, offers first-rate wages, and, once more, finds himself without a workforce. What happened this time, he wonders? The men, it turns out, feared that factory work would upset the balance of power within the family by giving the womenfolk an income of their own. The men were worried that they might lose their privileged position and, with it, undergo a drop in their real income. They thus refused to let the women take work in the factory, making use of religious and other taboos to justify their actions.

For historical researchers the implication of our scenario is that, in studying the economic features of household behavior, they must begin with the working hypothesis that whatever one observes has a good economic explanation. The hypothesis may prove to be incorrect but researchers should test it before they discard it. To return for the final time to our textile factory, if the argument that women refused factory work because it conflicted with religious beliefs were accepted, we may be hard pressed to explain why these same women, somewhat later but adhering to the same religion, eagerly accepted jobs in a new factory. The key this time around was the absence of the men, most of whom had gone off to work in the city and no longer had an interest in keeping the women in the home. Similarly, if we failed to take into account peak labor demands, as did our millowner, we might totally misinterpret the reason that women were reluctant to accept factory employment.

THE FARM

Let us look at organizational features of agricultural production within three sets of historical examples: French peasant farming in the nineteenth century, open fields and enclosures in Britain, and sharecropping, primarily in the southern United States after the Civil War. Once again, the economist begins with the simple assumption that agrarian institutions, which many dismiss as economically inefficient or irrational, may represent perfectly rational attempts by farm folk to resolve problems that markets cannot.

Peasant farming in France. An irrational attachment by French peasants to their small-scale, inefficiently run family farms has been held responsible for inhibiting migration from farm to factory, forcing up the cost of industrial labor, and slowing the pace of industrial expansion. Heywood (1981) argues that peasant agriculture, far from being the cause of slow economic growth, may have saved France from serious social and economic instability by offering income and employment to potentially excess workers. The problem was not labor's reluctance to leave the land but the slow growth of industrial activity that restricted demand for industrial workers. Family farms used techniques that required substantial amounts of labor relative to other inputs not because French peasants were ignorant or reluctant to take chances but simply because the labor was available. When industrial growth accelerated, especially toward the end of the nineteenth century and the first decade of the twentieth, the size of the farm population dropped, wages rose, farm size grew, and less labor-intensive techniques were adopted. The message for the historian is that understanding what was going on down on the farm requires finding out what was happening back in town too.

There is more to be learned from French peasant agriculture. As many note (Grantham 1978), attacks on the inefficient peasant farmer do not pinpoint the nature of this inefficiency. We may summarize the general picture as follows: the French peasant produced a crop mix too heavily weighted toward subsistence; he was unwilling to invest in new equipment (and, presumably, to borrow); he was a reluctant consumer of manufactured goods; and he and his kind were too attached to the land. Part of the problem may have been a lack of opportunities, as Heywood (1981) maintains, but there may have been other considerations as well. What is most striking about these "inefficiency" features is that they are exactly what we would expect if concern for security motivated the typical small-scale nineteenth-century French farmer (Wright and Kun-reuther 1975) as much as income and profit did.

Perhaps a more commercial crop mix would have yielded a higher income, but farming in nineteenth-century France was a risky business, so that the average peasant, given the option, may have traded income for security. To commit himself to commercial crops, he would be compelled to turn to the market for his necessities. If the commercial crops failed or did not generate the necessary income, the least the peasant faced was debts, the most, loss of his farm.

Only the boldest farmer would have been willing to take such risks. To exercise his taste for security, a peasant had to isolate himself from the money economy; taxes had to be moderate, he had to avoid debts, and he had to stifle desires for commodities produced off the farm. These features are likely to produce a farmer reluctant to borrow, to invest, or to consume manufactured goods. Other things being equal, safety first is more a characteristic of small than of large farms since a greater percentage of land on small farms must be devoted to meeting subsistence needs. And, of course, the more people down on the farm, the more true this will be.

At the same time, safety-first farming varies directly with the riskiness of farm operations. Thus, as long as farming risks were high and farms small, the French peasant had a strong incentive to opt for safety first. This preference should not be mistaken for irrationality or garden variety inefficiency.[3] Note that, had insurance been available to peasants, safety-first behavior might have been unnecessary. It may have been simply an effective institutional response to the lack of any other way for peasants to reduce the risks of farming.

There may be a further consideration. What many take to be unemployment or underemployment in the traditional sector may constitute a whole variety of activities such as marketing, transport, food and fuel processing, housework and child care (what Hymer and Resnick [1969] call Z goods) that contribute to total rural output and add to the well-being of country folk. These Z goods (and services) are similar to the household activities that our millowner overlooked. In the previous case, the millowner went broke while in this one, if substitutes are not forthcoming as peasants shift from the traditional to the modern sector, the whole development process may collapse. Z goods may be disdained by the rural population as inferior to manufactured goods but they are, nev-

3. For further discussion of risk see McCloskey, 72.

ertheless, often essential commodities and services. The reluctance of French farmers to leave the countryside for the city may have been, in part, a response to their inability to find affordable substitutes for Z goods.

The point is simply that institutional arrangements that appear unproductive or irrational may, upon closer examination, be perfectly understandable responses to unremovable constraints (Sjöstrand 1992). It is well to seek out the constraints before condemning peasants (or other groups) for what looks like stubborn irrationality.

Open-field farming and enclosures. How and why do alternative institutional arrangements of production in agriculture matter to the historian? Even for a scholar totally uninterested in open-field farming or sharecropping, this subject provides an excellent survey of how economists deal with institutions. The historian will have no trouble applying its techniques to other situations.[4]

Cohen and Weitzman (1975) argue that a predominant feature of unenclosed land is that property rights are ill defined so that no one has the power to exclude new entrants. Since everyone gets an equal share of output, the overriding objective of those on the land is to produce as much as possible, not to maximize profits. The argument, of course, is very similar to that associated with the common-pool problem described earlier. The result of this arrangement is that too many people work the land and profits or rents are below maximum. In other words, we have a case of excess labor (disguised unemployment) in agriculture, a positive and stable wage, and an institutional story to explain it.

The question is why such an arrangement exists. Some, such as Cohen and Weitzman and Marc Bloch, argue that for military and social reasons powerful English landowners were more preoccupied with maximizing the number of men under their control than with maximizing income from their land. When concern with income came to dominate interest in military might, pressures for institutional change mounted, and the struggle over the definition and assignment of property rights (the enclosure movement) intensified.

Not everyone agrees with this explanation of open fields or their demise. In one example, McCloskey (1975) asks why, if it is generally agreed that open-field farming was economically less efficient than enclosed fields, did open fields persist so long in so many areas of western

---

4. Research on enclosures will never cease. After this paper was completed, a major work by Allen (1992) appeared; it throws new light on many of the issues treated below.

Europe? Like the French peasants who opted for safety first (being unable to insure themselves against crop loss), English farmers may have viewed the economic cost in foregone output of scattering plots across the rural landscape as a kind of insurance premium.[5] Thus, anything that reduced the risks of farming—more disease-resistant crop strains or less weather-sensitive crops—or lowered the cost of alternative forms of insurance would promote a shift from open fields to enclosed ones.

While neither of these explanations may be compelling, both start from the premise that a durable, widely accepted institution (such as open-field farming) represents a rational response to particular economic and/or social conditions. The historian is well advised to adopt a similar starting point.

The next question is what happens when these conditions change. Cohen and Weitzman attempt to identify the economic costs of open fields and come up with the following: aside from too many workers on the land and below maximum rents, the crop mix was excessively weighted in favor of labor-intensive activities (for the obvious reason that there were too many farmers), and the national product was lower than it would have been if labor were allocated more efficiently. These results are perfectly in keeping with all common-pool situations. With enclosure (the assignment of property rights in land), numbers in agriculture dropped, output per worker rose, and the output mix moved toward greater land intensity, so that rents and the overall national product both went up.

McCloskey (1975) once again tells a rather different story. He argues that to understand the dramatic rise in the amount of land enclosed in the eighteenth and early nineteenth centuries, we must look at changes in the costs and benefits of enclosing. As one might anticipate, he shows that in the course of the eighteenth century costs fell and returns rose, pushing up net benefits and accelerating the pace of enclosure. He estimates the actual amount by which net benefits rose, but of more interest to us is his explanation of timing. One feature is that the risks associated with farming dropped, thus making open fields less necessary. But there was more. All observers, going back at least to the fifteenth century, maintained that rents on enclosed land were substantially above those on unenclosed land. Since there is no evidence that the rent differential jumped in the eighteenth century, the key to the increase in enclosures must rest with the decline in the costs of bringing them about.

5. For more on open fields and risk see McCloskey's essay, 74.

McCloskey maintains that costs fell for two reasons; first, because greater use was made of parliamentary acts, and second, because, during the course of the century, parliamentary enclosures, already less costly than private acts, became even less cumbersome and thus even cheaper. But why was this "cutting of the knot," as McCloskey calls it, delayed until the middle of the eighteenth century? The landed aristocracy had, by this time, tightened its grip on parliament and was thus in a position to use this institution to facilitate enclosures. We have, in effect, a decline in the transaction costs associated with the enclosing of land and, in consequence, an increase in the amount enclosed.

Sharecropping. Enclosures represented a major and often dramatic change in the way in which farming was organized in England. For Marx, it was the classic case of original accumulation; landlords gained clear title to their land while many small holders lost all possession and became wage laborers. Once the land was enclosed, it could be rented out on long-term leases to capitalist tenants. Why did this and not some other type of rental arrangement dominate the English countryside? Presumably because those who adopted it considered it to be the best of all possible systems and, under the circumstances, they must have been right. But what about alternatives such as sharecropping, a system practiced extensively in Italy and France at the time?

Consider what Arthur Young had to say about sharecropping on the continent.

> There is not one word to be said in favor of the practice [of sharecropping] and a thousand arguments that might be used against it. . . . In this most contemptible of all modes of letting land, the defrauded landlord receives a contemptible rent; the farmer is in the lowest state of poverty; the land is miserably cultivated; and the nation suffers as severely as the parties themselves. . . . There are but few districts [in Italy] where lands are let to occupying tenants at a money-rent; but wherever it is found, their crops are greater; a clear proof of the imbecility of the metaying system. (quoted in Mill 1871, 375–376)

If the system were indeed as contemptible as Young would have us believe, why would any rational landowner ever enter into such a contract—or, for that matter, why would any self-respecting tenant accept it? Young had an answer.

> The hard plea of necessity can alone be urged in its favor; the poverty of the farmers being so great, that the landlord must stock the farm; or it could not be stocked at all. This is a most cruel burden to a proprietor, who is thus obliged to run much of the hazard of farming in the most dangerous of all

methods, that of trusting his property absolutely in the hands of people who are generally ignorant, many careless, and some undoubtedly wicked. (376)

In other words, according to Young, landlords and tenants enter into share-tenancy arrangements because it is, given the poverty of the tenants, the best deal open to landlords. Most classical economists, including Marx, Mill, and Marshall, while aware as Young was of the drawbacks of sharecropping, also recognize its benefits. These include an incentive for share tenants to work harder than they would if hired as wage laborers, the chance to earn a return on their supervisory and managerial talents, an opportunity closed to wage workers, and finally access to assets that otherwise would be unavailable to them. "This plan [metayer] enables a man who has next to no capital of his own to obtain the use of it at a lower charge than he could in any other way, and to have more freedom and responsibility than he would as a hired laborer" (Marshall 1959, 353. See also Jaynes 1984).

In spite of this reasonable and insightful statement, Marshall has the dubious distinction of playing straw man in modern dramas enacted to discredit the idea that sharecropping is inefficient. Like all straw men before him, Marshall falls easily, in this case to Steven Cheung, a property-rights theorist. The problem, as Cheung (1969) sees it, is the following. If sharecropping is inefficient, why does it continue to coexist with other tenure systems in places where property rights are well defined? Competition should force it out of existence unless, of course, Marshall got it wrong. Since sharecropping thrives in many areas of the world, the problem lies not with sharecropping but with Marshall's argument.

Cheung shows that, with a suitable variation in plot size and division of output, landowners can achieve efficiency with sharecropping. In a nutshell, if the landowner controls the size of plot cultivated by each cropper, assuming the cropper has no other source of income and some minimum subsistence requirement, the owner will be able to dictate the amount of labor that the cropper devotes to farming; the smaller the plot, ceteris paribus, the more labor per acre. Yet even if sharecropping can be shown to be efficient, we still have no explanation for its existence. Moreover, all this manipulation of plot size and shares is costly; the contracts must be negotiated and enforced; the more complex the contract, the more costly these operations. So the question remains, why sharecropping? According to Cheung, in a world of risk-averse individuals, the chance to share risks more than offsets the higher transaction costs. That is, sharecropping facilitates risk sharing.

We now know enough to ask some questions about Cheung's argument. For example, is sharecropping the least costly (most economically efficient) way to obtain these risk-sharing features? Probably not, at least according to Cheung's critics. They maintain that a suitable combination of rental and wage contracts offers the same risk-sharing features as sharecropping without the costs associated with negotiating, writing, and enforcing share contracts (Newbery 1977). Cheung might respond that all types of tenure systems involve transaction costs. The objection is, of course, perfectly valid. But by the same token if all tenure systems have transaction costs and all, in some combination, come with risk-sharing features, the problem of tenure choice reduces to an exercise in comparative costs and benefits in which the system chosen provides the desired bundle of benefits at minimum cost. As it happens, this is exactly how most modern analyses of sharecropping (and, more generally, tenure choice) proceed.

If all the conditions of the general competitive equilibrium model are met (constant returns to scale, homogeneous commodities, perfect information, foresight, and markets), a fixed rent contract, English style, or a wage-labor system is ideal. If some of the conditions are violated, sharecropping becomes a viable alternative. Given the extensive literature on the rise of sharecropping in the U.S. South following the Civil War, this is the place to look for examples to illustrate these points.

Two questions dominate the literature: why did sharecropping come into existence when it did and what were its welfare implications? Any explanation of sharecropping must keep in mind one feature of the South: the general consensus that a tenure advancement ladder existed. At the bottom was wage labor followed by sharecropping, fixed rent, and, at the top, ownership (Reid 1979). The space between the rungs and speed of ascent may have differed for blacks and whites but a ladder existed for both groups (Reid 1979; Alston and Higgs 1982; Wright 1986). The literature focuses on black sharecroppers, and so will I.

The analyses can be divided, with poetic license, into two groups: those that stress the importance of credit (Ransom and Sutch 1977; Wright 1979) and those that focus on problems of labor management (Higgs 1974; Reid 1977, 1979; Alston and Higgs 1982). In spite of the bias against blacks owning or renting land, many scholars believe that it was not prejudice but their lack of wealth and access to credit that compelled blacks to start low on the tenure ladder. But why sharecropping? Blacks, particularly those with some supervisory skills and ambition, favored a share over a wage contract because the former offered a bonus to the superior worker while the latter did not. Sharecropping gave blacks a chance to establish their credentials and the opportunity to move up the tenure ladder. The problem was imperfect information; sharecropping acted as a kind of signaling or screening device to sort good from bad workers and thus established conditions for the good ones to obtain the credit that they needed to improve their lot (Newbery and Stiglitz 1979).

Sharecropping contracts appealed to the landowners as well: they spread risks, gave workers an incentive to work hard—relieving owners of the need to monitor field work—and discouraged tenants from leaving for greener, more lucrative pastures at periods of peak labor demand.

Although Ransom and Sutch contend, as does Cheung, that allocative efficiency was not a problem since a landowner could vary plot size and shares (broadly defined) to maximize profits (reduction in plot size or shares could prevent the cropper from undersupplying labor on the landowner's share), they do argue that sharecropping had a long-term negative impact on soil quality, innovative activity, and the welfare of croppers. The incentive to invest in land was low for both cropper and landowner; for the former because leases were very short, for the latter because he or she received only a fraction of the return on his or her investment. There was, instead, a tendency to overuse land and, as land quality dropped owing to soil exhaustion, to use more fertilizer. As a result, Southern agriculture remained backward with croppers trapped in a web of poverty. This argument implies that a more enlightened government policy might have rectified the situation.

Wright (1979) is more sanguine about the consequences of sharecropping. He maintains that the constraints on the system were real and that any attempt to sweep them away by land reform or some other government intervention was probably doomed. His argument recalls the attitude of the classical economists. As Mill noted, "The metayer system is not one which we should be anxious to introduce where exigencies of society had not naturally given birth to it; but neither ought we to be eager to abolish it on a mere *a priori* view of its disadvantages" (Mill 1871, 388; Jaynes 1984).

It is possible that imperfections in labor markets and not imperfect information on the quality of croppers gave rise to sharecropping (Reid 1977, 1979). Assume that the farming skills possessed by workers and landowners were different, specifically that potential croppers, because of their background, were first-rate supervisors of farm operations but poor managers; while landowners were good at managing the farm, handling accounts, and marketing output but not especially strong in overseeing actual farming activities. If markets in the South immediately after the Civil War for supervisory and managerial skills were poor (as Reid maintains), sharecropping may have been the most efficient way to organize farm operations. Both the cropper and the landowner could specialize in what they did best and, because they shared the output, each benefited from the effort of the other. The problem was one of incomplete or nonexistent markets for certain labor services.

If the above argument is correct, it would seem plausible to suppose that, *ceteris paribus,* farm size may have played an important role in determining the nature of contracts since the larger the farm, the more onerous supervision and thus the more attractive share arrangements, where incentives for self-supervision are strong (Higgs 1974). Attempts to test this hypothesis have met with modest success (Alston and Higgs 1982).

The message of this review for the historian is, once again, straightforward. Confronted with an institutional arrangement like sharecropping that has various flaws, the historian should follow the lead of the economist and try to identify the economic conditions (market imperfections or whatever) that may explain why this institutional setup, in spite of its drawbacks, dominates others. In a less than perfect world, less than perfect institutions are often the best.

THE FIRM

Economists often explore two related questions: first, how can we explain the existence of the capitalist (i.e., privately owned and managed) firm and second, what is the relation between transaction costs and technology, unemployment, and intraenterprise promotion ladders? Although these are neither the only nor necessarily the most important issues economists raise about firms, they do provide particularly useful insights into the way economists think about institutions.

The classical capitalist firm. To review briefly an argument presented earlier, Ronald Coase (1937) points out that because market transactions are costly, producers will seek to economize on them exactly as they would with any costly input. An employer may therefore find it more economical to sign a single, comprehensive employment contract with a worker than to renegotiate a contract with the worker each time he wants to modify slightly the character of the labor input. He, or his firm, replaces a series of costly market transactions with a series of less costly nonmarket ones.[6]

While Coase establishes a new and compelling way of looking at the firm, he does not provide a complete explanation of its existence. In particular, he fails to pinpoint those special features of the firm that give it a cost advantage over the market or over other institutional arrangements. Some maintain that the key lies with the assignment of property rights in the residual (profits) (Alchian and Demsetz 1972). The argument goes as follows. As we know, workers in equilibrium will be paid according to the extra value their work contributes to the product; anything more or less is incompatible with efficiency and with satisfaction for worker and employer alike.[7] Assume now that team production where producers work together in a group is more efficient than nonteam production. The assumption would lead us to predict, quite reasonably, that team production would replace nonteam production. The problem with team production is that observation of outputs may not measure the contribution of each team member.

A couple of examples may shed light on the problem. Two workers together load boxes onto a truck. To observe final output, the loaded truck, is easy enough; to separate out the contribution made by each would require a witness to the work process. The putting-out system or cottage industry provides a good example of nonteam production: individuals work separately in their isolated cottages and the merchant-capitalist unites the various parts of the process to produce final products; the link between inputs and outputs is reasonably clear. In a factory, by contrast, workers often engage in team production, in which final output is identifiable but each worker's contribution to it is not.

Before we look at a firm, its contribution, or its final output, we need to understand how economists identify workers' contributions to the firm. Assume, as economists always do, that workers derive satisfaction from both income and leisure and that it is costly to observe workers' behavior. Consider the following possibility. Since team production is more efficient than its nonteam counterpart, workers begin to produce as a team and, naturally enough, to divide the spoils equally among team

6. Simon emphasizes the "ubiquity of organizations" and suggests "organizational economy" as more appropriate than "market economy" to describe contemporary industrial nations (1991, 27–28).

7. For more on the relation between wages and labor productivity, see the chapter by Carter and Cullenberg, 91–95.

members. Each worker has an incentive to shirk (partake of on-the-job leisure), especially if he or she enjoys all the leisure but shares the costs (output loss) with other team members. The shirking can, of course, be controlled but only if the work process itself is monitored.

This is where the owner of the firm comes in. Workers hire a monitor but discover quickly that a problem remains. Who monitors the monitor? The solution is simple. Give the monitor full rights to the residual, that is, to what is left over after all expenses are covered, and he or she will have an incentive to work hard (note the close parallel with sharecropping). We thus have a rationale for the classic capitalist firm in which the monitor (owner-entrepreneur) is the residual claimant, a party to all contracts, has the power to hire and fire, liquidate operations, and supervise inputs. In other words, the monitor has property rights in the firm. Without such rights, inefficiencies exist; with them, all is as it should be. Workers (the monitored) submit to the monitor because it is in their interest to do so.

While provocative, the argument is not entirely compelling. Firms enter into a variety of contractual agreements—with suppliers, creditors, customers, as well as with workers; all agreements have to be monitored (Jensen and Meckling 1976). The worker-boss connection is thus not the only and perhaps not the principal contractual arrangement that the firm handles more cheaply than the market does. Even with team production, to link inputs and outputs may be less difficult than this argument would have us believe. Think of an automobile assembly line or a weaving mill or a brewery or practically any other type of manufacturing activity where it is easy to observe the link between inputs and outputs. Monitoring is still necessary but it is not a unique feature of team production. We now know much more about transaction costs than we did when Coase made his original contribution (Williamson and Winter 1993), but his fundamental insight stands: the market-firm choice depends on the relative costs of the two.

At this point let me put in a good word for Marx. Much of what he says about the benefits of firm (factory) production compared with "putting out" (what he calls petty commodity production), suitably translated, has a remarkably modern ring.

Marx stresses the benefits of hierarchy or team production (he calls it cooperation) and incorporates supervisory and contracting costs into his analysis. He is well aware that capitalists often brought workers together under one roof *before* the invention of the machines that we associate with factory production. The central figure in all this is the cap-

italist. He coordinates, plans, hires, supervises, and is the central contractual agent in all agreements. He has property rights in the firm and—
if it is in his economic interest to do so—centralizes production. Adding
to the gains from centralizing production, Marx says, was the introduction of modern machinery into a factory setting that truly revolutionized
capitalist production. "The starting point of Modern Industry is . . . the
revolution in the instruments of labour and this revolution attains its
most highly developed form in the organized system of machinery in the
factory" (1967, 394). With this change, the millowner gained the power
to regulate the speed, timing, and character of production and, in consequence, the unfettered ability to maximize profits or, as Marx would
have it, the rate of exploitation and surplus value. To put it in modern
terms, Marx reminds us that while transaction costs matter, we would
be unwise when trying to understand the success of the classical capitalist firm (factory) to ignore the enormous economies of scale associated with centralized production.

Technology, unemployment, and promotion. The cost of monitoring
cuts many ways. We assume that workers desire to loaf and that surveillance is costly; the introduction of a new production technique that
reduces monitoring costs increases employers' profits even if the old production technique employs fewer scarce resources (Bowles 1985). The
approach includes all the usual assumptions about rational behavior
and is thus perfectly compatible with neoclassical theory, but the conclusion is Marxist. The insight is significant for two reasons. It indicates,
first, that substantial transaction costs may cause a firm to pursue policies that increase profit but reduce economic welfare. Second, and perhaps more important, it suggests that technological change may harm
one social class and favor another.

Perhaps the assembly line increased output per worker, not because
it used scarce resources more efficiently than other techniques but because
it reduced supervisory costs and thus facilitated a speedup of the work
process. Or the factory system came to dominate cottage industry not
because it raised labor productivity, as most historians suggest, but because enhanced monitoring allowed the millowner to extract more labor
per hour from his workers. The workers' output did go up, but the apparent increase in productivity was nothing more than an increase in
work by employees (Marglin 1974).

Costly monitoring can explain unemployment. At the macroeconomic
level, Marx was perhaps the first to make this connection. He saw the

reserve army of the unemployed, the flip side of the accumulation process, as the lid that kept wages contained and workers disciplined. An increase in wages slowed accumulation, pushed up unemployment, and put downward pressure on wages. Modern analyses are different, but the consequences—unemployed workers in an economy with a positive, stable wage rate—are similar. If we assume, once again, that workers are inclined to shirk, that surveillance is costly, and that the costs of unemployment are borne by workers, an employer will have an incentive to offer a wage that exceeds what the worker could earn in his next best alternative but, because it is above the market wage, does not clear the market. The worker faces an unappealing alternative; if he shirks and is caught, he loses his job or at the very least faces a pay cut. Unemployment becomes a device that employers use to deter shirking (Shapiro and Stiglitz 1984; Bowles 1985).

Internal promotion ladders may also serve to discourage shirking and, like unemployment, cut monitoring costs. A worker dismissed from one firm for partaking in a little on-the-job leisure must return to the bottom rung of the ladder in another, taking a pay cut that is a price for shirking. Such promotion schemes may also create divisions among workers and reduce the costs of control of labor by capital (Gintis 1976; Gordon, Edwards, and Reich 1982, Williamson 1985).

In all these cases, the problem is shirking and the solution is some institutional arrangement that reduces it in the least costly manner. Marxists and non-Marxists draw different conclusions from these observations. The Marxists contend that it is in the nature of capitalism to pit capital against labor and to waste resources in its attempt to control labor. If you want to get rid of the problem, they say, change the system. The non-Marxists are less revolutionary. They also perceive that the interests of employers and employees differ but regard such conflict as an inherent feature of relations among the parties to economic contracts. The solution is not to change the system, since this would not remove the source of tension, but to trust the contracting parties to seek the least costly way to satisfy everyone.

CONCLUSION

Both Marxian and neoclassical economists explain the genesis of institutions in terms of problems associated with property rights and/or transaction costs that lead to outcomes in which markets fail to deliver the efficiencies predicted by the general competitive equilibrium approach.

The objectives of the economist concerned with institutions are to pinpoint the sources of market failure, to explain the institutional responses, and to evaluate their impact on the economic well-being of those involved. Why, for example, was sharecropping instead of the wage-labor contract so prevalent in the southern United States after the Civil War, in Tuscany in the nineteenth century, or in Taiwan in the twentieth? Why did women in some areas of rural China in the early twentieth century take factory jobs while others refused to do so? Imperfections in the market, not the institutions, influence distribution, accumulation, and people's well-being. But it is only through a study of institutions that the economist and the historian can evaluate the costs of these imperfections.

The historian may be justifiably wary of the economist's penchant to assume that behind every institution lurks a good economic reason. Such caution is to be admired. Yet the historian who sifts through the why and how of institutional arrangements and tries to explain them must make sure, before discarding these economic factors, that they are in fact inadequate. Where profit and loss are at issue, people usually look very carefully at the bottom line; without diminishing the importance of other considerations, we would be unwise to assume that they do otherwise.

Labor Economics
and the Historian

SUSAN B. CARTER
and STEPHEN CULLENBERG

Clio and Hades, two erudite and eminent professors of History and Economics, respectively, often discuss the relative merits of their disciplines over coffee. We transcribed, annotated, and added references to one such conversation and present it here.[1]

CLIO.   I just finished reading Alice Kessler-Harris's *A Woman's Wage* (1990). Very satisfying, I thought. She develops a historical perspective on the modern campaign for Comparable Worth, setting forth a view I have always found appealing. She argues that social norms are the key determinant in wage setting.

HADES: Gasp! That's quite a bit different from the view of most economists. As it happens, I just read Claudia Goldin's *Understanding the Gender Gap* (1990). Goldin explains women's increasing participation in the paid labor force and the persistence of a gender gap in pay with frequent references to *market forces*. Tell me, how does Kessler-Harris defend her position?

1. Clio is well known as the Greek muse of history. Hades is most often thought of as the Greek god of the netherworld though he was also responsible for dispensing earthly riches. We take delight in the way Hades' second function resonates with the new feminist definition of economics recently proposed by Julie Nelson. She argues that the central focus of economics is and has been "provisioning, or providing the necessities of life," not exchange (Nelson 1992, 118). You probably note that the historian is female and the economist male. This gendering of the scholars parallels the historic gendering of their respective disciplines (Nelson 1992; McCloskey 1993). Our hope is that the ensuing dialogue will make the strengths of each available to both. The authors would like to thank Lynda Bell, Jon Cohen, Roger Ransom, Thomas Rawski, Sharon Salinger, and Gavin Wright for valuable discussion and suggestions. All errors are their own.

CLIO: She begins by noting that normative qualifiers—"fair," "family," "living," and "women's," for example—have been key elements in all of this century's public policy debates over women's wages. These include the campaigns for protective legislation and the minimum wage, the debate over women's work in the Great Depression, and the disputes surrounding the Equal Pay Act of 1963. Her study of shifts in these normative qualifiers suggests that widely held notions of gender and justice moved in the direction of greater equality for women over time. Women's political struggles as well as their actions—they became family providers—led to these changes in social norms. Wage increases for women were the result.

HADES: That's interesting. Goldin, covering much the same territory, emphasizes the role of market forces such as an increased demand for educated, white-collar labor and improvements in household technology.

CLIO: I confess I haven't read Goldin's book. In all candor, however, I haven't read it because I thought I wouldn't like it. Women's issues cannot possibly be understood without considering custom, institutions, political power, and socialization—precisely the forces you economists ignore or trivialize. Economics calls itself the queen of the Social Sciences, but if you ask me, the discipline is nothing more than a collection of formal models, none of which have anything to do with *any* particular time or place. Moreover, the models are so narrow and technical they practically oblige their users to think small.

HADES: I most certainly agree—*by themselves* economists' models explain nothing. They are merely tools. Useful ones, though, because they call attention to logical implications of propositions that are sometimes overlooked.

CLIO: Fine. But you seem to suggest there's one obvious right tool for every question. We historians like to emphasize that almost all facts are subject to a variety of interpretations and that the art of writing good history is placing events in the appropriate context.

HADES: Ah! I couldn't agree with you more.
          I'm coming to believe that your negative opinion of economics may stem from a misunderstanding of the nature of our models and of their relation to the custom, institutions, social norms, and political power that figure so prominently in the stories historians tell. Economics—at least when it's being done well—is keenly concerned with these larger issues.
          Perhaps this concern is obscured by the *style* of our argumentation. Economists are sensitive to the fact that all analysis must begin somewhere, take some things as given. It's an epistemological necessity for historians as well as economists. Economists are simply more explicit about the boundaries of the questions they ask. I believe this explicitness is a good thing. By being clear we avoid many misunderstandings and move more quickly to the issues where we genuinely disagree (Davis 1971).

CLIO: I like what you're saying. Nonetheless, it's at odds with my casual impression of how economists operate.

HADES: The only way I know to defend my position is to work through some economists' models of the labor market and economic historians' application of them. I warn you, though, this may take a bit of time. Are you willing?

CLIO: All right. [*She utters this response with a bit of resignation in her voice. But Clio is nothing if not a good sport*][2]

HADES: For some questions economists find it useful to model the labor market like the market for any other input into the production process—iron ore, for example.

CLIO: You're kidding!

HADES   [*Ignoring this comment*]: Other things equal, the higher the price, the more iron ore will be supplied to the market and the less will be demanded.[3] Thus, in a conventional price-quantity diagram, the demand for iron ore is a downward-sloping function of the price; the supply of iron ore an upward-sloping function. If the quantity demanded is greater than the quantity supplied, prices tend to rise. If the quantity supplied is greater than the quantity demanded, prices tend to fall. The prevailing market price tends toward a level at which the quantity buyers are willing to purchase is exactly equal to the quantity iron ore mine operators are willing to supply. Economists say equilibrium occurs once these adjustments in price have worked themselves out, so that for the prevailing price, the quantity firms are willing to supply just equals the quantity that consumers are willing to purchase. The market clears. The equilibrium price and quantity, then, are just those prices and quantities where there's no tendency for change as there is no excess demand or excess supply.

          Again, this assumes everything else is constant, including the price of substitute and complementary goods, income, tastes, technology, wages, etc. [*Here Hades takes an envelope from his briefcase to make the proverbial sketch on the back. We reproduce this heuristic device*

---

2. Economic historians should not take Clio's amiability for granted. According to Richard Sutch, "Economic historians will have to do most of the changing" (1991, 277) because they need to take much more of the responsibility for integrating economic history into the discipline of history and for making it part of historiography.

3. If other things are constant, the supply curve slopes upwards—quantity supplied is an increasing function of price—because the rise in price makes it more profitable for firms to increase quantity supplied. The demand curve will normally slope downwards—quantity demanded is a decreasing function of the price—other things being constant. For certain products, however, quantity demanded increases as prices rise. Economists refer to these as Giffen goods after the nineteenth-century economist Robert Giffen who first called attention to them. The classic example of the Giffen good comes from the consumption of potatoes in Ireland in the 1880s. Because potatoes constituted such a large percentage of the diet, an increase in the price of potatoes caused people to cut back on the consumption of other high-cost foods such as meat and cheese and actually increase the amount of potatoes they consumed (Stiglitz 1993, 207).

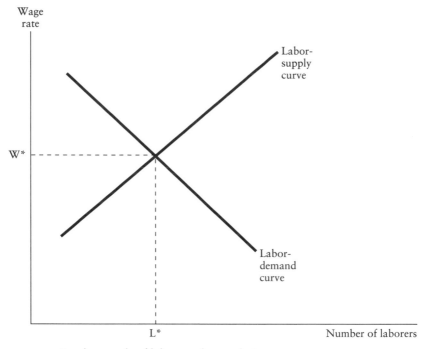

FIGURE 4. Fundamentals of labor market analysis.

as Figure 4] The same downward-sloping demand, upward-sloping supply with equilibrium at the intersection of the two curves may be said to characterize the market for labor. An astonishing array of labor-market phenomena can be understood with this one, very simple metaphor.

CLIO: Let's pause right here! I can already see two major objections to your analysis. I don't want to let you get too far ahead. I know if you grant an economist his assumptions, he will prove the moon must be made from blue cheese.

First, any historian knows that everything else is never equal. In fact, all the really interesting stories have quite a number of developments taking place all at the same time. To return to the case of change in women's social and economic roles with which we began this discussion, civil rights legislation, educational attainment, social norms, incomes, fertility, and more were *all* changing at the same time. This isn't an isolated example, either. It's the norm!

HADES: True enough, all things are changing simultaneously. But to be able to make sense of these changes an analysis must begin somewhere, take some things as given. The issue is not how the world really is but how we understand it and how we persuade others to think about it (Mc-

Closkey 1990). The *ceteris paribus* ("other things equal") assumption is necessary for all systematic inquiry. But I grant you that not all assumptions lead to great insights. In economics—and in history too, for that matter—the art is to know what aspects of economic and social life to take as given and what to highlight for further analysis. The conventional supply-demand graph that economists use so often highlights variations in price and quantity, holding everything else constant. It *is* a highly stylized picture of the world. Even so, you'd be surprised at how much it can explain. I know we'll come back to this issue later, so let's leave it there for now.

CLIO: Well, all right. Then let me raise a second objection. It seems to me that in presenting your model of the labor market you just gave a perfect example of a practice I criticized earlier. You seem to imply that markets exist everywhere and in all sectors. Historians would disagree. For example, while there may have been a market for iron ore, there was *no* market—or at best a poorly functioning market—for labor in British North America before, say, the early nineteenth century. A market for labor may not have appeared in the American South much before the twentieth century! The historical narrative is full of the complaint that reliable help was simply unavailable at any reasonable price.

HADES: You're of course right to point out that markets—especially well-functioning markets—cannot be assumed to exist at every time and place. As a matter of fact, economists have explored the consequences of missing markets in some detail.[4] Rothenberg, for example, dates the appearance of a well functioning labor market in America at about 1800 (1992, 162). Before that, she shows that spatial characteristics of the economy—low population density, relatively even population dispersion, and slow communication—made it difficult to assemble the requisite large number of buyers and sellers of labor services. Especially important, however, was land abundance. Because land was plentiful and cheap and because, by all accounts, people preferred farm ownership, a large fraction of the male population had an option they preferred over wage work. Men could and did farm for themselves.

The simple labor-market diagram I showed you earlier points up the implications. In this case the labor-demand curve would have the normal downward slope, its position determined by labor productivity and by the price the crop could fetch on the market. What's unusual in this case is the labor-supply curve. It has the normal upward slope, but its position is almost everywhere above the demand-for-labor curve. Only

4. Standard neoclassical general equilibrium models require that markets exist for all present and future commodities within the overall economy and that they be efficient. Economists recognize, however, that a large number of markets are missing. The presence of externalities and uncertain future contingencies make certain goods unavailable for purchase: a pollution-free environment, or house repair twenty-five years from now if the "big earthquake" were to strike southern California along the San Andreas fault. On the theory and implications of missing markets see Milgrom and Roberts (1992, 75–76).

young people desiring to earn the money to buy a farm of their own were willing to work for others. [*As is his wont, Hades sketches this configuration. We reproduce it as Figure 5*] Thus in equilibrium, the wage is high and the number of workers employed small. Note that this explanation also accounts for hired laborers' divided loyalties—another source of farm owners' complaints. Laborers were all looking forward to a day in the not-too-distant future when they'd be farm owners themselves (Wright 1978, 44–47).

CLIO: You're certainly clever in making that model appear to fit this circumstance. Of course, I suppose with sufficient cleverness a person could make any model fit any situation, especially if the model is simple and general enough. I wouldn't say that exercises of this sort have much to do with the writing of great history, however. What insights does it offer?

HADES: That's a fair question. I'd say there are two insights. One begins with an observation of Benjamin Franklin, who predicted that the United States would not develop a manufacturing sector. You no doubt recall, Franklin wrote: "But no man, who can have a piece of land of his own, sufficient by his labor to subsist his family in plenty, is poor enough to be a manufacturer, and work for a master. Hence, when there is land enough in America for our people there can never be manufactures to any amount of value" (Franklin 1840 [1760], 19). But yet manufactures *did* arise. The economist's approach suggests that the explanation for this unexpected development must be *either* a reduced ability to attain farm ownership *or* an outward shift in the demand for labor, or both. In other words, the model directs our attention to potentially fruitful areas for new research (Field 1978; Goldin and Sokoloff 1982, 1984; Craig and Field-Hendrey 1993).

         A second insight is that in economies where "people preferred farm ownership and were able to attain it," we'd also expect a demand for unfree labor (Domar 1970). In fact, we see just that. Indentured servants made up the principal nonfamily labor supply for many of the British North American colonies during the seventeenth and eighteenth centuries. Later, landowners began buying slaves as well (Galenson 1981). With a few more extensions I can even use the model to explain why slaves were used so much more extensively in the South than the North in the eighteenth century.

CLIO: I can see how those illustrations are logically consistent with your model. But I still fail to see how the model helps when you're trying to analyze a fresh, new problem.

HADES: The model helps because its logical nature rules out some possible explanations while suggesting the sort of evidence necessary to test others. Here's an example from our discussion of slavery. Suppose I want to understand why slaves were used so much more extensively in the South than in the North in the eighteenth century. It's quite a puzzle,

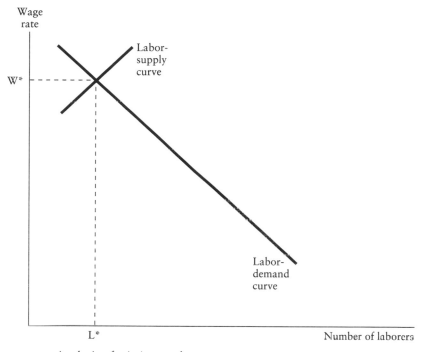

FIGURE 5. Analysis of missing markets.

actually! As you no doubt know, recent scholarship has shown that Northern society and culture were every bit as racist and, at least in the eighteenth century, there were no legal barriers to slavery in the North (Ransom 1989). So why didn't Northerners use more slaves?

Supply and demand analysis gives a straightforward economic reason why slaves were used so much more extensively in the South. [*Inevitably, he draws another figure. This one is reproduced as Figure 6*] I begin with a *supply* of slaves curve. Since the supply to the two regions was identical, I draw a single curve for both. By the way, I draw the supply curve as a horizontal line because the British North American colonies were small buyers in a large market. Doubling or even tripling the number of slaves purchased wouldn't have affected the price for potential slave buyers. Well, since the supply was the same, regional differences in the use of slaves had to be due to differences in the demand for labor. Let me use this occasion to talk a bit more about the demand for labor.

The demand for labor can be explained with the same framework used to analyze producers' choices with regard to any input into the production process. I mean, the demand for labor is a *derived demand*. It originates in the firm's desire to produce a product that can be sold

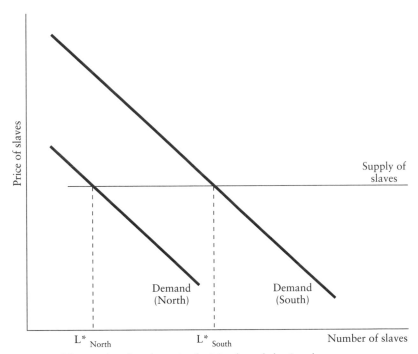

FIGURE 6. The market for slaves in the North and the South.

for profit.[5] A firm's demand for labor, then, is influenced by two considerations. First, a worker's productivity, or the number of units of output a worker can produce in a given time period. Second, the price those units can fetch on the product market. The more productive a worker is, the higher the profit and therefore the greater the demand for labor. Similarly, the higher the price of the final product, the greater the profit, and therefore the greater the demand for labor.

So, why did the South use so many more slaves? The productivity of slave labor in agriculture was probably higher in the South. The more temperate climate meant a longer growing season—and that meant a longer period of the year in which slave labor could be used to advantage. But the biggest difference between the labor demand of the North and the South was in the price their export crops could fetch on world markets. The South's tobacco fetched a high price on international markets compared with the North's timber and cod. Thus the demand for labor in the South was quite a bit greater than that in the North. In other words, the South's demand curve for slave labor was to the right

5. This point about derived demand also appears in the chapter by Rawski, 49–50.

of the North's. As my FIGURE [*Figure 6*] shows, this meant that the South used more slaves!

CLIO: So, you claim to explain the North-South difference in the use of slaves—a difference that later threatened the Union, a difference that had to be resolved by a bloody Civil War, and a difference that formed the basis for large racial differences that remain with us more than *two hundred years later*—in terms of a European fad for the noxious weed!?!

HADES: Well . . . it's a little more complicated than that. Some economic historians speculate that slavery might have been abandoned in the South around the end of the eighteenth century except for the dramatic increase in world demand for raw cotton. The profitability of tobacco was on the decline by then, you know. But the simple answer to your question is YES![6]

CLIO: [*Stunned silence*]

HADES: Since I seem to have your attention let me move forward and talk about what's more generally the most important determinant of the position of the demand-for-labor curve, what we economists call the marginal physical product of labor. This measure of worker productivity is affected by the quantity of other inputs into the production process, factors such as capital, land, and other natural resources. Since labor is generally used in combination with other inputs the level of these inputs affects labor productivity. For example, the number of bushels of apples that can be grown in a season depends on the number of acres of land and the quantity of other cooperating factors such as insecticide and pruning equipment. The more such capital inputs, the more productive each laborer will be and the greater will be the demand for labor.

Now, let's say the size of the apple orchard and the amount of equipment are given, fixed at a certain size. More apples can be harvested only by hiring more labor. The first worker hired—think of him as Johnny Appleseed—can produce a lot of apples by tossing seeds on the ground and then harvesting whatever the insects don't get. Adding workers increases the size of the apple harvest because more workers mean that trees can be pruned, insects fought, and the fruit picked in a timely fashion. *Increments* to the harvest decline with each worker hired, however: the easy pickings have all been taken. This decline in incremental output is what we economists call the law of diminishing returns. Now, a farmer may decide to hire more workers despite the workers' diminishing marginal productivity, but only if the farmer's costs—the hourly wage rate—do not exceed the farmer's benefits—the product of the number of bushels the worker can pick in an hour and the price of a bushel of apples. In fact, the profit-maximizing farmer

6. Hades' response may be a bit glib. A more careful reply would state that, in the absence of another high-price export crop like cotton, a decline in the price of tobacco would remove much of the economic motive for slave-holding.

will purchase labor just up to that point where the wage equals the value of the marginal product of apple picking. You see, the demand-for-labor curve is the same thing as the downward-sloping marginal product-of-labor curve.

CLIO: Give me some examples to bring this model to life. Even with your references to mythology and your evocation of apple orchards I find this discussion pretty abstract.

HADES: OK. Let's go back to Johnny Appleseed. He was my way of alluding to the enormous productivity of workers in the resource-rich American environment. Appleseed's approach exemplifies the sloppy agricultural techniques that were said to characterize American farmers generally (at least before, say, 1850). You recall the constant complaints of contemporary observers. I can, in fact, regale you with Percy Bidwell's summary of the criticisms since I quote him each time I teach my course in American economic history. I like to tell my students that economists are the only ones trained to appreciate the acumen of American farmers' apparently "irrational, custom-bound" response. Here's Bidwell's complaint:

> Although agriculture was the chief means whereby more than 90 percent of the inhabitants of southern New England got their living, yet it was most inefficiently, and, to all appearances, carelessly conducted. Very little improvement had been made over the primitive methods employed by the earliest settlers. . . . In the century and a half intervening between the settlement of New England and the opening of the nineteenth century, improvements of far-reaching significance had been introduced in English agriculture, through the work of Tull, Bakewell, Townshend, Coke, and Arthur Young. The knowledge of these changes had spread quickly to this side of the Atlantic, and yet the bulk of the farmers had shown no disposition to adopt the new methods. On their poorly cultivated fields little fertilizer of any sort was used, their implements were rough and clumsy, livestock was neglected, and the same grains and vegetables were raised year after year with little attempt at a rotation of crops, until the land was exhausted. (Bidwell 1916, 319)

But from the perspective of the model I just presented, the "apparent lack of intelligence, and of any progressive spirit, exhibited by the New England farmers" is an eminently sensible—indeed, brilliant—response to the fact that farmers had *a lot* of land. It wasn't great land. William Parker reminds us that the thinness of the soil and the harshness of the climate of New England prompted Arnold Toynbee to classify it together with such classic adverse environments as the "parched plains of Ceylon, the North Arabian Desert, Easter Island, and the Roman compagna" (Parker 1987, 21–23). Yet New England farmers were able to produce a surplus above subsistence by combining their sloppy labor with *lots* of this miserable land. In other words, the demand-for-

labor curve in New England was to the right of that in England, reflecting the abundance of land. As a consequence American farmers were
extremely productive, and workers were well paid.

CLIO: Wait! You began by talking about a profit-making capitalist's demand
            for labor. That was fine. But now you're using the same model to de-
            scribe the operation of owner-operated, largely self-sufficient farms.
            Doesn't that violate your own standard of good practice by using one
            of your simplistic models in an inappropriate way?

HADES: Gosh. You're right. As you can see it's really easy to get carried away.
            Good economics requires both an understanding of the economic mod-
            els and of the historical context. We economists tend not to appreci-
            ate the importance of historical context fully enough. But while I ac-
            cept your criticism regarding farmers' behavior, I want to insist that
            the model is appropriate in describing the experience of laborers. In
            fact, land abundance helps explain an enormous range of phenomena
            regarding wage laborers.
                Land abundance meant, as Festus Foster put it in 1812, that in
            America, "every necessary of life is sluttishly plentiful" (Lebergott
            1964, 38). The high productivity and wages in agriculture, in turn, led
            to developments in other sectors. Of course you know, Clio, about the
            American System of Manufactures. The distinctive features of that sys-
            tem—the raw-material intensity, skilled-labor saving, and modern
            forms of industrial organization—were all responses to the high price
            of labor (Habakkuk 1962; David 1975a; Field 1983; Wright 1990).
                If we consider *differences* in the position of the demand-for-labor
            curve then we can also explain the international and interregional labor
            flows so central to the history of the world economy in the nineteenth
            century. [*Figure 7 now appeared*] Strong labor demand meant a high
            wage in America relative to Europe. Festus Foster also noted that the
            sluttish plenitude of the necessities of life was an "allurement to emi-
            gration" (Lebergott 1964, 30). Later observers added, "bad times in
            Europe regularly increase, and bad times in America invariably di-
            minish, immigration" (quoted in Lebergott 1964, 40). Harry Jerome
            (1926) and Brinley Thomas (1954) confirmed these impressions with
            statistical studies demonstrating that regular outward shifts in the
            demand-for-labor curve in America raised the American wage relative
            to that in Europe and called forth a flow of labor to these shores.
                Shifts in labor demand account for the extensive interregional labor
            flows within the United States as well. The transportation revolution,
            resource discoveries, and the commercialization of agriculture all re-
            sulted in a relative increase in the demand for labor in the more west-
            ern cities. The quantity of labor supplied to these western locales grew
            in response, through migration from east to west (Easterlin 1960;
            Margo and Villaflor 1987; Rosenbloom 1990). We'd represent this
            movement up along the supply-of-labor curve as the demand for labor
            and therefore wage offers increase. The enormous magnitude of the en-

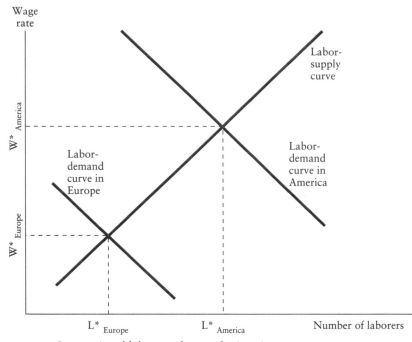

FIGURE 7. International labor markets and migration.

suing population shifts show up in the fact that whereas in 1790 East Coast states accounted for 97 percent of the population, their share was only 42 percent by 1890. Richard Easterlin concludes that the magnitude and direction of labor mobility was such "as to significantly alter the relative rates of growth of labor supply in the various regions in a direction that, other things being equal, would have made for convergence of relative income levels" (Easterlin 1960, 77, 142). Adjustments were not instantaneous, of course. Industrialization, land augmentation, and foreign immigration were constantly shifting the locus of relative opportunity. Yet, except for the special case of the South, the conclusion of scholars is that interregional wage differentials were the product of rapid shifts in opportunity (shifts in the demand for labor), not of workers' reluctance to respond.

CLIO: What *about* the South? Isn't that a case where culture, tradition, and perhaps politics were more powerful than market forces? It seems to me that the Special Case of the South is an excellent example of the limitations of your model.

HADES: Well, I'd put it rather differently. I'd say it's an example of how the simple model frames the questions to be asked. It *is* puzzling that low-wage Southern workers did not move north and west to take better-paying jobs before the World War I period. But I would reject an explanation framed simply in terms of culture, tradition, or even politics. Recall that once the migratory flow began, it was extremely large. It seems implausible that culture and tradition could change so dramatically in a five-year period. Maybe some unusual barriers to migration were acting like a cork to keep the population bottled up. Once the cork was released, the usual forces could act. This isn't the place to speculate on what that cork might have been. My real point is that the simple labor-market model identifies the absence of migration out of the South before World War I as an anomaly *and* suggests the kinds of places we might look for an explanation.

CLIO: That *is* rather clever.

HADES: The labor-market model can also shed light on a more complex and controversial phenomenon   the rise of a manufacturing labor force. We spoke earlier of Benjamin Franklin's doubts that the United States would ever develop a manufacturing sector. And yet an industrial sector *did* appear in the North in the first half of the nineteenth century. Many of the recruits were the daughters and sons of farm families. Daughters appeared at the factory gates first. They were less likely than their brothers to migrate west. As competition from the West reduced the profitability of New England's grain farms these young women became increasingly eager to enter factories (Field 1978; Goldin and Sokoloff 1982; Craig and Field-Hendrey 1993). By the latter part of the nineteenth century thousands of former farm boys entered the industrial labor force as well (Lebergott 1964)—despite a substantial rise in agricultural productivity and wages. These young men chose factory work because industrial productivity and wages were higher still (Hatton and Williamson 1991). In our diagrams of labor supply and demand, this shows up as an increased demand for manufactured goods and improvements in manufacturing techniques shifting the demand for manufacturing labor outward, causing the wage rate to rise (Long 1960; Rees 1961; David and Solar 1977; and Adams 1982). Those in the economically active population moved along their stable supply-of-labor curves and became factory workers—just as Figure 7 predicts!

CLIO: Whoa! You're talking here about what historians call the proletarianization of labor! Herbert Gutman (1977) and others show that this movement of workers along their stable supply-of-labor curve was a distinctly *unstable* process. This creation of a factory labor force, as we historians would have it, involved the substitution of factory automation for natural work rhythms, the abandonment of self-employment, subjugation to a boss, loss of control over major decisions about how the work was done, periods of involuntary unemployment, and the possibility of wage-rate cuts. Sometimes the process wrenched apart an older way of life. Please don't forget the Enclosures. Or, ask yourself, could the U.S. have industrialized as rapidly as it did without the enormous influx of immigrants uprooted—sometimes violently— from more traditional economies? I noticed, for example, Hades, that you omitted all references to foreign immigration from your saccharine account of the growth of manufacturing. Historians rightly emphasize the resistance of workers—and of the larger society—to these trends. I see none of this in your analysis. Where's the passion? Where's the struggle? Where's the glory?

HADES: Movement along a stable labor-supply curve needn't be smooth and passionless. Demand and supply curves are only metaphors, after all. They're part of the overall rhetorical tetrad that characterizes all argument. As Donald McCloskey (1990) reminds us, rhetoric—or the art of persuasion—always involves fact, logic, story, and metaphor. My use of demand and supply curves is a way to metaphorically capture the logic of what you call the proletarianization of labor.

I do understand your complaint, though. Since the 1960s, when the systematic application of economic theory to the analysis of labor markets was begun in earnest, labor economics has focused on the scientific half of the persuasion tetrad—the fact and logic. We, ourselves, may have lost sight of the way we use metaphor and story. It's certainly not a surprise that those in other disciplines have trouble seeing these elements of persuasion in our work. It may also be the case that we have too many *poor* metaphors and tell too many *bad* stories. In any case, I believe things are changing. McCloskey (1985b, 1990) has inspired a lot of economists to examine and improve their rhetoric. Feminist economists such as Marianne Ferber and Julie Nelson (1993) have led a parallel initiative. Today almost every aspect of economists' method is being reexamined (Cullenberg 1988; Klamer 1988; Klamer, McCloskey, and Solow 1988; Summers 1991). Among other things we're beginning to see how economics and history are complementary not competing styles of explanation. But let's go on.

Now, I don't want to deny that the prominence of young women and then Irish-famine refugees in the early American factory labor force is a sign that the choice of industrial work was influenced by distress. The fact that nativeborn white men did not enter factory employment in large numbers until later in the century certainly fits the view that factory work exhibited disamenities. I *am* insisting on the salience of the fact that the manufacturing wage rate rose while the numbers (and fraction of the labor force) employed in manufacturing was growing. In terms of the supply-and-demand diagram we've been using, these twin facts mean that the proximate cause of the transfer of labor out of agriculture (in the U.S. and abroad) and domestic work was an outward shift in the demand for labor. It may be that the supply-of-labor curve shifted outward (as nonindustrial opportunities diminished). But the wage rate can rise while the supply of factory labor is rising only if an outward shift in the demand-for-labor curve dominates the outward shift in the supply-of-labor curve.[7] This suggests that

---

7. On the relation of demand to supply see Lindert's chapter, 212–213.

the reason workers abandoned nonindustrial work habits was because the monetary rewards to wage labor compensated workers for their loss of autonomy. You know, Clio, it always seemed odd to me that we can read all the great histories of American labor written by historians without realizing that the real wage—that is, the purchasing power of an hour of wage labor—rose dramatically over the course of the nineteenth century!

CLIO: Well, certainly it's true that the long-term rise in the real wage doesn't stand out in the stories labor historians tell about this period. Perhaps the problem is that you are talking about something that never figured prominently in contemporary *discussions* of the nineteenth-century labor market. Laborers, trade unionists, employers, and observers talked about many labor-market issues—the length of the workday; the employment of women and children; education, training, and the skill content of jobs; control of the work process; workplace safety—in fact, almost everything about the employment relation *except* the wage rate. I return to my earlier stance—Hades, your model is irrelevant to the history of labor in nineteenth-century America!

HADES: It *is* relevant! You just have to know how to use it. Let me show you the model's relevance for each of the phenomena you listed, beginning with the length of the workday. To talk about that properly, though, I will need to say more about the supply of labor.

CLIO: I promised to allow you to develop your model fully. Proceed, by all means.

HADES: Labor supply can be explained with reference to the framework economists use to analyze consumers' choice between any two commodities. For the decision about whether to participate in the paid labor force, we define the commodities as income and leisure. Consumers choose the combination of income and leisure that makes them as well off as possible from among the combinations that are affordable. We show affordable combinations as the budget constraint. [*Figure 8 now appears!*] The budget constraint is drawn on a graph in which the vertical axis shows increasing levels of income and the horizontal axis increasing levels of leisure. I draw the budget constraint by first considering the income of someone devoting all of her time to generating money income. That income is the product of her market wage and her total available hours [*point C in Figure 8*]. My second point marks maximum leisure. It is given by the number of available hours [*point F*]. If our hypothetical person can receive the same wage rate no matter how many hours of market work she chooses, up to the maximum hours available, then the full budget constraint is the straight line connecting points C and F. Since time not consumed as leisure is spent in the labor market, the individual's labor-market hours can be seen in the graph as well. It is the difference between point F—full leisure time—and the actual number of actual hours spent in leisure, say F^A in the graph.

In terms of the graph, the length of the workday can be thought of

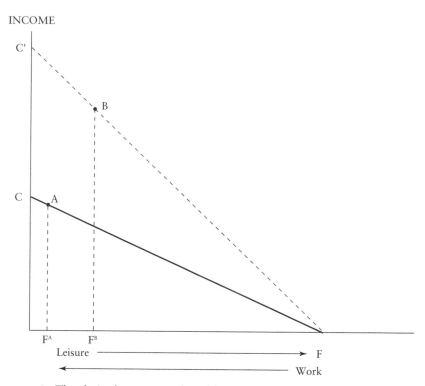

FIGURE 8. The choice between work and leisure.

as the individual's labor-market hours. Most economic historians would argue that the long-term reduction in the length of the workday—or the growth of leisure time—was the result of an increase in the wage rate. A rise in the wage rate is shown by an outward pivot of the budget constraint along the vertical axis. With a higher wage rate, the individual who spends all available time in the market will enjoy a higher income and therefore the vertical intercept, or maximum income, will increase from C to C'. But if all time goes to leisure the rise in the wage rate is irrelevant, so the horizontal intercept remains the same. In sum, the budget line pivots up and to the right [*the dotted line in Figure 8 shows this*].

An increase in the wage rate actually has two effects on the individual's choice of how much labor to offer. An increase in the wage rate raises the quantity of goods the worker can purchase in exchange for an hour of work. This encourages individuals to increase the amount of labor supplied by substituting work for leisure. Economists call this the *substitution effect*. But an increase in the wage rate also increases income, assuming people work the same number of hours as before. At a higher level of income more of all goods—including leisure—becomes available. If some of the extra income does go to purchase more leisure, it reduces time in the labor market, since the total number of hours doesn't change. This is the *income effect.*

When wage rates and incomes are low the substitution effect generally dominates; that is, increases in the wage rate lead to increases in the amount of labor supplied. As wage rates and incomes rise the income effect comes to dominate; increases in the wage rate lead to reductions in the amount of labor supplied. This overall pattern is often called the backward-bending labor-supply curve.[8]

At the beginning of the industrial era hours of work were very long. Textile firms had thirteen-hour days; eleven or twelve hours were common in other industries (Lebergott 1964, 48). The model worker was probably at a point like A in Figure 8, at a wage rate that called forth relatively long work hours. As wage rates and incomes rose above this point, the income effect dominated the substitution effect. Workers demanded more leisure. This is shown in the graph as the worker's movement to point B. By 1976 estimated weekly hours averaged only 8.1 per day (Owen 1976).[9] Thus, over the past century and a half daily hours declined by about *a third!* The decline in weekly hours was even greater. Let me emphasize that this is a *huge* decline in world-historic perspective.

CLIO: You explain why workers might *want* a shorter workday, but your account makes the long-term decline seem like a smooth, inevitable process. That's certainly not the way it happened. Workers had to go on strike to win the Ten-Hour Day. They had to go on strike again to win the Eight-Hour Day. In fact the Haymarket Riots, arguably one of the most important events in nineteenth-century American labor history, began as a protest by the shorter-hours movement (Roediger and Foner 1989). In the American iron and steel industry the *twelve*-hour day was not overturned until 1923! Even then the Interchurch World Movement and a direct entreaty from then-President Warren G. Harding had to weigh in on the side of the unions before steel companies capitulated to workers' demands. The resistance of the steel companies is no surprise from a Marxist perspective. Indeed, as Marx argued long ago, it was in the direct interest of employers to *lengthen* the workday as this would increase the amount of surplus value produced by each worker. A lot more is certainly involved here than can be captured by your supply and demand economics.

---

8. Hades did not want to interrupt the argument's flow to mention a distinction between the shape of the labor-supply curve of individuals and that of an entire economy: individuals' curves may each bend backward yet the aggregate labor-supply curve of a population can (and generally does) slope upward at each point. As wage rates rise, the reduction in hours for current labor-market participants is swamped by increases in hours for individuals new to the labor force. This point is sometimes important but does not directly concern discussions of the average length of the workday for current labor-market participants.

9. The statistics on weekly hours are for non-student males.

HADES: You're right, of course. More than simply the demand for shorter
        hours is required to explain the pace and pattern of the long-term de-
        cline in the length of the workday. But in defense of the power of the
        supply and demand framework I'd like to point out that my model does
        help explain why protests from church groups and pressure from the
        president of the United States did not appear until the 1920s. By then
        high wages had made short hours the desired norm. A hundred years
        earlier thirteen-hour days were the rule, yet no one complained!

        But I will admit that employers' apparent reluctance to grant work-
        ers' demands for shorter and shorter workdays is a puzzle for my sup-
        ply and demand economics, as you put it. Like Marx, economists today
        approach this puzzle by trying to understand why employers would
        care how many hours their workers worked each day. In an innova-
        tive paper, Martha Shiells pursues this approach. She suggests that em-
        ployer reluctance may have stemmed from a possible "public good"
        aspect of work hours. That is, if there were efficiency gains associated
        with having all workers work the same hours, then the length of the
        workday would be expected to decrease discontinuously and then only
        after the preferences of a substantial fraction of workers had changed.
        Under these circumstances the more modern workers—well-paid work-
        ers?—would perpetually find themselves wanting shorter hours than
        employers were offering (Shiells 1990. See also Whaples 1990).

CLIO: Well, that's a *consistent* explanation within your framework, but then
        so is the Marxian one I put forward. Deciding between competing
        plausible stories is a complicated issue, as we both know . . . [*Decid-
        ing to move on*] I suppose the same model can be used to explain the
        exit of children and entry of women into the paid labor force.

HADES: Right you are! The entry of women is most straightforward. Much of
        the long-term increase in the labor force participation rate of married
        women can be explained by the rise in the market wage rate. Over time
        productivity rose faster in the marketplace than in the home. This rel-
        ative rise in the market wage rate induced women to shift the locus of
        their energies into market work.

CLIO: Things were a lot more complicated than that! Why, before the 1940s
        a working wife stigmatized her husband as inept, immoral, or both!
        Even if she and her husband thought they could withstand those social
        pressures they had to contend with social opprobrium that plagued
        women who didn't spend full time caring for their own children. In
        other words, public acceptance of paid child care was a requirement
        for the wholesale entry of wives and mothers into wage labor as well.
        I believe that these social and cultural changes were extremely impor-
        tant determinants of change in the locus of women's work over this cen-
        tury.

HADES: I agree. Nonetheless, your objections do not refute my case. My point
        is that the rise in the wage rate was very important as well. In fact, if
        you just look at the numbers you'll see that I've got to be right. Recall

that the labor force participation rate of married women was only 4.0 percent in 1890 and only 15.2 percent in 1940. But then, over the next twenty years it jumped to 31.2 percent. That pattern in the labor force participation rate of married women is matched by the pattern of real wage rate change. The wage rate available to women really soared beginning in the 1940s. Over the fifty-year period starting in 1890 real wages for women had doubled—not a small change by any means. But in the next *twenty* years they nearly doubled again! By 1970 women's real wage was 230 percent of its 1940 level (Goldin 1990, 129 [table 5.1]). Goldin argues that the pace and pattern of change in women's real wages can explain over half of the increase in the participation rate of married women between 1890 and 1980 (Goldin 1990, 126–128). She goes on to argue that quantitative studies of the long-term increase in labor supply "overturn the conventional wisdom that women entered the labor force as a result of a more complex set of factors—changes in social norms, declining barriers to their paid work, increasing work flexibility, smaller numbers of children and the diffusion of labor-saving devices in the home, to mention a few of the most cited" (126).

CLIO: I remain unconvinced. Your story is too simple. I just can't believe that the conventional wisdom you so quickly discard did not, in fact, play a more important role.

HADES: Perhaps the source of your discomfort is the phrase, over half the increase, but it has a perfectly straightforward definition. Since the actual increase in married women's labor force participation rate was 45.3 percentage points between 1890 and 1940, Goldin's claim that the rise in the wage rate accounted for over half the rise means that even in the absence of any of the social changes you emphasize the participation rate of married women in 1980 would have been about 30 percent, in other words its rate in the mid- to late 1950s. The difficulty may be that to say "over half" makes the contribution of the rise in wages seem very large. And no one, neither Goldin nor anyone else, for that matter, proposes a standard for judging whether "half" is a large or small fraction (McCloskey 1985, 154–173). Historians, with their sensitivity to context, could no doubt improve the work of economists by suggesting appropriate standards for evaluating these quantitative results. I'll confess that even I find it fairly difficult to relate the quantitative work on women's issues to the more descriptive social histories I read.

CLIO: Well, good. Why don't you go on, then. We were talking about labor-market entry. What about the kids? It seems that if the wage rate was increasing, youthful workers should have been motivated to enter the labor market as well.—Am I making sense? Is this an accurate prediction based on the logic of your model? But of course we know this hasn't happened as one might expect. How do you explain this anomaly?

HADES: Oh, you *are* making sense, up to a point, at least! You're correct in predicting that a high wage should draw youths into the labor market. The reason that didn't happen is that even more powerful forces drew children and youths to school instead. People increasingly found that the costs of school attendance were more than offset by an increased income stream when their children finally did enter the labor force. Moreover, higher incomes meant that their families could increasingly afford to allow children to take advantage of these opportunities. Even though youths' wage rates rose, their labor force participation rates fell.

CLIO: You speak of schooling as if it were an investment.

HADES: Right! I do. You certainly are catching on to this approach! The economic analysis of the demand for education is sometimes called the Human Capital model precisely because of its similarity to the demand for physical investment goods (Becker 1993). Just like the metaphor of supply and demand used to explain market transactions, the human capital metaphor has been extremely useful in understanding the economic importance of investments in education, job training, and so on. In the case of both physical and human capital, individuals endure costs in one period in expectation of receiving benefits in some future period.[10] For the decision to attend school, costs include books and tuition plus the wages that could have been earned had classroom time been spent at work instead. By the way, this latter cost—foregone earnings or the opportunity cost of time—is, by far, the largest cost of school attendance.

CLIO: Your argument implies, if I understand you correctly, that the cost of schooling should *rise* as the economy develops, as the opportunity cost of foregone earnings rise together with increased capital, improved technology, and so forth.

HADES: You *have* understood the argument. Excellent! I suppose you were going to ask, why then, if the cost of education was rising, was there an increase in the quantity of education in the economy.

CLIO: Yes, that's the question I was planning to ask. You know, before we began this conversation I hadn't considered the long-term rise in educational attainment as something that needed to be explained. It seemed so naturally a part of the complex set of changes we historians refer to as modernization. But as I think about the things you've been saying, all kinds of developments I'd taken for granted now seem less obvious than they did.

HADES: Good! Back to your excellent question. You asked why youths extended their schooling at a time when the cost of schooling was on the rise. The answer is that even though the costs of schooling were rising,

10. The costs and benefits occur in different time periods, and to bring them into equivalence requires "discounting" the earning stream (McCloskey 1985b, chap. 26). That is, money now is always worth more than the same amount of money promised later because you can take that money, put it in the bank to earn interest, and have a larger sum at a later date. "Discounting" an earnings stream takes account of this problem. Hades decided to leave this issue for another conversation.

the benefits and the ability to finance the investment were rising more rapidly still. Remember, the actual outcome we observe in a market, whether for tomatoes, iron ore, labor hours, or education depends both on the supply and demand for those goods. In the same way here, the actual amount of schooling demanded will depend on both the costs and benefits of schooling.

One example of the power of the model is its ability to explain the rise in schooling in the twentieth century. First, there were outward shifts in the demand for educated labor. The growth in large-scale business organizations (Chandler 1977) increased the demand for coordination and record keeping inside the firm, which led to an increased demand for managerial, clerical, and technical skills. Scientific breakthroughs in medicine together with the growth of family income led to an increased demand for medical services. One crude measure of the magnitude of the transformation is the fraction of the labor force employed in the white-collar sector. In 1900 this fraction was about one in six; by 1950 it was more than one in three (U.S. Bureau of the Census 1975, series D216 and D217). Another crude measure is the fraction of the labor force employed in the professional and technical sector. This fraction rose from one in twelve to one in seven over the same period (U.S. Bureau of the Census 1975, series D216 and D218).

Not all children did or could respond to these opportunities, of course. The dilemma facing the potential student was that education was costly. A major portion of total costs was the earnings foregone while the child was in school. Thus, the improved ability of parents to finance their children's schooling was an important contribution to the trend as well. Poor parents can't afford to let their children attend school. Children's earnings are necessary for the family's support. The long-term rise in parents' real wages made it possible for more families to forego the earnings of their children and allow them to make lucrative investments by attending school.

CLIO: OK. What about the high rates of school attendance—and literacy—in eighteenth-century America? The majority of white men of that era could read and write, and literacy rates for women were quite high as well (Kaestle 1983, 3). Are you claiming that children and their parents made investments in these skills because they thought they would lead to more income? The economy of that era was certainly not technologically sophisticated and over 90 percent of the labor force was engaged in agriculture.

HADES: You're right, of course. School attendance rates were high even though the economy was not technologically advanced and there were no mandatory school attendance laws in effect, at least not for those fourteen years of age and older. I am arguing that the desire to acquire job-related skills is an important reason for school attendance, especially for school attendance on a large scale. It is certainly not the *only* reason, however. In the case of eighteenth- and early nineteenth-century

America individualistic, Protestant religious values—the importance of Bible reading—and republican, egalitarian political goals are thought to be the reason why so many children—girls as well as boys—attended school.

The prospect of acquiring job-related skills doesn't seem to have been responsible for the substantial increase in educational attainment known as the Common School Revival, either. Alex Field (1980) could find no evidence of any increase in the demand for skilled or educated labor during the half century following 1820. Perhaps schooling expanded in response to the growth of incomes. Education is a good, it's desired for its own intrinsic worth. At the higher levels of income families are able to make more of this good available to their children. Alternatively, Field's results may be thought to support the view put forth by Samuel Bowles and Herbert Gintis (1976), that the expansion of public schooling in this period was motivated by a concern to socialize workers into factory discipline. In other words, this is another case where a negative finding—a development which takes place without the normal stimulus—directs our attention to new areas of investigation.

But I don't want to overlook the very many *positive* findings of the human capital model. For example, did you know that during the forty years bracketing 1900 *girls* predominated in the high schools? Girls outnumbered boys by over four to three among whites and three to two among blacks (Carter and Prus 1982)! This is surprising because literary evidence suggests that these girls faced more barriers than boys in their pursuit of education. Surely you've read quotes such as the following: "Had I been a boy instead of a girl, with my natural love for my studies, Mother might have struggled to send me ahead, much as she needed what little I could earn. But a girl didn't need an education. In fact, it might be a mistake to teach her too much" (Wolfe 1922 quoted in Tentler 1979, 102). So you see, girls' greater high-school attendance rate can be explained by reference to a differentially high rate of return to women's education! It's not that female schoolteachers made more than their male colleagues. Rather, the high rate of return to female education was due to the fact that the wage premium associated with schoolteaching was huge compared to women's next-best option—say working as an operative in some manufacturing plant. Men who wanted high-paying jobs could apprentice themselves in a trade. This option was closed to women. When boys' apprenticeship opportunities disappeared around World War I, their high-school enrollments rose to match those of girls.

Used another way, the human-capital model also sheds light on the pace and pattern in the improvement in the relative earnings of blacks over the twentieth century. As I'm sure you know, Clio, the relative economic status of black Americans remained low and essentially unchanged over the half century before World War II but improved substantially since then. Robert Margo shows that racial differences in access to schooling played an important role in explaining these patterns (Margo 1990). About the turn of the century the disenfranchisement of blacks and an increase in white demand for better schooling led to a *growing* racial inequality in access to education. Educational inequalities led to income inequalities. Poor education for blacks limited their movement out of agriculture and into the better-paid blue- and white-collar occupations, it inhibited their migration to the North, and it limited the educational attainment of the next generation. Political and legal changes in the 1940s and 1950s that moved in the direction of reducing racial differences in educational opportunities helped equalize earning opportunities as well.

CLIO: Let me take up another topic, then. I pointed out that union organization was a key development in the nineteenth-century and especially the twentieth-century labor force. Until now I've thought about the successes and failures in terms of worker consciousness. What can your economic model add to that?

HADES: Lots! The study of labor unions is a popular topic in the field of labor economics. If you let me introduce just one more concept—the *price elasticity* of labor demand—I can explain the long-term rise and fall in the unionization rate as well as differences in unionization rates across industries and across demographic groups.

CLIO: Reticence is not a problem for you, I see.

HADES: [*Plunging forward*]: The concept of price elasticity refers to the sensitivity of quantity supplied or quantity demanded to price changes.[11] For example, as the relative wage—the price of labor—of domestic workers began to rise because more and more young women found better-paid employment opportunities in manufacturing, clerical, and trade occupations, the quantity demanded of domestic labor fell dramatically. In 1900 almost 30 percent of the female labor force was employed as domestics. Twenty years later only 15 percent were so occupied (U.S. Bureau of the Census 1975, series D216 and D228). Because a *small* increase in the price of domestic labor led to a *large* decrease in the quantity of domestic labor demanded, we say that the demand for domestic labor was price *elastic*.

At the opposite extreme, the demand for the labor of physicians is

---

11. The price elasticity of demand is defined as the percentage change in quantity demanded divided by the percentage change in price. If the percentage change in quantity demanded is greater than the percentage change in price, elasticity is greater than one and demand is called relatively elastic. If the percentage change in the quantity demanded is less than the percentage change in quantity supplied, elasticity is less than one and demand is called relatively inelastic. Finally, if the percentage change in quantity demanded is the same as the percentage change in the price, the elasticity is equal to one and demand is called unit-elastic. Elastic demand curves typically characterize goods whose demand is highly sensitive to changes in price, such as restaurant meals or CD's. Inelastic demand curves characterize those goods considered necessities, and therefore less sensitive to price, such as milk, medicine, and housing.

price *inelastic*. Patients want the services of physicians and are willing to pay for them even when the price rises. As a consequence, since the time of the Great Depression when the American Medical Association first became effective in keeping the number of physicians growing at a rate below that of national income, medical fees have risen faster than almost any others (Rayack 1967; Berlant 1975).[12]

The elasticity of labor demand helps explain why unionization efforts succeed at some times and places but not at others. Successful unions raise the wage rates of their members above the market equilibrium. By looking at different elasticities of labor demand we can see the employment consequences of this action. Take a look at these two figures [*shown together in Figure 9*]. Both show labor markets with the same equilibrium wage and the same supply-of-labor curve. The difference is that in the upper figure labor demand is inelastic while in the lower the demand for labor is elastic. Now consider the employment consequences of setting the wage above the market equilibrium in each case. In the upper panel where demand is inelastic a rise in the wage rate results in only a small reduction in the quantity demanded and a small increase in unemployment. At the higher union wage rate there is an excess supply, but it is small. In the lower panel where demand is elastic, the same wage increase produces a large excess supply of labor. Since a large excess supply means large numbers of unemployed workers wanting jobs at the union rate, unions have difficulty surviving. Thus, *elastic* labor demand is not conducive to unionization whereas *inelastic* demand is.

CLIO: Fine. But how do I know whether labor demand is elastic?

HADES: A good first question to ask yourself when thinking about the elasticity of labor demand is whether the employer has close substitutes for the labor in question. For the services of domestics there *are* close substitutes. As the wage rates of domestic servants rose, housewives were able to use washing machines, vacuum cleaners, prepared foods, and simpler home designs to get the work done. The availability of close substitutes makes the demand for domestic servants elastic. For the

---

12. Graphically we show elastic supply or demand as relatively flat lines; lines closer to a vertical position represent inelastic demand or supply. There is an important relationship between elasticity and total revenue. Total revenue is defined simply as price times quantity. If price falls by 1 percent and quantity demanded stays the same, total revenue will fall by 1 percent as well. But as price falls, the quantity demanded will usually rise. The amount the quantity demanded rises will depend on the elasticity of demand. If the elasticity of demand is greater than one (demand is relatively elastic), the percentage increase in the quantity demanded will be greater than the percentage decrease in the price and total revenue will increase. If the elasticity of demand is less than one (demand is relatively inelastic), the percentage increase in quantity demanded will be less than the percentage decrease in price and total revenue will fall. If the elasticity of demand equals one (demand has unitary elasticity), the percentage increase in quantity demanded will just equal the percentage decrease in prices and total revenue will remain the same. Similar logic applies to the revenue consequences of a price increase.

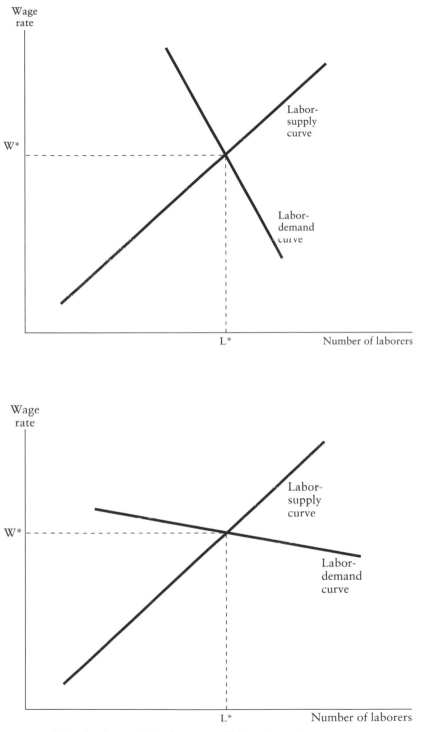

FIGURE 9. Unionization and the elasticity of labor demand.

services of physicians there are *no* close substitutes. As physicians' fees rose, patients found it difficult to do anything but pay the higher costs. The unavailability of close substitutes makes the demand curve for physician services inelastic or insensitive to wage changes.

CLIO: But wait a minute! Good substitutes for physician services were far more common in the past than they are today. For example, until the mid-nineteenth century most babies were delivered by midwives. Today there are a lot of restrictions that prevent anyone other than a licensed practitioner from assisting in childbirth. The development of legal regulations surrounding medical practice is largely responsible for the absence of close substitutes for the many services of regular physicians today.

HADES: I take your point. You've just identified one of the forces that change the elasticity of labor demand over time. Remember the *ceteris paribus* assumption? Once again, it comes into play. Legal changes restricted the public's opportunity to consult with homeopaths, hydropaths, eclectics, and other "irregular" sectarian healers as well (Walsh 1977). I'm sure you are aware of the work of scholars who argue that the development of professional licensing was a conscious effort on the part of the American Medical Association to raise the incomes of its members (Rayack 1967; Berlant 1975).

          Other forces affect the substitutability of labor as well. One is the capital-to-labor ratio. Where this ratio is low—that is, where there's relatively little capital—it is easy to find substitutes for labor should the wage rate rise. For example, in midwestern agriculture in the mid-nineteenth century a small rise in the wage rate led to a large reduction in the number of farm laborers employed. Farmers simply switched from hand- to machine-harvesting methods (David 1975b; Olmstead 1975). At high capital-to-labor ratios, by contrast, labor demand is inelastic. Oil rigs, for example, require at least *some* staff. Oil companies must continue to employ a skeleton crew almost no matter how high wage rates go. This suggests that as the capital-to-labor ratio rises labor demand becomes more inelastic and the possibility of unionization rises. It also suggests that the capital-intensive sectors will be more highly unionized as employers will be less willing to resist the payment of high wages.

CLIO: All right. But what confuses me is that your logic seems to imply that Henry Ford's automotive plant should have become unionized at the time he introduced his famous highly capital-intensive, assembly-line, mass-production techniques. After all, Ford's method of making cars certainly involved far more machines than that of any other automobile manufacturer of the period. Instead of a union, however, Ford voluntarily offered the Five-Dollar Day and pioneered an extremely elaborate set of paternalistic personnel policies—his famous Sociological Department (Raff 1988). How does an economist account for that?

HADES: Good question. You are prompting me to move beyond my simple comparison of the labor market with the market for iron ore. I believe I demonstrated its usefulness by showing how it provides insights into questions ranging from slavery to agricultural practice; from migration to technological choice; from the long-term growth of real wages to the entry of women into the paid labor force. I certainly do not mean to leave you with the impression that economists believe that *all* labor-market issues can be treated in this way. You brought up Ford's Five-Dollar Day. I agree with you that saying the labor market is just like the market for iron ore offers little insight into why Ford—or any employer for that matter—would voluntarily pay a wage in excess of the market-clearing one.

    The answer to why Ford offered to pay an enormously high relative wage is related to another puzzle—wage stickiness, or the failure of wages to adjust to disequilibrium in the labor market. As you mentioned earlier, the wage rate was relatively little discussed among nineteenth-century workers. They talked about the length of the workday, lost time, and so forth. As you pointed out, almost everything about the employment relationship *except* the wage rate was being discussed. Perhaps that was because the nominal wage rate remained remarkably stable over the nineteenth century.

CLIO: Thank you for reminding me. You're right, of course. The stability of nominal wages was noted by quite a large number of observers. Then-U.S. Commissioner of Labor Carroll Wright observed that the price of labor fluctuated far less freely than other prices: "Whenever prices of commodities rise, they rise higher, relatively, than does the price of labor, and . . . when prices go down they go down much lower, relatively, than does the price of labor, which remains ordinarily very nearly at its inflated price" (Wright 1893, 228).

    Shortly later Wesley Clair Mitchell called attention to the common practice of paying "conventional sums" (Mitchell 1908). Employer testimony seemed to confirm the practice. You recall, no doubt, the testimony of a Maine lime plant owner offered during a state labor bureau investigation of the severe depression of 1893–94: "The working force has been reduced 70 per cent on account of no demand for lime, with no prospect of returning to full capacity at present. What men are retained are paid the old rate of wages, yet it would be easy to hire a crew at much lower rates" (Maine 1895).[13]

    In fact, noticeable changes in nominal wage rates occurred only during the three episodes of general inflation during the century—1812–15,

---

13. Quoted in Carter and Sutch (1991, 23), who develop statistical evidence on wage-rate stickiness consistent with this literary evidence. On wage-rate stickiness in the 1890s see Sundstrom 1990, 1992; and Hanes 1992, 1993.

1830–37, and 1860–65.[14] As I think about this evidence in light of our current discussion it seems to me to be powerful proof of the view that labor markets simply did not work.

HADES: Hold on a minute! Wage rates *were* remarkably sticky, I certainly grant you that. Just because variations in the wage rate didn't equate supply and demand in the labor market doesn't mean that the labor market wasn't working and that economics should be thrown out the window. The full price of labor may include many different types of compensation.[15] Gavin Wright noted that the process of adjustment to a new labor market equilibrium often took the form of a modification to the *nonwage* components:

> they may change the workload, as the Waltham mills did after the coming of the Irish (Lazonick and Brush 1985); they may change the length of the standard workday, as employers did during World War I; they may change their hiring standards, or the criteria by which workers are promoted to more advanced jobs, as the Ford Motor Company did at the time of the Five Dollar Day (Meyer 1981); they may institute night shifts (Shiells and Wright 1983); they may offer binding promises of job security, such as seniority systems, as numerous employers did well before unionization (Slichter 1929; Schatz 1983); and so on (Wright 1987, 323).

Additional mechanisms might include direct recruitment of workers to meet labor shortages (David 1987; Wright 1987), adjustments of the length of the pay period, and the award of bonuses (De Vries 1991). When you think of it in this way, the imagination employers used in order to avoid using the wage rate to make labor market adjustments is truly remarkable!

CLIO: Don't you think it's significant that firm owners went to such great pains to avoid using the wage to make labor market adjustments? Their heavy reliance on nonprice adjustment mechanisms is certainly different from their handling of the market for other inputs such as iron ore. I still think it's time you gave up that metaphor.

HADES: Yes, I think you're right on that point. Up until now I've tried to show you how the labor market can be thought of as if it were the market for iron ore. However, as you point out, this is not always the case. In fact, in recent years economists have paid a lot of attention to markets

---

14. Because the cost of living was falling, the real wage was rising; see Wright (1987, 328–329). Carter 1993 shows that the rise in the real wage exceeded the growth of labor productivity between 1870 and 1900—for Clio, further proof that the labor market didn't "work." On wage-rate stickiness in other times and places see Phelps-Brown and Hopkins 1981, Wright 1987, and De Vries 1991.

15. The response of the wage to the presence of other forms of remuneration is called a "compensating differential" in the economics literature. For a recent paper measuring the size of a compensating differential see Rees 1993.

for labor, which are very unlike the market for iron ore. Efficiency-wage theory is one of a number of new models in which the *social nature* of the labor market is placed at the center of the analysis (Akerlof and Yellen 1986; Solow 1990). It does just what you want; it emphasizes the ways in which the labor market is different from other markets. There is, however, an important, fundamental *similarity* between this model and the ones I described earlier. In all cases, the objective of these models is to see whether phenomena such as sticky and above-market wages—like Ford's Five-Dollar Day—can be explained in the context of *rational economic behavior*. In my description I'll try to highlight the advantages of this characteristic of the model.[16]

Up to this point, I assumed that the market for labor is just like the market for any other input. Indeed, standard economic theory treats all inputs completely symmetrically in the production process. There is, however, a crucial difference between the labor input and all other inputs. It's not simply the hours of labor worked that matter. The actual *effort* performed is critical to the productivity and therefore the profitability of the firm. If we could write a complete contract—specify all possible future contingencies, as well as all the duties and tasks workers would be expected to carry out, and the payment associated with each contingency—then we'd have no problem of effort extraction. The optimal labor effort would be automatically forthcoming. However, such contracts are impossible to write. Employers fear what economists call the "moral hazard problem"—the workers may take a full day's pay but deliver less than a full day's effort unless bosses employ monitoring mechanisms. A further difficulty is that monitoring is expensive, furthermore, if it makes the workers resentful, they may retaliate by slowing the pace of work, thus creating additional cost increases.[17]

Because incomplete contracts are inevitable, wage-rate cuts tend to reduce firms' productivity and therefore profitability. One link between wage-rate cuts and profitability derives from the moral hazard problem. If workers respond to a reduction in wages with an equal or

16. Efficiency-wage models focus on the connection between wage and effort and the interaction between institutions such as the family or labor unions and public policies such as social security or unemployment insurance—topics of interest to an earlier generation of labor economists and, of course, to historians all along. Their elaboration today makes ours an especially auspicious time for historians to make an acquaintance with labor economics. See Sutch 1991 and Wright 1991 for more discussion of these new initiatives by economic historians.

17. Moral hazard is the term economists use to designate situations where there is the possibility of one party to a contract engaging in postcontractual opportunism. The concept comes from the literature on writing insurance contracts in the recognition that the content of certain contracts gave individuals they insured incentives to behave differently. A classic example would be an insured individual who drives less carefully, knowing that the insurance contract will cover any damages. Moral hazard problems are an instance of what can be called in general information problems. On this topic see Cohen's chapter, 64–65; and Stiglitz 1987.

greater reduction in work effort then a firm's efforts at cost savings might have the paradoxical effect of *reducing* profits. A second link is that a wage-rate cut might induce workers to seek alternative employment. If there are costs to hiring and training replacements then this labor turnover would reduce profits, perhaps offsetting the savings from reduced wages. Finally, if better-qualified workers are more prone to leave—economists use the term "adverse selection" to describe such phenomena—then a wage-rate cut would lead to a lower-quality workforce—perhaps one not even worth the new low wage rate being offered, again frustrating the firm's efforts to achieve a cost saving.

One advantage of this formulation over explanations of wage stickiness cast in terms of culture or tradition is that it yields a set of predictions about where and when efficiency wage considerations would be most salient. In other words, in an efficiency-wage world it is perfectly possible that a worker would enjoy above-market wages in one firm but not in its neighbor. It is perfectly possible that market-clearing wages would be paid one day, efficiency wages the next. Differences and changes of these types are hard to explain with culture-based or tradition-based approaches.

Since the problem that gives rise to efficiency-wage payments is the possibility of a worker-initiated reduction in work effort, made possible in part by the inability of the employer to monitor and maintain work intensity, we would expect efficiency-wage considerations to be most salient where problems of worker morale pose the biggest threat to profits. We would thus expect efficiency wages in the heavily capitalized, mass-production Ford automotive plant, for example, where the consequences of shirking or generally low morale among workers would be more costly than in a small shop. Should Ford's workers go out on strike or stage a slowdown, millions of dollars' worth of capital would be idled. It may be easy to discipline or replace a single worker, but groups of disgruntled workers make more complex issues. As Daniel Raff put it:

> [Groups] might or might not be easier to identify; but swooping down on them, plucking them out of the circuit, and instantaneously replacing them with another group that knew exactly what to do and would do it without hesitation would have been another matter entirely, for there were many fewer supervisors than jobs. (Raff 1988, 396)

Efficiency-wage theory identifies Henry Ford's profit-related motive for keeping his workers happy, or at least grateful for their jobs.

Ford is not the only example. The predicament of Southern cotton textile-mill owners in the 1920s, as described by Wright (1986, 138–155), can be understood with reference to efficiency-wage theory as well. By way of background information, you recall that the Southern textile mills employed whole families whom they recruited off the farm.[18] In order to make use of the age/sex distribution of workers brought forth by this labor recruitment process, the mills *redesigned* their jobs. More than half of all jobs were designated for the young, since families who came to the mill villages tended to have a lot of teenage workers.

Unfortunately for the plan, the age/sex distribution of the village labor force changed over time. This was because the men, at least, tended to stay with the firm over their entire life cycle. As the village matured, the fraction of the mill labor force who were older men also grew. By the 1920s the structure was top-heavy. There were too many older men relative to the number of senior positions. Since older men were paid high wages, labor costs rose. Eventually they became too high to be consistent with profitability. The mills had two choices—they could cut wages, especially the wages of older, more senior male workers, or they could raise the productivity of the men to a level where the high wages were warranted. Wright explains why a wage cut was definitely ruled out.

> It was sure to trigger labor revolt, to say nothing of adverse outside attention. . . . Even the nominal wage cut of 1920–21, when the general price level fell by more than 35 percent, caused the "largest, bitterest strike" in southern textiles to that time, involving 9,000 workers in nine towns. And replacing an older experienced group of workers with a set of new recruits off the farm was tantamount to throwing away fifty years of progress in labor skills and socialization. (Wright 1986, 153–154)

Southern textile mills therefore undertook investment in new plant and equipment even though the world market for textiles was depressed. As the efficiency-wage model makes clear, this was their only viable option.

Generalizing these stories—we expect above-market wages in more capital-intensive, oligopolistic industries. For example, the efficiency-wage model predicts that the wages of secretaries working for a steel manufacturer would be higher than those of secretaries doing exactly the same sort of work in, say, the child care industry. It also suggests that efficiency-wage payments should be more common in the twentieth century than they were in the nineteenth. This is exactly what we find (Krueger and Summers 1987; Carter and Philips 1990).

There are other interesting implications as well. Did you know, for example, that in the otherwise racist South in the late nineteenth century black farm laborers were paid the same wage rate as whites (Wright 1986)? In the 1880s, when most Southern wage laborers worked in unmechanized agriculture, employers paid the market

---

18. Wright notes (1986, 138) that initial efforts to recruit a textile-factory labor force in the South focused on unmarried females—a self-conscious attempt to replicate the success of the Waltham model. Only after these efforts failed did employers begin to recruit entire farm families.

wage—not an efficiency wage—just as the theory would predict. This was because in this agricultural labor market it was fairly easy to monitor employees' work effort—there were almost as many supervisors as laborers. A shirker could be easily identified and fired and an adequate replacement found. Training costs were nonexistent and therefore hiring and turnover costs extremely low. Finally, there was little concern over worker quality. Two slow workers, each paid half the wage rate, could substitute for one fast one. Because conditions in Southern agriculture displayed none of the special attributes of Ford's assembly-line automobile plant, market wages prevailed. No equivalent of Ford's Five-Dollar Day was offered, not even by racist white farm owners trying to attract white farm laborers.

All of this changed as the more capital-intensive textile industry grew in importance in the Southern labor market. Because whites were initially employed at such firms and because experience was an important contributor to worker productivity in this industry, employers were inclined to *continue* employing whites *and* to respect whites' resistance to working with blacks. Any effort to integrate blacks would have reduced profits. Since textiles paid more than agriculture, the growing importance of white-only textile employment and the virtual absence of any other sorts of industrial employment meant the appearance and then growth of a race-based wage differential in that economy.[19]

CLIO: Well, I've learned a lot. But I wonder if we can go back to the issue with which we began this discussion, the long-term change in women's employment patterns. Are you saying that supply and demand, perhaps supplemented by some of these new models incorporating moral hazard and so forth, can explain the long-term change in women's employment without reference to custom, institutions, political power, or social norms?

HADES: Well, no, not exactly. History may matter as well . . .

CLIO: How can you say *may?* I should think it's obvious that history matters. We tell our stories in chronological order, after all. Dates are of some interest.

HADES: In the standard models used by economists, history is in fact **irrelevant!** Current prices are all I invoked in the many examples I put before you

---

19. Another model that takes the consciousness of workers as a serious datum is the "fairness" model developed by George Akerlof and Janet Yellen (1990). Here workers' notions of the appropriate degree of inequality of rewards within the firm explain an otherwise puzzling phenomenon—the fact that low-paid workers bear a disproportionate share of the unemployment during downturns. This well documented phenomenon does not fit the context of the standard model, which assumes that workers are paid their marginal products. If workers are all paid exactly what they're "worth," an employer should be indifferent as to which workers are dismissed when downsizing is required. Yet we observe that employers are much more likely to dismiss workers who are relatively poorly paid. The point of departure for the fairness model is the observation that in real workplaces employees of low productivity tend to get more than their marginal product while those of high productivity tend to get less. The rationale that workers offer for this relation is that it is more "fair." Within a given workplace workers dislike large wage disparities.

this afternoon. Think about it. When I explained the small number of wage laborers in eighteenth-century U.S. agriculture I talked about a prevailing wage rate that was high relative to the demand-for-labor curve. When I explained the westward shift of the population I did so in terms of an outward shift in the demand-for-labor curve in the west.

CLIO: True, but you didn't claim that adjustment was instantaneous.

HADES: That's right. In these models "history"—past prices, really—can enter the analysis in the form of lags. The larger the shift in relative prices and the more sluggish the response, the longer it may take the economy to reach its new equilibrium values. In other words, history matters, but only in the "short run."[20]

CLIO   [*Stifling a gasp*]: But to play devil's advocate for a bit, what about institutions? I know that you economists take at least some account of institutions in your work. Since institutions embody structures from the past they would seem to open up another possible role for history.

HADES: Actually, for a long time many economists took almost *no* account of institutions nor of culture or consciousness either. The assumption was that change—and this is the *stuff* of history, after all—could be understood as a result of the workings of competition. Competition in the context of scarcity selects efficient institutions, cultures, and ideologies. The rest just go the way of the dinosaurs. In the long run the past is irrelevant.[21]

CLIO: Gasp! I had no idea things were this bad.

HADES: In defense of my colleagues I repeat: the ahistorical supply-and-demand metaphor has provided valuable insights into a variety of issues. Nonetheless, the art to doing good economics or history is knowing when such models are inappropriate. Better data, bigger and faster computers, and, I hope, an increasing attention to ecological issues heighten economists' sensitivity to self-reinforcing mechanisms in complex systems. We know about the ecology of marshes and interactions between rain forests and rainfall. We're beginning to notice self-reinforcement and "lock-ins" in social and economic systems as well (Arthur 1994). Historians have been well aware of such processes all along, of course.

          One example of a lock-in is the "trap of debt peonage" in postbellum Southern agriculture, described by Roger Ransom and Richard Sutch (1977). The story begins with the failure of the federal govern-

20. Economists define the short run as the time during which some inputs such as the plant or equipment cannot be changed. The short run may be as brief as a day—as in the case of a hot dog vendor—or as long as a century or more—as in the case of a city's streets, buildings, sanitation, and transportation systems.

21. See Douglass North 1981 for a review and critique of this approach to competition in the context of scarcity. A new economics of organizations has flowered in recent years. Its point of departure is an explicit recognition that intangibles such as information and transactions are nonetheless costly. For an introduction to this literature see Cohen's chapter, 79–83; and Stiglitz 1991. North 1981 offers additional historical applications.

ment to make good on its promise to fortify newly emancipated slaves with "forty acres and a mule." Their lack of these or any other assets meant that those who wanted to farm had to become tenants *and* needed credit to get started. Credit was available only from the local merchant who used his territorial monopoly powers to insist that cotton—a cash crop—be planted. Since cotton couldn't be eaten, creditors' ability to set the price of cotton *and* the price of provisions enabled them to prevent debtors from accumulating savings and freeing themselves from the system. Once a debtor you were locked in for life! The system didn't end until an exogenous event—an infestation of boll weevils—destroyed the cotton crop and its profitability to creditors.

Kessler-Harris's (1990) story about the low wage rate for women also involves feedbacks. The typical turn-of-the-century female wage earner was young, single, and inexperienced. This was because a relatively low female wage and a generally adequate male wage led many women to choose to withdraw from the wage-labor force at the time of their marriage, never to return. But it was also because women who might have preferred to remain faced considerable obstacles. Apprenticeships, on-the-job training, promotions, and the pay increases that went along with them were generally denied to women, often with the argument that women wouldn't be in the labor force long enough to make proper use of these opportunities (Carter and Savoca 1991). A young woman might easily conclude that the obstacles to a career were insurmountable and choose marriage. In doing so, of course, she lent support to the status quo. Only pressure from organized groups could cut through these self-reinforcing tendencies. Note the fundamentally *historical* character of both of these stories. To understand tenant indebtedness in 1890 or the low level of the female wage in 1950 you have to know how they got to be that way.

The interest of the economics profession in processes with an essentially historical character is due in large part to Paul David's (1985) discussion of the QWERTY typewriter keyboard. As you no doubt know, Clio, the familiar QWERTY arrangement of letters on typewriter and now personal computer keyboard is extremely awkward. Speed-typing records are all held by users of other systems. In fact, QWERTY was *designed* to slow the fingers of the typist. From the point of view of standard economic theory the persistence of QWERTY is puzzling. Why hasn't it been replaced by one of the more efficient arrangements? David offered a historical explanation.

The QWERTY arrangement was featured on the first typewriter to gain commercial success. When initially developed, the typebars had a tendency to "clash and jam if struck in rapid succession." This was a particularly serious defect because, as David explained:

the printing point was located underneath the paper carriage, [where] it was quite invisible to the operator. . . . When a typebar stuck at or near the printing point, every succeeding stroke merely hammered the same impression onto the paper, resulting in a string of repeated letters that would be discovered only when the typist bothered to raise the carriage to inspect what had been printed. (David 1985, 333)

By making the typebar arrangement as awkward as possible, clashes were minimized and overall speed was increased.

After its introduction practically every aspect of the original design was modified. Only the QWERTY keyboard arrangement persisted. David argued that this persistence was due to three qualities—technical interrelatedness, economies of scale, and quasi irreversibility. Technical interrelatedness refers to the fact that firms' decisions about whether to adopt QWERTY or some other keyboard arrangement depend not only upon each keyboard's technical efficiency—"lets you type 20–40% faster"—but also on the price and availability of typists qualified to use the keyboard. The overall cost of a typed page is lowest for a typewriter keyboard arrangement that most trained typists know. The relatively low wage of the already trained typist more than offsets his relatively slow typing speed. Economies of scale mean that each decision in favor of the QWERTY keyboard arrangement—an adoption decision by either a firm or a typist—reduces the cost of that arrangement to subsequent decisionmakers. Each QWERTY purchase by some firm increases the probability that the next typing student will choose to learn QWERTY. Each typist's decision to learn QWERTY reduces the cost of the QWERTY system to firms deciding which system to adopt. And the third quality, quasi irreversibility, refers to an asymmetry in the costs of converting to an alternative system. Improvements in the technical design of typewriters eliminated the tendency of typebars to clash and jam. This made it increasingly easy for typewriter manufacturers to install any keyboard design they might choose. The same was not true of QWERTY-trained typists, however. QWERTY was difficult to unlearn.

Technical interrelatedness, economies of scale, and quasi irreversibility meant that a historical accident—the typewriter that achieved initial commercial success happened to have a QWERTY keyboard—had far-reaching consequences. As David put it, typewriter designers "adapt machines to the habits of men (or to women, as was increasingly the case) rather than the other way around. And things have been that way ever since" (1985, 336).

If technical interrelatedness, economies of scale, and quasi irreversibility make for historical stories, then we'd certainly expect history to "matter" in many labor-market outcomes. One recent effort to develop a historical explanation for a pressing labor issue of our times is the hysteresis unemployment notion developed by Olivier Blanchard and Lawrence Summers (1990). Standard ahistorical labor-market models have had a difficult time explaining the very high levels of European unemployment since the early 1970s. Blanchard and Summers suggest that if *insiders*—currently employed workers—play a substantially larger role in wage determination than *outsiders*—the unemployed—then the high European unemployment might be explained as an enduring effect of the Arab oil embargo![22] When workers lost their jobs in the dislocation following the rapid rise in oil prices in 1972 and 1973, they argue, they also lost their voice in the wage-setting process of firms. As outsiders, they preferred that firms lower wage rates and expand employment. But because insiders naturally preferred to keep wages up *and* the insiders were the ones with the votes, wages remained high. Double-digit unemployment was the result.

CLIO: As you remind me, good rhetoric in any discipline involves the entire rhetorical tetrad: fact, logic, metaphor, and story. "Pieces of it are not enough" (McCloskey 1990, 1). I believe this afternoon I learned quite a lot about how the logic and metaphors of labor economics might improve the rhetoric of historians.

HADES: Well I'm delighted! Now, if only economists prove to be such adept students of history, we may soon see better stories in both disciplines.

As they got up to pay the bill and return to their respective departments, Clio and Hades felt energized. Clio was thinking of ways in which the metaphors of economics might help answer the "whys" raised at the end of her last talk. Hades was thinking about the stories of historians and their relevance to his current work. Both sensed breakthroughs to a new, more satisfying type of scholarship.

22. For a fuller description of the insider-outsider theory see Lindbeck and Snower 1986.

For those with an interest in some particular topic in labor economics and for those wanting some help in seeing the forest for the trees we provide this annotated guide to the topics covered. The technical discussion was deliberately kept to a minimum (there is only so much one can impose upon a luncheon partner, even one as agreeable as Clio). For those who would like a more complete, though still accessible, treatment of the formal material we recommend Stiglitz 1993.

Topic	Illustrations	Pages
The Labor Market Is Like Other Markets		
Law of supply and demand	thin, high-wage labor market in the British North American colonies	85–90
Labor-demand curve	use of unfree labor in colonial America, differential use of slaves in the South, sloppy agricultural practices, appearance of American System of Manufactures, international and interregional labor flows, Special Case of the South, movement of labor out of agriculture and into manufacturing (proletarianization of the labor force)	90–97
Labor-supply curve	declining length of the workday, entry of women into the wage-labor force	97–103
Supply of and demand for skills	increase in educational attainment over the twentieth century, gender differences in school attendance at the turn of the century, improvement in the relative earnings of blacks	103–108
Elasticity of labor supply and demand	declining employment in domestic service, high incomes of physicians, long-term change in the unionization rate, differential unionization rates by industry and demographic group	108–110
The Labor Market Is Different from Other Markets		
Moral hazard, adverse selection, asymmetric information, and efficiency wages	nonwage labor-market adjustments, nominal wage stickiness, Ford's Five-Dollar Day, productivity improvements in Southern cotton textile mills, interindustry wage differences, the emergence of a racial wage gap	110–117
History Matters		
"Lock-ins"	trap of debt peonage in postbellum Southern agriculture, social norms and women's wages	117–118
Path dependency	QWERTY typewriter keyboard, high European unemployment	118–120

FIGURE 10. A reader's guide to the conversation of Clio and Hades.

The Economics of Choice
Neoclassical Supply and Demand

DONALD N. McCLOSKEY

NEOCLASSICAL ECONOMICS
IS THE STUDY OF CHOICE

A century ago the English economist Alfred Marshall began his exposition of what is now called neoclassical economics with a definition: economics, he said, is the study of humankind in the ordinary business of life. The definition covers the non-neoclassical approaches, too—Marxist, Austrian, Gandhian, institutionalist. All these are part of the conversation of economics since the seventeenth century about the business of humankind. Marx was a follower of David Ricardo, who was in turn a follower of Smith. Marshall himself and the neoclassicals are another branch of this tree, the dominant branch in modern economics.

The specifically neoclassical definition, which was made central in British economics in the 1920s and was committed to mathematics in the 1940s, is that economics is the study of *choice* in the ordinary business of life. To study choice is to fail to study other things (which is in fact a neoclassical way of putting the matter). Neoclassical economists are fond of preaching that to take one road in a yellow wood is to sacrifice the other. Intellectual choices are no exception. The Marxist study of Power, the institutionalist study of Habit, the Austrian study of Creativity are more or less subordinated in the neoclassical approach to what the neoclassicals are pleased to call "maximization under constraints."

Neoclassicals are obsessed with Choice, and see choice where others see subordination or necessity. They would urge the historian not to jump hastily to a diagnosis that peasants follow their plows by custom alone or that traders trust each other on grounds of solidarity alone.

That is the main payoff to thinking neoclassically about history. The historian will be able to see choices where she did not before. The businessperson must choose between markets at home and abroad; the consumer must choose between buying in the village or in the town; the male laborer must choose between a factory or an apprenticeship; the female homeworker must choose between making homespun or entering the market.

Neoclassical economics, in other words, completes sociology and anthropology, because it studies a motivation unattractive to those fields: choice under constraint. Whether analysis of choice under constraint is more useful for writing history than the analysis of symbols in the late medieval French monarchy or the analysis of tension between the classes in late nineteenth-century Massachusetts towns remains to be seen. But it can be part of most histories.

The economists are not the only students of society to emphasize choice. Their parables were anticipated by writers of fiction in the age of the bourgeoisie. Charles Dickens peopled his novels with monsters of calculation among whom his prerational and Pickwickian heroes swim. Jane Austen was writing novels of domestic maximization—marriage-seeking mothers and status-seeking fathers—about the same time that Jeremy Bentham was holding forth on the maximizing model of man.

And Daniel Defoe, a pioneer of the genre, saw in Robinson Crusoe a Choosing Man: "having considered well what I most wanted, I first got three of the Seamen's Chests" (41). Crusoe's raft is not of infinite size; at any moment the weather can change, and sink the wreck; this may be the only trip. Crusoe cannot have everything, and so must make choices. He takes only the clothing "wanted for present use," because there were "other things which my eye was more upon" (42). That is, he chose to have fewer clothes and more carpenter's tools. He could not in the circumstances have both. He is a commercial man making choices under conditions of scarcity.

Details of the style reinforce scarcity in *Robinson Crusoe*—a contrast to the stories of shipwrecks in the *Odyssey* or the *Aeneid,* over which hover gods willing to perform miracles of abundance. The miracles in Crusoe's world are naturalistic, reflecting always Adam's Curse. The story is filled with realistic disappointment, signalled often by an ominous "but." "There had been some Barly and Wheat together" on the wreck, "but, to my great Disappointment, I found afterwards that the Rats had eaten or spoil'd it all" (41). The wreck had "a great Roll of Sheet Lead: But this last was so heavy, I could not hoise [*sic*] it up to get it over the Ship's Side" (45). He takes a kid from a she-goat, and "hopes to have bred it up tame, but it would not eat, so I was forc'd to kill it and eat it myself" (50). The "but" is unsentimental, aware of life's scarcity. It is the economist's master conjunction.

To emphasize a *free* choice is of course to take seriously a certain political agenda. Neoclassical economics, like the novel, has never fully recovered from its origins in the bourgeois revolutions of the eighteenth and nineteenth centuries. The alternatives to mainstream, bourgeois economics—above all Marxist economics, but also institutionalist and other smaller schools—spend a good deal of their time attacking the reality of free choice. They argue that the free choice that matters is choosing the institution within which the so-called freedom is exercised, not choosing from inside a given institution. Freedom in such a view consists not in being free to sleep under the bridges but in being free to change the society that allows people to be homeless.

To this the bourgeois economist—who in truth is not overburdened by such worries—can reply as follows. Yes, the wider choices of reform and revolution are important. (Incidentally, the choices of reform and revolution are also subject to scarcity, and therefore to the economist's calculus of choice. A version of the well-worn phrase "political economy" has recently brought politics itself under the economist's way of reasoning, and is applicable to history—see Root 1994, Hoffman 1995.) But the Marxists and institutionalists, says the neoclassical, underestimate how powerful are the small choices. The individual choices by rice buyers and factory owners in the economy are like the movement of air molecules in a balloon. The economics of choice examines the single molecules, with an eye on their behavior in the mass. It is a Tolstoyan point, that even Napoleon's history needs to be told from the point of view of the common soldier on the battlefield, who in a mass sets the conditions under which the Great Man maximizes or fails to maximize.

The purpose here is to indicate how choice can drive an economy. The wider, institutional choice is treated in some of the other chapters. Here I can do no more than sketch a few of the main themes in the neoclassical theory of choice under constraints—known to its friends as "price theory." Price theory, most economists agree, is one of the characteristic gifts of economics to the study of society. No more than psychoanalytic technique or thick description, it cannot be learned in a day. Most economists themselves do not master it until they have been teaching it for some years.

CHOICES OFTEN TAKE PLACE IN A MARKET SOUP

Economic molecules in the modern world huddle, of course, in markets, which gives another sense in which economics is bourgeois, the townsman's science. But the markets operate beyond the town walls. Markets in the economist's way of looking at it are arrangements and attitudes, not necessarily single places. A market is merely the group of people who are willing to buy and sell things that they are willing to treat as reasonably close substitutes. Notice how much judgment and psychology goes into the definition. The market in wheat, for example, is located in a million places, wherever wheat might be bought and sold. It is contained in human minds wherever bread is grown and milled and eaten. Considering the narrow limits of transport cost nowadays, the world has essentially one price and one market for wheat. On the other hand the housing market of Manchester is confined to Manchester, because houses and especially locations cannot by their nature move, and few people in Los Angeles view a house in Manchester as much of a substitute for their shake-shingled paradise.

Historians have been accustomed by anti-neoclassical writers such as Karl Polanyi to think of the market as something new, born in 1795 or thereabouts, or at the earliest in the years a few centuries before of sheep-eating men. Polanyi's work has not survived scrutiny in the many fields of economic history he touched. But even if Polanyi were correct the conclusion would not follow that modern, neoclassical economics applies *only* to market economies. Choice has nothing in particular to do with markets, perfect or otherwise. Many choices are made outside markets: in families most of all; in governments; and in other institutions. Even a business firm is dominated internally by the "visible hand" of conscious planning, rather than by anonymous instructions from a market. The business firm must in any case make choices. Robinson Crusoe made choices wholly outside the market, but his choices were no less economic on that account. Centrally planned economies make their choices Robinson-Crusoe style outside a market, too.

Yet many choices are made in markets. It is therefore impossible to talk long about choice without mentioning markets if lots of them are around. And in an economy with markets the values they generate will influence many of the decisions made outside the market. To this extent Polanyi was surely right. Markets pervade when they exist. A wife may choose to work inside the home rather than to sell her labor in the market, but the size of her potential market wage will influence the choice. A king may choose in the royal bedchamber a strategy of conquest, but the market in ships and cannon will determine whether it succeeds or fails.

ENTRY AND EXIT TELL THE ECONOMIC STORY

The simplest way to extend the notion is to say that the molecules in the economy make their choices with profit in mind. The profit, however, is not some vulgar cash balance. Somewhat surprisingly, economics is not primarily about money. The profit can be inward and spiritual as well as outward and corporeal, as wide as utility or as narrow as what the stockholders want. The notion of the pursuit of profit is therefore reasonably innocent. It commits the historian who adopts it to offering reasons why his subjects behave as they do, but not much more. The reasons can always be translated into a sort of profit.

Broad or narrow, the idea of profit has been a device for telling stories that would otherwise not get told. Economists since Adam Smith have emphasized the obvious point that unprofitable businesses fail, called in the modern jargon "exit." The observation is of course not surprising to historians. The wheat growers of Europe faced low prices in the 1870s, pushed down by competition from Russia and America. When their governments did not protect them, as they did not in Denmark and Britain, the wheat growers shifted to milk and vegetables. In the early nineteenth century the weavers of cotton cloth in India had a profitable domestic industry. But in time the cheaper cloth from the factories of Lancashire drove them to failure. The north-south railroads came to Texas by way of Dennison in 1881, and soon the Long Drive to Kansas ended and mythmaking began.

One can see the uses of this notion of profit for historical narration. After all, unprofitability and exit figure in history as much as success and entry. When faced with a story of failure a noneconomist is likely to look for a cultural flaw. The overindulgence in social graces by English wheat farmers would be one, for example, or the traditional values of the Indian cotton weavers or the careless nobility of the Texan cowboys, all pursuing something other than profit. Victorian businessmen in England are sometimes said to have "failed" because they are claimed to have been the grandsons of successful men or because they are supposed to have been addicted to Greek verse. As David Landes put it long ago, "Thus the Britain of the late nineteenth century basked complacently in the sunset of economic hegemony. . . . Now it was the turn of the third generation, the children of affluence, tired of the tedium and trade and flushed with the bucolic aspirations of the country gentleman. . . . They worked at play and played at work" (1965, 563).

Neoclassical economics wants to tell the story another way, emphasizing circumstances of profit rather than features of culture. It is again a complement to what is missing from an anthropological approach.

A business in trouble will not remain in business long—there's a simple plot line. Ecologists and evolutionists have been using it since Darwin, noting that a white pigeon sticking out in a Black Country of factory smoke is not long for this world. Economic history uses it, too. As a Dickens character famously put it: Annual income twenty pounds, annual expenditure twenty pounds ought and six: result misery. And exit.

The other side of the story of exit is the story of entry. Profitable businesses do well, and may often do good. Andrew Carnegie was profitable at making steel and John D. Rockefeller was profitable at marketing oil. Their businesses grew. What is more, their profitability attracted imitators. Their whole industries grew. To state the obvious, industries that are profitable will expand, attracting entry. An ecological niche profitable for black pigeons will become thronged with them. Similarly, regions that are profitable will expand, attracting entry, as did the American Midwest in the second half of the nineteenth century. Nations that are profitable will expand, attracting entry, as did China from Chou to T'ang to Ming. Profit is nectar to the bees of industry.

Profitability is a way of replacing the overused metaphor of growth, a handy metaphor to start with, but not rich in the questions it suggests. It suggests the historian ask whether the field for growth was fertile, say; but it does not show how to answer it. The profit metaphor, by contrast, no less a metaphor, guides the historian to calculations of profit or loss, suggesting an account of action. Early in its trading history, Athens and its countryside exited from producing wheat, expanding olive oil and the manufacture of urns to carry it to Egypt (Lévy 1967, 24). The olive-oil industry did not merely grow like a plant. People supplied more oil because it was profitable to do so. They entered.

The economistic story of entry and exit is told in two acts, a short run and a long. The sensitivity to time should be attractive to historians. Profitability or unprofitability is not forever, because entry spoils what causes it. The bees use up the nectar. Carnegie and Rockefeller made their killings in a few years before wide entry, but they lived to see steel and petroleum selling cheap. Likewise, as Egyptians and Italians and others entered the olive-oil trade in the ancient world the temporary advantage of Attica faded. The price of olive oil fell, reducing profits to normally low levels. The Roman Cato the Elder earned merely 6 percent per year on his olive trees. The price of Rockefeller's oil or Cato's could not have stayed abnormally low or abnormally high for long. Entry spoils profitability, exit cures unprofitability.

The story of profit, with the corresponding entry and exit, is a self-regulating one, a historical thermostat. Earnings in the end are kept not too high and not too low because the one attracts entry and the other causes exit. As in scholarship, unusually high returns attract entry to the fashionable specialities, which in the end become routine.

A characteristic bit of economic reasoning, then, as characteristic of Marxist as of neoclassical economics, is to conclude that entry and exit force profits to hover around "normal" in "the long run," by the end of the second act of the two-act play. "Normal" is what one can earn in the alternative occupations one might choose (note the role for choice again). The "long run" lasts as long as it takes the activity to get back to normal profit.[1]

AN EXAMPLE: TAXATION

A pension scheme is proposed for the nation, in which "the employer will pay half." It will say in the law and on the worker's salary check that the worker contributes 5 percent of his wages to the pension fund but that the employer contributes the other 5 percent. A law is passed "designed" (as it is put) to have such and such an effect. The lawyerly mind goes this far, urging us therefore to limit the hours of women workers or to subsidize American flag shipping. The women, the lawyer thinks, will be made better off—as will the American ships. Under the pension scheme the workers will be 5 percent better off, getting half of their pension free.

---

1. Note that the reasoning is circular. The long run is as long as the long run takes. The circularity closes off a hemorrhage in the analysis. The tourniquet is necessary because economics cannot say much about the traverse to the long run. A sensitivity to how long the long run should be in any particular case is the main skill of applying economics, but unhappily there is no general rule. The long run today in the market for foreign exchange among major financial centers may be milliseconds; the long run yesterday in the market for women's labor may have been decades.

No neoclassical economist, however, will want to leave the story of the pension plan in the first act, the lawyer's and legislator's act of laws "designed" to split the costs. She will want to go further in the drama. She will say: At the higher cost of labor the employers will hire fewer workers. In the second act the situation created by the law will begin to dissolve. At the old terms more workers will want to work than the employers wish to hire. Jostling queues will form outside the factory gates. The competition of the workers will drive down wages. By the end of the play a part of the "employer's" share—maybe even all of it—will sit on the workers themselves, in the form of lower wages. The intent of the law is frustrated, because what matters in neoclassical economics is actual incidence, not the legislative intent.

Thus in Chicago under Mayor Daley the elder when a tax on employment was proposed the reporters asked who would pay the tax. Alderman Thomas Keane (who later went to jail, though not for misappropriation of economics) declared that the City had been careful to draft the law so that only the employers paid it. "The City of Chicago," said Keane, "will never tax the working man." Thus too in 1987, when Senator Kennedy proposed a plan for workers and employers to share the cost of health insurance, the newspapers reported Kennedy as estimating "the overall cost at $25 billion—$20 billion paid by employers and $5 billion by workers." Senator Kennedy will never tax the working man. The manager of employee relations at the U.S. Chamber of Commerce (who apparently agreed with Senator Kennedy's lawyerly analysis of where the tax would fall) said, "It is ridiculous to believe that every company . . . can afford to provide such a generous array of health care benefits." The U.S. Chamber of Commerce will never tax the company.

The ironies of the case illustrates the delight economists take in unforeseen consequences, a delight shared by other social scientists. It illustrates, too, the picking of a few consequences for special attention. An accountant or political scientist or institutionalist economist would want to hear how the 5 percent pension was funded, because the manner of funding could affect the behavior of politicians and businesspeople in the future. Neoclassical economists usually set such institutional consequences to the side. It illustrates also the way economists draw on typical scenes—the queues in front of the factory—and typical metaphors—workers as commodities to be bought and sold. Especially it illustrates the way stories support economic argument. Since Adam Smith and David Ricardo economists have been addicted to little analytic stories, called by Joseph Schumpeter "the Ricardian vice." The economist muses, Yes, I see how the story starts; but I see dramatic possibilities here; I see how events will develop away from the situation given in the first act.

The rule of art is to push the analysis to the later acts of the play. For instance, a calculation by Peter Mathias and Patrick O'Brien (1976) of the tax burden in eighteenth-century Britain stopped in the first act. It reckoned ingeniously the *legal* incidence of the taxes, finding that the British government relied more than did the French on taxes imposed on things purchased by the poor—beer, for example. But in the next act a tax on beer could move away from where it was placed. True, a tax on beer in the first instance increases the price of beer to drinkers, many of whom are poor, unless the poor brew their own or drink untaxed beer purchased behind the shed. But it also *decreases* the price to brewers. (Economists speak expressively of taxes on goods inserting a "wedge" between what the makers get and what the buyers pay, the width of the wedge going to the government.) The lower price would cause a little exit from brewing, which would in turn—we are into the third or fourth act by now—somewhat reduce the rewards to land used for hops and buildings used for malting. The owners of land and buildings are rich, not poor, yet they are paying some of the tax nominally imposed on the poor man's drink.

The correct calculation of tax incidence may or may not reverse the merely legal incidence. It will reverse it if the legal bearer of the tax can easily exit from under it. Thus an Iowa corporation can easily exit from under an Iowan tax on corporate profits, and so Iowa cannot count on the tax falling on the owners of the corporation.

In general the ultimate, long-run incidence need have nothing to do with the legal, short-run incidence. That's a finding of neoclassical economics that can be applied immediately to historical taxes and subsidies. But this result goes deeper, since it is applicable to any local cost or benefit. The argument is for example the equitable basis for the property tax as the way of supporting local government expenditure. The net beneficiary of public expenditure on roads and schools is not the tenant. The tenant is willing to pay in higher rents exactly as much as the better schools or roads are worth to him. Competition assures that he will pay it over to the landlord in rent. The neoclassical economist suggests that in general the immobile input cannot escape taxes. But the immobile input also extracts all the benefits. The owners of land, therefore, collect the benefits from city expenditure and therefore should pay the taxes.

ENTRY AND EXIT TO MISERY

Entry and exit drive all manner of historical argument. For instance, a serf who can run away is not much of a serf. In frontier areas, such as southern Russia in the eighteenth century, serfdom did not work well, because a serf could escape from Voronezh to Rostov and to the wild Cossack life. The internal frontiers of settled societies have a similar effect: town air makes one free. A serf who could exit, therefore, could not be exploited. Even if the place to which he exited was merely another manor, as was common in the European middle ages (Raftis 1964), the competition among manors helped. The exploitation from de jure serfdom—or de jure debt peonage or de jure slavery or de jure subordination to the great power of a capitalist mill owner—depends on the de facto immobility of the victim. A society able to impose internal passports, as in Russia until recently, in Japan until the Meiji Restoration, and in the United States, effectively, around the time of the Dred Scott decision—can pin people down and suppress competition for their services. Stories of exploitation depend on a lack of exit.

A story of exploitation, the neoclassical economist avers, should tell why exit did not work. Roger Ransom and Richard Sutch (1977) tell a story of the reenslavement of American freedmen after the Civil War by elites in charge of country stores. They argue that during the 1870s and 1880s the sharecroppers became peons in a system of rolling indebtedness. But the question is why the freedmen did not merely walk away. The answer is that sometimes they did, not to the Northern industrial cities, a later development, but to other counties beyond the reach of the sheriff, in the style of serfs disappearing from the rent rolls of one English manor to reappear on the rolls of another.

Of course the freedmen who fled from Washington to Jefferson County had not escaped to heaven. Conditions were bad in Jefferson County, too. Nothing in the argument says that American blacks were not damaged by their experience after the Civil War. It suggests merely that the powerful mechanism of oppression was not debt peonage. The powerful mechanism was directly political, it would seem: the hooded bands, and then the gradual reassertion of white political control in the South, the strange career of Jim Crow. The ability to walk put the freedman in a quite different position from a slave (as those so positioned said). A slave was subject to the oppression of his individual master. A freedman had to be oppressed by the entire community acting in concert, a more difficult trick, though in fact accomplished. The story is radically different. It is not more optimistic, merely different.

A similar question can be asked about speedups in nineteenth-century factories (Lazonick and Brush 1985) or about owing one's soul to the company store in mining towns (Fishback 1992): where is the obstacle to exit? The economist will argue that the market pushes businesspeople back to normal behavior while it pushes them back to normal profits. As much as the wicked capitalist would like to exploit workers and earn more than normal profits, the market will tend to force him to conform to the average degree of nastiness. In the market the nice guys, to be sure, finish last. But so do unusually nasty guys, who find it hard to get employees and business partners.

It is for this reason that economists do not moralize about the behavior of people in markets. The journalistic way of telling a story about a successful business is to ask whether the success was achieved morally or not. The economic way, by contrast, asks about the conditions of entry and exit. The argument is that the conditions determine the results and have little to do with the character or culture of the people involved. Good or bad, the competition of other businesses is what matters to what happens.

The Ransom and Sutch argument about the freedman illustrates the entry side, too. They calculate that the owners of country stores earned high interest rates. This would suggest that the stores were profitable undertakings—profitable, that is, unless the high interest rates were merely offsets for the sharecroppers who did not pay back their loans at all, walking away to borrow in the next county next year. Other evidence suggests that country stores were in fact not especially profitable enterprises. They went out of business from time to time in the usual way and they did not increase in number. If the flowers were so rich and the nectar so ready for the taking it is odd that the bees did not prosper. In telling a story of high profitability sustained over a long time—the story of pawn shops in rural China or of Dutch conquests in the Spice Islands or of Venice serving as the hinge of Europe—the historian faces the question: why was there not competing entry? It is often an important question.

To ask why competitors did not enter, say, pawnbroking if the business was so exploitatively profitable is not to suppose that the entry will always work wonderfully well. Entry can after all be prevented, by governmental or private violence, or by private barriers to entry, such as secret knowledge of industrial technique. Abraham Darby, the inventor of coke smelting of iron, was able for decades to keep the secret that made coke smelting profitable, the technique for casting the iron into thin-walled pots (Hyde 1977, 40–41). A company town in Maine around 1930 with its single wool mill may in fact have been a miserable place, because the company may in fact have been able to prevent people from exiting its grip. It is for a good reason that dictatorial governments turn the guns inward. The neoclassical logic of entry and exit merely directs attention to the facts of how such situations came to pass.

A fixation on entry and exit typifies neoclassical (and "Austrian") economic narrative, and is not foreign to Marxists, either. Economic science was named "dismal" not because the scientists were dreary or the subject boring but because its earliest conclusions, based on consideration of entry, were dismally Malthusian. If the society permits free entry to the laboring classes by excessive births, then the laboring classes will never rise for long above subsistence, said the classical economists. The modern neoclassical economists are not so confident that the laws of motion of a capitalist society are this simple. But they agree with Malthus and Marx that entry and exit matter.

Entry and exit underlie most important arguments in neoclassical economics. The economist's belief in competition, for example, comes from a lively appreciation of entry and exit. A Chinese historian explains why in the modern Chinese textile industry no one could establish monopolies or, for that matter, suffer long from unprofitability:

> Most cloth merchants were also money-changers or grain dealers, or both; they were thus in a position to close up shop without much hardship anytime they felt the profits were too low or the risks too high in the textile market. Furthermore, their high mobility permitted them to shift operations from one site to another with comparative ease. (Kang Chao quoted in Rawski 1989, 54)

Entry and exit is a way of telling a story, a drama with the classical unities. The hero can be the manufacturing of pots, the growing of rice, the teaching of children, the giving of protection. When the curtain comes down the rate of profit in all these activities has been driven back to normal.

AN EXAMPLE:
ECONOMIC RENT AS A FAILURE OF ENTRY

Free entry and exit does not mean that profits need be identical and routinely normal everywhere in an industry. The olive grove next door to Cato's might have earned 10 percent rather than only 6 percent because its land was better. Some farmers have better land than others, some have better technique, some are just smarter or harder working. Only routine land and routine technique earn the routine reward. As long as there is no way that the poor land can be made fertile and the poor technique made intelligent the lucky few will go on making high profits. The lucky few are protected from entry by their special fertility and intelligence.

The argument explains the wide variation in rents of land, which are in the economist's way of thinking pure profits. Land close to London or Peking earns high rents for its location. A good location, close to the consuming masses of the metropolis, is just a form of fertility. The rent falls as the land becomes less extraordinary in location. Finally, out in nineteenth-century Montana or Tsinghai at "the margin of cultivation" (beyond which the land is not worth cultivating at all, because it earns no profit), the rent is zero and the land is free for the taking. The gradient from Peking to wildest Tsinghai illustrates the economist's "theory of rent," a theory of permanently abnormal profit.

The theory of rent applies to more than land. It applies to slavery and serfdom, for example. When labor is scarce relative to land, the labor will earn "profits" above subsistence—in the way that bottom land earns profits above the cost of cultivation compared with the poorer and more remote land in the hills. If new labor cannot enter by birth or migration— which would drive down the "profit" to zero—then a man with a sword will form the idea of taking the labor. Abundant labor is not worth taking, which suggests why successful slavery is associated with labor scarcity, on the frontiers. The high wages of the white-settler colonies in America put the notion into the head of merchants and plantation owners to import white indentured servants and later, when these proved able to exit, African slaves (Galenson 1981, 1986). Only profits above normal attract the bees.

Neoclassical economics says in other words that people seek rents, which is more of their talk of "maximization." "Rents" mean to an economist "rewards to someone above what he could earn elsewhere." A nobleman earns rents by acquiring the favor of the king, getting a monopoly of playing cards or the County of Leicester. His pursuit of place may be taken as a typical example of "rent seeking." All manner of striving may be called "rent seeking." The ward heeler looking for a sinecure or the inventor looking for a cheaper way to make iron are both seeking rents, which is to say, seeking profits above normal. In the neoclassical fiction it is profit not love that makes the world go round.

The point of talking this way is to draw attention to the competition for rents. A royal court is populated by rent seekers, each of whom cancels out the efforts of the others. If fresh rents are available from drilling into an underground lake of oil, many will do so. The many bees, as the neoclassical jargon has it, will "dissipate the rents." That is, so many people will be drilling into the oil that no one will make much money out of it.

The result has been called "the tragedy of the commons." Overfishing or overgrazing by people facing a common pool or a common field will ruin the catch and incidentally drive returns back to normal. The neoclassical economist points out that the play only reaches its last, tragic act if the resource cannot be owned. Ownership is justified, the economists note, by the evils of its absence. As William Bradford remarked in his *History of the Plimouth Plantation,* common ownership of land "was found to breed much confusion & discontent, and retard much imployment that would have been to their benefite and conforte" (Bogart and Thompson 1929, 5). And so the Pilgrim fathers abandoned common ownership in favor of private property. Buffalo were exterminated, to be replaced on the Great Plains by European cattle ill adapted to the environment, because no one owned them.

Beyond ownership there is the common sense of a small group. If the group is too large, as Mancur Olson points out in one of the founding volumes of the new political economy (Olson 1965), collective action to prevent the tragedy of overuse may be impossible. But if it is small then various punishments can easily be arranged for those who defect from the social good—or social bad, for as Olson also points out the same logic of collective action applies to forming monopolies against the public interest. In actual fact the tragedy of the commons is averted by collective action as much as by private property (Feeny et al. 1990).

Rent seeking is the life of capitalism—and when you come to think of it, of aristocracy, too. It is the reason for striving for gains, and the reason for the good that comes of it:

> By directing that industry in such a manner as its produce may be of the greatest value, he intends only his own gain, and he is in this, and in many other cases, led by an invisible hand to promote an end which was no part of his intention. . . . By pursuing his own interest he frequently promotes that of the society more effectually than when he really intends to promote it. (Smith 1937 [1776], 423)

Marx believed that rent seeking would end in the death of capitalism. The neoclassicals agree, if the rents attract the bees in the wrong direction. If institutions are such that people are attracted into *useless* rent seeking (the court of the French kings from Louis XIV being the classic case, designed for just this purpose), seeking monopolies and other obstructions to trade, the energies of society can be dissipated along with the rents. The modern case in point is the American federal income tax, which economists know as the Tax Accountant's and Lawyer's Welfare Act.

The theory of rent, in short, is a powerful tool, derived from the neoclassical economist's notion that people choose what is best for them. It explains differential rents and the consequences of pursuing them. And it goes further. Consider that renters of something to be used commercially, such as agricultural land, will pay what they can earn from it. Why? Because if they do not other people will spring forward gladly to pay a trifle less. Competition assures it. (The competition does not have to be some fantastic ruck of millions in order to work; two buyers of land are enough, if they can't find a way of conspiring together.) The thing to be rented can be a slave or a patent or an acre of land. A farmer renting land will be willing to pay more rent to the landlord if the land improves in profitability. The result is that the owners of the land, not the farmers renting from landowners, get the benefit from an improvement.

Some historical insight follows at once. If leases of land are short, improvement needs to come from the landlord, as in England in the nineteenth century on rack-rented land. A similar issue arose in Ireland at the time, the issue being whether tenants should be compensated for improvements to the land, such as ditching and fencing. If they were not compensated (and in fact they were not), the landlord theoretically could evict them and get a higher rent from a new tenant for the land improved by the late tenants' money and sweat. Realizing this the tenants would be reluctant to invest in improvements. Without long leases and fixed rents, it is said, improvements were ignored and Irish agriculture in the late nineteenth century decayed. Barbara Solow, however, argues that the tenants had virtual security of tenure. Though leases were officially annual, they were routinely renewed, providing the same incentives as owner-occupation to improve the land (Solow 1971).

The benefit from canals built in Ohio in the early nineteenth century looks at first impossible to measure. The benefit to the canal companies themselves may be known, because the accounts have survived. But the accounting is incomplete (an economic analysis starts and often finishes with accounting). What of the benefits to the people of Ohio, from lower costs of transport? It appears that one would need to know how much the costs fell and how much was transported. That is, one would need detailed statistics, which do not exist, on how much was carried on the canals. But in "Social Returns from Public Transport Investment: A Case Study of the Ohio Canal" (1970) Roger Ransom uses the theory of rent to measure the benefit indirectly. He reasons that lower costs of transport would have raised the rent that farmers were willing to pay for land close to a new canal. The price of land would therefore have risen. By examining the prices of a sample of land before and after the canals Ransom is able to estimate the elusive social returns.

The theory of rent allows the measurement of the apparently unmeasurable, providing the historian with a sensitive index of local improvements in law enforcement, transportation, crop varieties, irrigation, or whatever. The index that measures all these things is the rise in the rewards to immobile inputs, especially rents on land. The landlord in the first instance gets it all, and so land rents are a good, and neglected, historical source on improvements.

Similar notions have been applied to the benefit from English enclosures in the eighteenth century (McCloskey 1972), to American slavery (Yasuba 1961), to African slavery (Thomas and Bean 1974; Gemery and Hogendorn 1974), and to many other matters. The owners of immobile resources such as land or slaves or urban building sites are the sole beneficiaries of improvements that increase their desirability. The desirability can be measured from their benefit.

The economist's favorite argument, then, is Darwinian. Entry and exit to a market play the role of natural selection. The horse is the best horse he can be, because if he was not his ancestors would have changed by natural selection until he was. The hippologist can then "explain" the modern horse, which is to say, give a story satisfying to us about how horses came to walk on their toenails. The reasoning is backward looking, showing how what actually happened is natural. It is the commonest device of historical writing, to show how the events leading up to World War I or to the partition of India were natural (after all, they happened). Likewise one can base an economic story on a premise that American oil regulation (Libecap 1984) or the choice of tenure in the South (Reid 1973) was natural.

There is little harm in this so long as it is recognized as a convention of storytelling. The talk of "preconditions" for economic growth or "continuity" in history generally (on these see Gerschenkron 1962, 1968; McCloskey 1987a) or "modeling" economic behavior is harmless so long as it is understood to suggest merely that we should hunt for the connections among things, especially among earlier and later things. True, such talk flirts with vacuity, a hazard of determinism. Tellers of stories about economic development will offer "models" that abstract a particular piece of history. The phrase "Urbanization leads to industrialization," for instance (marked by the gnomic present) has a scientific air. But it is false, as the cases of Lancashire and the Netherlands suggest, or vacuous, if a mill site is always reckoned "urban."

Historians sometimes imagine that economics can provide "models" in the sense of typical patterns that apply to all history. But a chronological pattern that Karl Marx or Ester Boserup or Walt Rostow believed they discerned in the past, useful though it may be, is not the most useful economics for historical scholars. The most useful will change the metaphors and other conventions with which historians tell stories. Neoclassical economics can provide, in a word, another and more self-conscious rhetoric for history (Megill and McCloskey 1987).

AN APPLICATION OF
ENTRY AND EXIT TO PRICE STATISTICS

A historian imbued with economic rhetoric, then, would tell stories of failure by recourse to unprofitability more than to cultural flaws; she would replace metaphors of "growth" with metaphors of "profitability" and "entry"; she would portray unusually bad or good conditions as being on their way to normality; she would discipline her judgments about exploitation by considerations of entry and exit; and she would make use of the fruitful if deterministic myth of efficiency to explain how institutions arose.

Here is a more elaborate example, a showing of how the economist's rhetoric of entry and exit can tell a better story. It is not chosen as transcendentally important, but merely as an example in detail of why thinking neoclassically is worth the historian's time.

The raw economic fact we know in greatest bulk about any economy is price. Though not collected and indexed (in either the mathematical or the bibliographical sense of the word), prices in ancient Mesopotamia can be collected from tablets in unlimited quantities, given peace in Iraq and a large enough budget for excavation. Medieval Europe (that non-market economy) has prices of grain, labor, grazing rights, bail bonds, beer, oxen, land, wives, husbands, manors, ecclesiastical benefices, kingdoms, and eternal salvation from the tenth century in rising volume, to be retrieved from manorial accounts, cathedral records, and the letters of Italian merchants. China is particularly well endowed with such records. From times of famine there survive market quotations even for human flesh.

Prices are fundamental to market economies, and telling. The difference between the price of wheat in exporting Poland and importing Venice from the fifteenth to the eighteenth century tells of falling transport costs (Braudel and Spooner 1967). The real wage in England from the thirteenth to the twentieth century, a ratio of two prices (Phelps-Brown and Hopkins 1956), tells of rising human rewards.

The noneconomic way of using these riches is typified in the *Annales* school, which treats price as the pulse of the economy. A pulse rate seems a natural metaphor to a noneconomist.

A neoclassical economist sees different ways to use the prices. The primary sources for prices are commonly quotations as specific as a particular day—for instance, a sale of six quarters of barley from the manorial grange of Great Durnford, Wiltshire on Ladyday 1334—but most historians will present them as part of a yearly average. The rise and fall of grain prices *from month to month,* for example, is not of much interest to an *annaliste* in pursuit of *la longue durée.* The yearly average is the right treatment if daily or monthly figures have no use. But they do, as follows.

One may ask what the pattern of grain prices during the year was and what explains it. (The Baconian way of putting it is misleading, because, as is common in scholarship, scanning of the data was *not* how the argument was discovered.) Consider for example James Lee's work on eighteenth-century prices of rice in his (1993) study of Southwest China. He kept the monthly detail because the official statistics from which he works were in lunar months. In Lijiang prefecture in Yunnan province average monthly prices (in taels of silver per shi of white rice) moved like this over the twelve months:

Month	1	2	3	4	5	6
Price	1.97	1.95	2.01	2.09	2.10	1.99
Month	7	8	9	10	11	12
Price	2.24	2.21	2.06	2.08	2.12	1.91

The price is lowest in month 12, rising more or less steadily to a peak in month 7. The nineteen other prefectures recorded in Lee's study show the same pattern. The twelfth month always has the lowest price, substantially lower than the months before or after. The seventh month or sometimes the eighth has the highest price.

What is happening? Plainly, rice is being harvested in month 12 (a late variety, it seems), making rice on average abundant and driving down its price. Probably an earlier-ripening variety is being harvested in month 9, breaking the peak. (This is deduced entirely from the price statistics, without knowledge of Chinese agriculture; the pattern in neighboring Kweichow province is the same but unfolded a month or so earlier: was Kweichow differently favored by climate?)

So far we have learned what we already might have known from non-quantitative sources about the agricultural year in Southwest China. Month 12 was the harvest. If neoclassical economics could offer no more than routine confirmations of what we already knew then the historian could safely ignore it.

But watch the entry and exit, and the tale it tells. Rice could be stored, which is to say that it could be "transported" from month 6, say, to month 7. That is, an owner of rice in month 6 could *enter* the market in month 7 (by storing rice bought in month 6 and then waiting a month) and would do so if he believed the price in 7 was going to be far above that in 6. Consequently, if storage were costless (contrary to fact) there could be no persistent and predictable difference between prices in month 6 and month 7. A flat price from month to month is a neoclassical implication of costless entry.

Yet there was in fact a persistent difference. The price was not flat. Apparently therefore entry was *not* costless. To put it the other way, apparently storage *was* costly. No wonder. There would be the cost of the jars and buildings to hold it, the guards to keep it safe, depreciation of its quality during storage. Call these d per month, still unknown. Additionally, to store a quantity of rice for a month required the tying up of funds. The funds could have been invested at some interest rate in projects of money lending or paddy making, at say i per month. The economy does not need to be thoroughly capitalistic for alternative investments to be possible and to yield a return. Crusoe could build pens for goats or build a canoe to escape, and each had its "internal rate of return" to be compared with each other in a world of scarce effort. So the economist's accounting says this: the monthly cost of doing the storage instead of some other moneymaking project is both the ordinary storage cost and the cost of interest forgone. It is $d+i$.

Now use the logic of entry and exit. If the actual growth of price per month had exceeded this $d+i$ then new storers of rice would have entered the business. Focus for example on month 12 (the big harvest and the low point) and month 7 of the next calendar year (the month just before the first harvest, the high point). Suppose that in a particular month 12 the grain dealers expect the month 7 will have an unusually high price. The weather is expected to be poor or the politics disrupted. If the dealers try to get more rice in month 12, taking advantage of what they believe will be an opportunity for profit from resale when month 7 arrives, the price will in fact rise immediately in month 12. Later, in month 7, when the dealers sell the twelfth-month rice the price will fall, since more will be supplied. In other words, entry to the profitable business of storing grain will cause the price to rise in month 12 and fall in month 7. The growth in price from 12 to 7 will be lower than it was before entry. That is, it will be forced down toward the normal differential, the normal cost of "transporting" rice across months, $d+i$ per month.

Entry therefore governs the growth of prices, ensuring that on average (and only on average) no abnormal profits above costs can be earned by storing rice. The effect of exit is symmetrical. If the actual growth in prices is not expected to compensate people for holding rice at a monthly cost of $d+i$, then people will exit from the storage business, twisting the prices the other way. The equilibrium, or normal, price differential just pays for the normally expected costs. At such rewards no one exits or enters. The nectar is exhausted.

In other words, the actual rise in price (averaged over a series of years to eliminate extraneous disturbances) measures $d+i$. That is, the whole cost of storage can be measured from the price statistics. This is the payoff. An economic metaphor extracts meaning from an unused source.

The calculations are simple. In the case of Lijiang prefecture the cost is 2.24−1.91=0.33 taels per shi over seven months, or a rise of .33/7=0.047 taels per shi over a single month. Taking the midpoint ([2.24+1.91]/2=2.075) as the typical price per shi, the monthly increase is typically 0.047/2.075=2.27 percent per month. The price of rice goes up at about 2.25 percent per month between harvests on account of the full costliness of storage.

In southern England during the thirteenth and fourteenth centuries the rate of rise for wheat was similar, and for inferior grains it was higher (McCloskey and Nash 1984). The wheat estimate, based on 1,075 pairs of dated prices, is about 2.5 percent per month. A sum growing at 2.5 percent per month will grow by 34 percent a year (the figure for Lijiang implies 31 percent per year).

All this is to say that the cost of storage for a year in medieval England

and eighteenth-century China was about a third of the crop. It is therefore unsurprising that storage was inadequate to prevent famine in England until the seventeenth century, and that in China only extraordinary governmental intervention and great stores of grain could prevent it.

The technique can be used, further, to tell of storage costs over time. In England they fell sharply in the sixteenth century. Since barns did not improve much (and the cost of keeping grain, d, therefore did not change) the fall must have come from the other component, the interest rate. The interest rate fell by the sixteenth century to a half of its medieval level.

Noneconomists think of interest as one tiny item in their bank account. Economists think of it as permeating the economy. Interest is the price at which present resources are exchanged for future resources. You lend $100 this year and get $110 back next year. A dollar's worth of resources this year is worth $1.10 next year, expressing both the impatience for seizing the fruit now and the productivity of waiting until it ripens. Every decision that involves the future will involve the rate of interest. (This is true whether or not the economy is capitalistic, or even monetary. Impatience and the productivity of waiting, as in Crusoe's case, are not uniquely capitalistic or monetary.) Because the interest rate in America was higher, the American railways were built more flimsily than British railways. In countries with a history of higher interest rates, veal is more common than beef. Tying up one's money in a growing steer is a poor project if other projects yield especially high returns.

Falling interest rates from medieval to early modern times, detected in the neglected statistics of monthly movements of grain prices, can account for all manner of changes, from greater investment in agriculture to a longer perspective on the future. The fall can be confirmed in other prices that reflect interest rates, such as the relationship between the prices of wool and mutton and the prices of hay, shepherds, and land; or in the relationship between animal products and the prices of the animals (see again McCloskey and Nash 1984; Clark 1988, 1992). The logic of entry and exit applied to otherwise useless statistics on prices can give a technique for measuring interest rates, watching them fall on the eve of modern economic growth. It is a way of telling a new story.

TESTING RATIONALITY, SECOND-GUESSING THE FARMERS

Someone not socialized within economics will worry that such a technique (and all neoclassical economic techniques run this way) "assumes rationality" in choice. He is accustomed to dealing with complicated and confusing choices. To reduce the humans in the rice market to single-minded seekers after profit does not seem to accord with common sense.

It does not. We see ourselves failing every day to make the best decision about which food to buy or whether to change jobs. Considering that most of us wander in a fog of indecision and emotion the bright sunlight in which the rational man strides toward his goal is difficult to credit.

Various replies are possible. The "rationality" in question means the "sensible apportioning of means to ends." It is another word for the pursuit of profit, defined broadly. The economist does not mean anything very deep by asserting that people behave rationally. He means something like "approximately calculating." Rationality depends on circumstances. Someone who rushed out into the street in Iowa City in a non-revolutionary year, such as the present, waving his hands and shouting "Overthrow the government!" would rightly be considered irrational, a bad calculator. His means would be poorly adjusted to his announced ends. On the other hand, different circumstances might make the identical action thoroughly rational: Petrograd in late October 1917, for instance.

The amount of light needed for rationality is easy to exaggerate. An English farmer choosing a reaping machine (David 1971) did not need detailed engineering specifications for each of the dozens of machines available in order to make up his mind to buy. Nor did he need perfect foresight about the future price of harvest labor. A crude decision is rational if information to make a more subtle one is expensive. If it were profitable to do so the market itself would make available some of the information, with catalogues and commercial travelers. The decision-maker here was not a consumer making many little decisions about toothpaste and tea; he was a producer making a few decisions about what big machine to buy, decisions on which his livelihood depended. Such a man would have every incentive to think clearly.

The clarity, furthermore, need characterize only some of the decisionmakers. Most could have been lumpish and driven by habit, letting their livelier cousins show the way. The point is not wholly one of imitation. The great entrepreneur, of course, can influence thousands to emulate his trick. He can also persuade them to absurdities, such as gold mines in Louisiana or machines for perpetual motion. But the sober, firm pressure of the invisible hand is at work, too. The price of bread is determined by the cheapest source that can make enough money to stay in business, not by the average. This is what economists mean when they talk about the importance of "the margin." It is the tiny, cutting edge of profitable participation, not the sluggish majority, that sets the price. The majority has to be there, in the background. But the last player calls the tune.

Now of course many decisions are wholly private, shielded from the scorn or competition of the neighborhood. These can persist as irrational. It may be irrational to put one's trousers on both feet at once, but some people do it. When Ouija boards or tarot cards are used to make important economic decisions, however, they will do badly against more rational methods. Rational methods have survival value, even for the least prosperous. A peasant near starvation will seek any comfort he can get, through a diverse crop or through the village wizard. But if he makes a mistake, by trusting the wizard (or the local econometrician, for that matter) beyond reason, he will die. In the backwaters of an economy and in good weather life can go on without troubling overmuch about its rationality; in the main channel at tempest's height the currents of rationality run strong. (And yet it is reported that 10 percent of French companies make some use of astrologers.)

Above all the assumption of rationality can be tested. It is not an assumption removed from scrutiny. Indeed, if the leading question in historical economics to date had to be put in one sentence it would be, how well does the assumption of close calculation fit the economic past? The answer has been, pretty well; at any rate better than earlier students of the matter have believed.

In other words, the assumption of rationality in economics is not an axiom in the Euclidean sense, an indubitable premise from which irrefutable conclusions can be drawn. It serves merely as a working proposition, subject to testing and revision to suit the case at hand.

It is, to say it again, a way of telling a story. Economics looks from the outside a deductive field, filled with words like "therefore" and "suppose," an instance of the deductive certitude that Western intellectuals have pursued since Plato. But for practical purposes the deductive chains of reasoning in economics are short, beginning and ending with links of fact. Think of grain storage. An economic argument is mistaken or irrelevant most usually because it got the facts wrong. The objection that economics "assumes" or "postulates" rationality is naive. The facts can speak to the assumption.

For example, one can test the rationality of British businessmen in the late nineteenth century (Sandberg and McCloskey 1971) or of Chinese peasants on the lower Yangtze in the early twentieth century (Bell 1992), by second-guessing. Putting oneself in the position of the businessman or peasant, one can ask whether the decision made to spurn ring spinning or to adopt sericulture was sound. In the British and Chinese cases the rationality itself is of historical interest: once rationality has been established all manner of storytelling follows.

One must, however, second-guess intelligently. The economist like the historian needs some of the knack of the novelist in getting inside other people's decisions. The retrospective accounting again is crucial. It will not help in understanding the situation of British business in 1910 to imagine what the decisions would have been with perfect foresight. A businessman in 1910 who could anticipate the decline in demand for British cotton textiles that would occur by 1925 would not have invested in any spinning machinery at all, whether modern ring spinning or old-fashioned mule. But no one in 1910 could reasonably have anticipated the catastrophes of 1925 (after all, many wise politicians and princes did not). To be useful for understanding business decisions the accounting must look forward from the perspective of 1910.

The "irony of history" is of course a legitimate theme, and economics can help make the joke stick. It was surely an irony of history that building new British blast furnaces or cotton mills in 1910, whatever the technology, turned out to be a terrible idea, considering the business slump lasting in those industries from 1920 virtually down to the Second World War. Economic accounting of profit and loss can measure how terrible. That history has many cunning passages and contrived corridors, however, does not justify scorning its victims. That economic actors make mistakes does not mean necessarily that they were irrational to make them.

Second-guessing children and fools is easier than second-guessing adults with an incentive to decide intelligently and with the mental equipment to do so. We do not expect Iowa farmers with advanced degrees in agronomy to make decisions about soil conservation that the average newspaper columnist could profitably second-guess. The American Question is relevant here as elsewhere in historiography: If you're so smart why aren't you rich? The historian who spends his time refighting Grant's battles better than Grant himself is not telling us much about Grant or about battles, a point made about battle history by Keegan (1977, 75).

Chinese farmers, to take an economic case, were not wholly uneducated (30 percent of males were literate around 1930 [Buck 1930]) and gave other signs of being able to respond quickly to incentives. One therefore doubts Han-seng Chen's argument that in North China the peasants did not choose rationally to cultivate tobacco, which, according to Chen, "certainly reduced the standard of living among the peasantry of the tobacco regions" (1939, 85). What is at stake here is the sensible disposition of family labor, "penny capitalism" (as the anthropologist Sol Tax once put it). Perhaps the better word is "prudence." There is no reason to suppose that farmers would not have done it right. One doubts the result because so many others have found farmers of all types, "peasant" or not, to be rational (Helleiner 1975; Popkin 1979). The peasant who indulges a taste for bad old ways or for meritless novelties pays at harvest time.

Explaining modernity in the economy depends on what came before. If human character changed in the sixteenth century, if the Protestant ethic was important to the spirit of capitalism, or if

> [it was a] utopian endeavor of economic liberalism to set up a self-regulating market system (29) . . . market economy is an institutional structure which, as we all too easily forget, has been present at no time except our own (37). . . . In no case can we assume the functioning of market laws unless a self-regulating market is shown to exist (38). . . . The alleged propensity of man to truck, barter, and exchange is almost entirely apocryphal (44). . . . Local markets proper are of little consequence (58). . . . Individual acts of "truck, barter, and exchange" are only exceptionally practiced in primitive society (274). . . . The countryside was cut out of trade in the Middle Ages (277), (Polanyi 1944)

it would be easy to believe in irrationality.

But a world in which neoclassical economics is supposed *not* to work at all would be a paradise for the stray wise man. In such a world there would be unclaimed profits everywhere, as for example from making land private (a good example of this sort of reasoning is Cohen and Weitzman 1975). An economy filled with people as irrational as some historians have believed, under the baleful influence of Karl Polanyi and A. V. Chayanov and James C. Scott, would be filled with opportunities to buy low from one set of fools in order to sell high to another.

Such a view, I would say, does not treat the dead with due respect. It entails assuming that our ancestors were heedless and, if asked, would not prefer a little more bread to a little less. If true it provides a program for research in history. The second-guessing ought to be easy in such an economy, because the mistakes would be so egregious. They would compound one another, the foolishness of peasants allowing the lords to engage in still greater foolishness. The world imagined by one strand of historical opinion—against that of medievalists such as David Herlihy or

Ambrose Raftis, for example—would be a paradise for professors of history, who would be able to spot opportunities better than the people at the time. They would be in the position of Addison: "Thus I live in the world rather as a SPECTATOR of mankind than as one of the species. . . . I am very well versed in the theory of a husband or a father, and can discern the errors in the economy, business, and diversion of others better than those engaged in them."

SUBSTITUTING THE FACTORS OF PRODUCTION

The respectful second-guessing of economic actors often involves the notion of "factor substitution." "Factor" is the economic jargon for inputs—the land, labor, machines, and materials used up to satisfy human demands. The ultimate factors of production are land, labor, and capital, from which everything else is made. But in dealing with something less than the ultimate it is reasonable to speak of materials, fertilizer, lumber, and coal as factors, too. One factor can substitute for another. America in the nineteenth century, for example, substituted abundant land for men and machines. Americans making guns used machines that made gun stocks quickly, saving labor, but were notably wasteful of wood. Americans had wood to burn from their lands in forest, but no labor to waste. British gun makers carved the stocks by hand, since wood was expensive in Europe relative to skilled labor. Again the economics comes down to a choice under constraints.

The crucial deduction is that nations or regions can have different ways of doing something without either being worse. The constraints differ. It is no evidence of American vigor to mention the gun stocks and to talk of Yankee ingenuity in "saving labor." The Americans were merely trading off cheap wood for expensive labor, as any profit-making business would do, in South Asia or south Connecticut. The British making gun stocks by their own, labor-intensive methods were being no less businesslike. They were as vigorous in saving wood as the Americans were in saving labor. One region can of course be uniformly more vigorous or intelligent or educated or capitalistic or up-to-date than another. The big differences in productivity between countries and historically is testimony to "higher production functions," as the economists say. But commonly the evidence for vigor will be mixed with evidence for merely rational substitutions, doing what one can do best. In the jargon, two regions can have "the same production function," or book of recipes, yet choose differing "factor proportions."

It is sometimes argued, for example, that low wages imply a low incentive to adopt labor-saving innovations. Strictly this is true: if labor is relatively the abundant factor, it would be irrational to substitute away from it. But what is often meant is that low wages reduce the incentive to do better *on balance, overall.* In the neoclassical way of thinking, and historically, it is false. Someone who thinks otherwise has to explain why people would not act rationally, or why China was the world leader in technology around the year 1000. A dollar saved is a dollar earned, regardless of whether the saving comes from a factor in large or small supply. That labor was cheap in eleventh-century Yorkshire was no disincentive to adopt the windmill, which saved labor and oxen, too. What cheap labor does discourage is the substitution of an expensive piece of capital equipment for a cheap gang of laborers—but that is good, not bad, if labor is so very cheap. One does not want a nation investing in modern steel mills when backyard furnaces, under the constraints that the nation faces, are a better choice.

Historically speaking the notion that low wages lead to low innovation is doubtful. For all its energetic pursuit of novelty the United States had fewer innovations to its credit than low-wage Europe in the nineteenth century. Japan developed through low wages, as did Belgium and the Netherlands.

THE DISTASTE FOR RISK

In its very simplest form the "assumption" of rationality amounts to saying that people pursue average profit alone. To put it in the quaint jargon of economics, the "utility" of people is supposed to be a function of dollars alone. If mere dollars account for investment in slaves in the American South (note the image of "accounting" here again), without adding in the alleged benefits from a feudal social position as a slave owner or from the sexual exploitation of the slaves, then the historian is justified in drawing the inference that slave owners were businesslike (Conrad and Meyer 1958).

This simplest of "utility functions" will often fail. Yet often the failure itself speaks. An example is the return from landed estates in England during the eighteenth century. If land were merely another asset, with no social and political consequences to its ownership, then entry and exit would force its return into equality with government bonds, which earned 5 percent. But land in large estates in fact earned only 3 percent per year, because with large estates came social status and political power. The businesslike accounting reveals the 2 percent per year that the landed class was prepared to pay to maintain its privilege. "Irrationality" by a strict business definition leaves measurable footprints in the snow of rationality.

One important item that would make average income a poor description of why people did things is risk. Peasants in North Africa have proven suspicious of new high-yield wheats; but their suspicion has turned out to be justified by the greater *variability* of yields from the new seeds. In a world of less than perfect insurance it is not irrational to seek a safe income as well as a high average income. Philip Huang (1990) argues persuasively that cotton was a risky crop in northern China, and *therefore* earned high average returns.

The logic of entry and exit is at work again. If cotton was risky without a compensating benefit from a higher average return, no one would grow it. Since it was in fact grown, the growers must have had a two-item utility function, getting pleasure from a lower variability of return around the average as well as from the average itself.

An example of using the two-item utility function historically is the explanation of scattered farms. In Europe, India, Latin America, China, and in most farming communities long ago few farms were perfectly consolidated. They were inconveniently scattered in little plots, which is to say that some output on average was lost. The neoclassical economist looking at such a system instantly thinks of "portfolio balance" (and in different language anthropologists have thought similar thoughts, trained as they are to see rationality in apparently outlandish behavior). They turn over in their minds an image of medieval peasants as mutual funds, holding dry land and wet as the Dreyfus Fund holds General Motors and Raytheon. In the medieval English case it can be shown in fact that the number of plots was about right to achieve safety first, which starving peasants might well think a good thing (McCloskey 1989).

THE TASTES OF HOUSEHOLDERS

The complicating of the utility function leads finally to one containing average income, variance of income, *and tastes*. Thus an "irrationally" conservative peasant, whose degree of scattering could not even be explained by the insuring effect, would have to be portrayed as having a "taste" for holding onto ancestral land, perhaps, or indulging in equitable inheritance practices. At this point the idea of a utility function stops being refutable. That is no shame. It can still be a persuasive way to tell a story, a device of orderly accounting.

Economists use a governing metaphor of the household as a little business. As the economist George Stigler remarked ironically, "It would of course be bizarre to look upon the typical family—that complex mixture of love, convenience, and frustration—as a business enterprise. Therefore economists have devoted much skill and ingenuity to elaborating this approach" (1966, 21). Thus do economists enrich their stories of one market by comparing it with another: the household as an "enterprise"; the "market" for "human capital"; the "industry" of crime.

To have one utility function, though, does force an assumption about household governance. The most routine kind of neoclassical economics, to be sure, holds that The Household is one unified decisionmaker. Inside the household, in other words, someone is king (more rarely queen), or else all parties in the household miraculously agree on every choice. A historian who wants to get inside the household will often find she has to go further, allowing for non-agreement. But there is nothing to prevent an analysis of conflict inside the household, and in fact neoclassical game theory permits something like this (McElroy and Horney 1981).

The neoclassical economist sees the historical shift out of home production as a matter of choice in the presence of markets, that is, a matter of profitability. The spinning and weaving and sewing that occupied such blocks of female time in the eighteenth century moved into the market by stages in the nineteenth century in Europe and its offshoots, just as food preparation moved into the market in the middle of the twentieth century, and child care late in the century. Readymade clothes and processed food radically altered the little factory of the home, altering the status of women for better and for worse inside marriage and outside.

The economist's idea of the consumer suggests that the word "need" is not needed. One means by "need" that which is insensitive to price. At any price, one needs oxygen. But most choices are not matters of need. The peasant "needs" food but does not need the particular bundle of food he acquires. The needfulness explains why he tramps to the field each morning but does not explain the fine detail of his behavior. It is the latter that is in need of illumination. Economics claims that most things *are* sensitive to the price charged for them, that if white bread is more expensive to make than black, black bread will be the peasant's fare.

Certain associated ideas fall when need does. For example, "surplus" does not make sense without a need. To say that the Greeks exported olive oil because it was "surplus" in Greece is a non-neoclassical way of speaking. In the opinion of neoclassicals it does not lead to interesting questions. The economist would say that the Greeks exported olive oil because Greece was an inexpensive source of it relative to its competitors; and that the price of olive oil (relative to wheat) that faced Greek merchants was high enough to entice the Greeks into the sale. The inquiry proceeds along these lines. The neoclassical talk leads to more history, not less.

SUPPLY AND DEMAND

The consumer is the ultimate demander. So on one side stand the suppliers (ultimately the factors of production), and on the other side the demanders. The exemplar of economic analysis is of course this very situation, supply and demand. An economist, it is said, is a parrot taught to answer any question with "Supply and demand! Supply and demand!" The mere phrase in truth does a lot of work of an accounting sort.

For instance, it affirms that the quantity sold and the price of, say, cotton textiles in New England from 1815 to 1860 were determined not by bargaining or conspiracy or class power but by competition in an anonymous market, that is, by supply and demand (what follows is a summary of Zevin 1971). For better or worse, no one intended the price; no one was to blame. So the theory says. According to the neoclassical economist's way of talking it was no central plan that caused the quantity of American cotton textiles to rise by a factor of 363 and the price to fall by 75 percent between 1815 and 1860. The outcome was the sum of individual predictions, ambitions, and failures; in a word, choice under market constraints.

A more definite version of the theory will talk of supply-and-demand curves moving out and in. The geometry is attractive to economists, and its beauties explain much of their enthusiasm for the argument. Since the price of cotton textiles from 1815 to 1860 fell relative to other goods, and the demand for cotton textiles certainly moved out, the supply curve must have moved out even faster. An outward-moving supply curve means simply that a given quantity of cotton textiles could be offered at a lower price, the sort of lower price that comes from better ways of making the textiles. The theory draws attention to the possible reasons that a supply curve can move out, such as the cheapening of raw cotton and the mechanization of weaving. The theory draws attention to possible reasons, such as rises in the incomes of Americans, the cheapening of transport costs (by those same Ohio canals, for instance), and the substitution of American for British cloth. The commonest use of supply and demand is this: to give the historian an orderly list of factors fixing quantities and prices. The list will vary with the product and the date, but again the mere idea of the list will discipline the history.

A still more definite and complex version of the theory will give quantitative weights to the supply-and-demand curves, as did Robert Brooke Zevin in his essay on the production of cotton textiles after 1815 (1971). The theory needs first to be put in algebraic form, in order to accept numbers from the historical record that express how much the rise of income affected demand or how much the fall in raw cotton prices affected supply. Zevin did this, concluding from the calculations that expansions of demand more than supply caused output to grow, especially in the first decade; that four-fifths of the fall in price was caused by technological progress (the outward movement of the supply curve), especially again in the early years; and that the initial disturbances to the industry smoothed out by the 1830s. Supply and demand at its most concrete provides a narrative framework for the history of an industry.

THE GENERAL EQUILIBRIUM OF ALL MARKETS

The final neoclassical idea I want to mention here is that the markets reflecting and altering individual choices are all *connected*. The thought is a commonplace: No man is an island, entire of itself. The men and women are one economy, one general equilibrium of markets. If you think of the history of a single industry as the outcome of competition in an anonymous market it is natural to think of an entire economy as a collection of such industries. Says the neoclassical economist, and for that matter every other kind of economist, this point being almost a defining doctrine of the economic conversation, everything depends on everything else. Such a point does not make the *partial* equilibrium analysis of single markets or single decisions wrong. Sometimes it is not worthwhile including all the indirect effects through markets remote from the one in question. But sometimes it is.

Looked at from a great height the participants in an economy are all households, all families from emperor to coolie. From a nineteenth-century liberal point of view the utility of households is the raison d'être for the economy—this in contrast to a corporatist view, medieval or modern, which elevates the company, the group, the nation, or the race to the position of honor.

An economist (and again most schools of economics would agree) holds the Wheel of Wealth, shown in Figure 11, constantly before his mind:

Consumers buy goods (and, always, services too: the notion that services are not real products is from the neoclassical point of view bad accounting, present to this day in left-wing thought). They buy them from firms in the "goods market," which might be a literal place, like the *mercato centrale* in an Italian town, but as was noted earlier is not necessarily so. Households purchase rice in the market even when the sellers are as varied as official market stalls and one's country uncle down the Delhi Road. Competition and substitutability make it one market. If a sufficient number of consumers can move from one outlet to another they will keep the price more or less unified within the market. Entry and exit will work again. In the unusually densely settled parts of northwestern Europe or lowland China or North India during recent centuries the variety of sellers available to most customers made for competition—never literally perfect but always present. The density of competition kept prices close to each other, at any rate by international standards.

On the other side of the wheel of wealth is the "factor market," which is to say the market in which households sell their labor and land and capital to the firms. A factor of production, I have noted, is something used to make something else. Economists take the view that some factors are more basic than others, that ultimately a lump of coal or a piece of financial advice is produced with labor or land or capital. Such a distinction is not written in the stars. Even labor itself is produced ultimately, one might say, by rice for food and by roofing tiles for shelter. One could cut into the wheel of wealth at some other point, perhaps by choosing the market for raw materials as the basic market (this is the way oil has been treated in most policy discussions by noneconomists since 1973; and institutional economists tend to think this way). But it does no harm to go along with the neoclassical economist's choice for the nonce, and for the story.

The main point is that money spins around the wheel one way and goods and services (for instance, the services of the basic factors of production) spin around the other. Furthermore, the households "own" the firms. A corporation is literally owned by its stockholders, partnerships

Households earn income by supplying services to firms, which demand the services of households to produce goods that households demand.

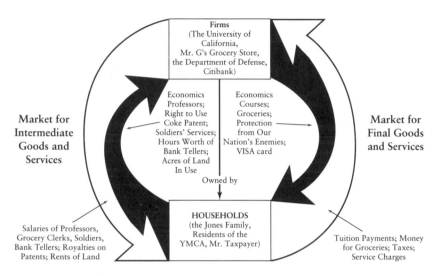

One must follow around the wheel the consequences of a shock. For example, a rise in meat prices that is a *demand pull* (consumers demand more) may look like a *cost push* if the rise is not traced to its source. Suppose that meat consumers demand more, perhaps because they have become richer. The grocer does not at first raise prices to match. Meat supplies on the grocer's shelves run out unusually fast; the butcher will order unusually large amounts from the supplier, who will order in turn unusually large amounts from the packer and, finally, from the farmer. The farmer will only supply more meat at a higher price. He charges it. The higher price will now be passed back around the wheel of wealth through packer, wholesaler, and grocer. Each will believe, quite reasonably, that the rise in price came from "costs." No one, least of all the consumers and their outraged representatives, will realize that the rise came from the demands of the consumers themselves. Firms hide the underlying transactions. The economist must look around the wheel of wealth to the households of farmers and meat consumers transacting with each other.

FIGURE 11. The wheel of wealth. (McCloskey 1985a, 286; reprinted by permission of Simon and Schuster, © Macmillan.)

by their partners. But governments, too, are "owned" by households, which is to say that certain households have rights to streams of income generated by the government (during the Napoleonic Wars William Cobbett called them "tax eaters") and the government is run by people who retire at night to households. Firms are not outside entities that can be taxed, for example, without affecting humans. The bumper sticker Tax Profits, Not People is mistaken. In the words of Pogo the Possum, "We have met the enemy and he is us."

The wheel shows, for example, that the income of the nation or any part of the nation can be measured in at least two ways, by the goods and services purchased or by the factors paid, since the wheel is in balance, by accounting convention. The double-entry character of national income gives the historian two shots at the same figure. In national accounts for developed countries the two figures differ as little as 1 percent. In Charles Feinstein's careful reconstruction of the British national accounts the discrepancy is 6 percent in 1920–26 and 14 percent in 1870–1887 (Feinstein 1972, 13). That the two measures move in parallel over time, however, makes one confident about the true trend.

It is significant that all payments are ultimately payments to some person, not to institutions. The tax of inflation will help someone who earns the higher price at the same time that it hurts someone else who pays it. Inflation does not reduce income as a whole (though it does of course change who gets the income). The lag of wages behind prices can be a cause of rising profits for a little while (though in actual cases wages have proven quick to catch up [Mokyr and Savin 1976]), but it does not change income as a whole.

An example in detail of the advantages of thinking in terms of the wheel of wealth and general equilibrium concerns the early years of the British industrial revolution. In the 1960s two groups of economic historians fell to quarreling about the effects of a series of good harvests in Britain from 1730 to 1750. They quarreled over how the good harvests would affect the demand for industrial products like cloth and iron. One group pointed out that the good harvests drove down the price of grain, reducing on balance the income of the farming community. Since the farming community was one part of the demand for industrial goods, the demand for industrial goods on that account would be lower. According to one partial equilibrium argument, then, the years of good harvests were a drag on the industrial revolution.

The other group, however, pointed out that on the contrary the fall in price would increase the real income of the *non*-farming community. Their higher income would result in *more* purchases of industrial goods, not less. According to this other partial equilibrium argument, then, the good harvests were on the contrary an impetus to the industrial revolution.

In 1975 Richard Ippolito noted that the two groups of historians were pulling at opposite ends of the same bone. Raised to contemplate whole economies at once, and to recognize that the income of one part is the expenditure of another, an economist can see that the farmers' loss was precisely the non-farmers' gain. It is no great mental trick. The fall in the farmers' revenue was what non-farmers therefore did not need to pay to acquire grain. The lower income of farmers *was* the higher income of non-farmers. The nation as a whole did not lose or gain income. Therefore industrial goods did not lose or gain. What the demand for industry gained on the swings it lost on the roundabouts. As a first approximation the argument of the first group of historians plus the argument of the second equaled zero.

As a second approximation, to which Ippolito then turned, good harvests increased a little the income of the nation. The nation as a whole, speaking of the general equilibrium, is plainly better off when the weather is better. Ippolito concluded that the small increase worked to increase demand for industry, but not by much.

The pioneer in using the idea of general equilibrium to write history has been Jeffrey Williamson, an expert in the study of present-day poor countries and of the economic history of the nineteenth century. In 1974 Williamson published *Late Nineteenth Century American Development: A General Equilibrium History,* which displayed the economy of the United States in seventy-two equations (he has subsequently applied similar methods to British and Japanese history). Seventy-two equations sounds like a lot, but in fact, as Williamson himself noted, they do not capture much detail. Since Williamson's main interest was in the contrasts between eastern and western regions he distinguished only East and West for most variables, requiring him to leave out the American South. And to keep the argument calculable and lucid he had to confine attention to the markets in labor, capital, part of land, all manufactured goods taken together, and all agricultural goods taken together (leaving out services). Two goods and three factors of production are made to stand for all the riches of America in cowboys, coal mines, cotton mills, slum housing, iron deposits, ocean fisheries, books, beer, wheat, cheese, office space, primary education, train journeys, and the means to wage war.

But one cannot think about an economy without simplifying. One cannot deal with everything at once. Even a study of the "partial" equilibrium of supply and demand in an isolated market throws the rest of the economy into a single category of "all other goods." The question is not whether to simplify. One must. The question is whether the particular simplification is useful, that is, whether it illuminates or obscures important historical questions.

IS IT GOOD?

The analysis here has moved from the mundanities of individual choice to the grandeur of general equilibrium. I said earlier that neoclassical economics is at heart bourgeois. I might add "liberal," for one of the reasons that the analysis of choice and markets holds such fascination is that it is claimed to model a liberal society.

Whether or not the vision of liberal capitalism is attractive to everyone, everyone should recognize its charm, if only to question the charm intelligently. Suppose that you are reasonably well satisfied with the present distribution of income and rights. That is a conservative supposition, but widely held after all. And suppose now you look on the choices made in the market. They are by their nature mutually advantageous. No one enters a deal if he expects to lose from it. If both sides are moderately well informed, then the deals in the market will make both sides better off. They will not be made better off every single time they go to market, of course, but most of the time. Being made better off does not mean being made perfectly well off, as in the best conceivable society. If someone is poor when she goes to the market she is probably going to be poor, if a little better off, when she comes home. But from a satisfactory situation all have been made somewhat better off (all at least who participate). What could be more pleasant to behold? An economy moves from strength to strength by way of mutual satisfaction.

No adult needs to be told that there are flaws in this vision, though neoclassical and Austrian economists can show that some of the putative flaws are less serious than the average left-liberal academic might assume. Economics reached its peak of intellectual influence in the early nineteenth century. Since then most intellectuals have resisted reading any of it and are therefore filled with mainly idiotic complaints about what they suppose, without reading, to be its content and arguments. But anyway, that economics fits an early-nineteenth century view of the free society is not irrelevant to its attractions, nor to some of the illiberal hostility toward it.

The issue is not wholly philosophical. The liberal philosophy supports for example cost/benefit analysis—which is just what it sounds like, a careful accounting of the costs and benefits of a project, viewed from the whole society's point of view. Such calculations have stood near the heart

of economics since the political arithmeticians and improving pamphle-
teers of the late seventeenth century (among them Daniel Defoe). The balance sheet is sometimes an interesting historical question.

Imperialism, for example, was long viewed through a checklist of costs
and benefits, to colony and to metropolis. Such history has fallen out of
favor, but it would seem unwise to simply discard all its findings. Recently Lance Davis and Robert Huttenback (1989), for example, have
confirmed what many economic historians long suspected: that from the
British point of view British imperialism was a bust; that Britain extracted
practically nothing by way of booty from its nineteenth-century colonies;
that half of British defense expenditures, supported mainly on the backs
of home not colonial taxpayers (remember the Boston Tea Party) protected the routes to India to no *economic* purpose; and that only particular individuals in Britain benefited from the Empire, again at the expense
of other British citizens. Such calculations are similar to second-guessing
farmers or businesspeople, and again can be made more complex by
adding other items to the utility function. If the British people in 1900
got enough pleasure from seeing the world map splotched with red, then
their lower income may have been justified. Income is not necessarily all
there is to happiness. But the neoclassical economist, in his liberal and
literal way, would want to know whether the people would have voluntarily paid for the empire, with open eyes. He doubts it.

•   •   •   •   •

It goes without saying that political issues are raised when the historian
reaches for the choice-as-economics tool. The tool is of course shaped
by ideology. But then it would be naive to claim that some other tool is
not. Carefully handled the tool can inscribe good history, without in-
juring the writer or the reader. The neoclassical theory of choice is a sweet
little saw and hammer set, just the one to take for many historical uses,
like the tools that rational Crusoe chose to take in his few, scarce hours
on the wreck.

Macroeconomics

An Introduction for Historians

RICHARD SUTCH

Anyone who has made the acquaintance of the science of economics knows she has two faces. Each expresses its own personality. We call them microeconomics and macroeconomics. *Micro*economics examines economic behavior in a small part or small sector of the economy iso lated from the larger whole. Describing how prices are determined in the market for rice or analyzing the effect of a tax on the work effort of artisans are illustrative microeconomic topics. *Macro*economics, by contrast, is the study of the economy as an entity, as a complete functioning system of economic institutions. Establishing what determines the total quantity of output produced by the economy and analyzing the problems of unemployment and inflation are typical macroeconomic issues.

There are two branches of economic methodology, not because economists suffer with dual personalities but because there have to be. To answer macroeconomic questions the economy must be analyzed as a system—not on a piecemeal basis, but as a whole. This imperative can be attributed to three facts of life. The three points are closely related, but it helps—certainly so, at the outset—to discuss them individually. Each

I wish to thank all the participants in this enterprise for their critical, helpful, and attentive comments. The historians of China helped me set the tone and level of my argument and clear away muddle. Particular thanks are due to Thomas Rawski, Donald McCloskey, and Susan Carter for their constant belief in the value of presenting an introduction to economics for historians.

helps in a different way to explain why microeconomic methods, if applied to a macroeconomic problem, would fail.

    1.   With a macroeconomic problem the microeconomic assumption of *ceteris paribus* is unrealistic.

    2.   The behavior of the whole cannot reliably be deduced from the behavior of its component parts. Reasoning by analogy from the part to the whole often fails.

    3.   There are constraints that do not bind individual behavior but work at the aggregate level.

CETERIS PARIBUS FAILS

When studying a small segment of the whole economy, microeconomists assume that the influences emanating from all the other parts of the economy are known and unchanging. As a vestige of the long-lost classical heritage of economics, this simplifying assumption still bears its Latin name: *ceteris paribus* (other things being equal). The assumption of an unchanging context simplifies most microeconomic problems into tractability. Indeed, microeconomic methodology is based on *ceteris paribus* and in that branch of economics it is employed universally.

    When *ceteris paribus* can be said to hold, each economic segment of the economic system can be examined separately in isolation from the others. When supply and demand in the village market for rice is discussed, for example, we mentally freeze all other activity going on in the economy. Everything relevant to the market participants' behavior other than the price of rice is assumed to remain unchanged. The assumption that the outside influences are unchanging in such cases is often an excellent approximation to reality. The price of gold, recent medical advances in treating infections, the volume of river traffic on the Mississippi, and so on are very unlikely to be much influenced *by* the village rice market. Thus, whatever their influence *on* the rice market might be, that influence is unlikely to change as a result of what goes on there. But not every economic problem can be dealt with in this simplified way. Some phenomena are so bound up with the rest of the world that one cannot usefully separate them from the wider economy.

    Macroeconomics deals with economic problems where the *ceteris paribus* assumption is unrealistic. Dispensing with this assumption is often necessary when the economic changes under examination affect a large number of people. In such cases the collective response to the economic change may have a significant *indirect* influence on the phenomenon under study that is distinct from its direct impact. For example, suppose you are interested in the implications of a reduction in the rate of income taxation on your well-being. The direct impact on your take-home pay is obvious, but a tax cut affects many other people as well. Since a general tax reduction would put more spendable income in nearly everyone's hands, you should expect an indirect influence on your welfare from the general increase in spending that would result. To assume that the rest of the economy stood still when you analyzed such problems would be to make an error that could have serious consequence for the conclusion.

In macroeconomics human behavior is examined, as I said at the outset, within the context of a "complete functioning system of economic institutions." But a simultaneous examination of each and every economic institution in the economy could not be very fruitful. Macroeconomics concentrates on the entire economy, rather than the separate institutions that are its constituent parts, by using what is sometimes called a systemic approach. In so doing, macroeconomic analysis focuses more attention on the interactions between the various parts than on the separate parts themselves.

It may take some experience working with economic problems before one is able to recognize immediately when a microeconomic analysis will suffice and when a macroeconomic approach is more appropriate. Two examples at this point may help to clarify the distinction.

UNEMPLOYMENT

If a historian is unemployed, it is because, temporarily at least, there are more historians wishing to have a job than there are history positions offered by employers at the established wage. A microeconomic analysis would note the disequilibrium in the market for historians implied by the labor surplus and predict as a consequence that the relative wage would begin to fall. As the going wage declines, the number of historians demanded by employers should increase slightly while at the same time the number of people who wish to be employed as historians should decline slightly. Sooner or later the unemployed person will be hired as a historian or alternatively will take a job in some other occupation. In either case, equilibrium is restored and the unemployment is eliminated. In other words, a decline in the relative wage ought to help eliminate the unemployment in this particular labor market. Or so goes the microeconomic reasoning.

Macroeconomic reasoning is different. If unemployment is spread throughout the economy involving many people and many occupations, a general fall in wages will *not* have the same equilibrating effect. In that case, every worker in the economy will receive less income and as a result the consumption of many products will be curtailed. When the producers of these products discover that sales are declining, they might decide to reduce production and lay off workers. Thus, in a situation of widespread unemployment—essentially a macroeconomic problem—a reduction in wages across the board will probably aggravate, rather than cure, the unemployment problem.

Notice that the relation between the income of laborers (set by one economic institution, the labor market) and the demand for the products of labor (determined within another set of institutions, the product markets) is a central part of the analysis of widespread unemployment. Whenever such interrelations between segments of the economy are important, a macroeconomic approach is necessary.

INFLATION

If the price of an ax rises at a time when other prices generally remain unchanged, the supply and demand model of microeconomics is an appropriate analytical tool to explain why the price changed. In this case the *ceteris paribus* assumption of microeconomics is a good approximation to reality because changes in the price of axes are unlikely to have a significant effect on the incomes of consumers or the technology of ax production.

If the price of an ax were to rise during the course of a general inflation (when all prices were rising), then the *ceteris paribus* assumption would no longer be reasonable. Other prices and thus the incomes of consumers would rise during an inflation: to assume otherwise would be misleading. Indeed, in this case the price of an ax *relative to all other prices* would not even change. The model of supply and demand, which is designed to explain relative price changes, would therefore be inappropriate. A macroeconomic model is required to explain inflation.

THE FALLACY OF COMPOSITION

The macroeconomic approach is necessary to avoid a common logical error that logicians call the "fallacy of composition." This consists of deducing the behavior of a system from the behavior of its component parts, claiming that what is true for a part is *necessarily* true for the whole. Sometimes described as "arguing from the specific to the general," this way of thinking quite often yields incorrect conclusions. A few examples should suffice to illustrate the problem:

> During the early 1950s the average wage of male workers in Japan rose. At the same time the average wage of working women also rose. It might seem natural to conclude from these facts that the overall average wage in Japan rose. Actually, though, it fell in several industries. Women were paid substantially less than men at the time and during this period the number of women working in these industries increased so much that the shift in composition lowered the average wage despite the increases measured for both men and women. What is true for the individuals in society may not be true for the society as a whole.[1]
>
> If you cannot see well at a football game, you might think of standing up to get a better view. Yet if everyone stands up during an exciting play, no one sees very well. What is good advice for an individual is often bad advice for a group.
>
> Local community studies often reveal very stable socioeconomic stratification of the population, yet the society as a whole may have had abundant opportunities for social and economic mobility. The local studies may miss this fluidity if socioeconomic mobility was accompanied by geographic mobility; that is, if people had to leave their native village to change their status.

Once explained, the fallacy of composition in these examples probably seems obvious, but in many cases it appears in more subtle ways. In economics (and in history!) the fallacy is encountered surprisingly often and the scholar must be constantly on guard against fallacious generalization. Several famous errors of this type have led economists' thinking astray. We have already introduced one such instance, their early thinking about unemployment.

RETHINKING UNEMPLOYMENT

It was once believed on the basis of misapplied microeconomic logic that the general unemployment associated with a depression could be eliminated by a reduction in wages. Each employer, the argument went, would want to hire more workers if labor could be obtained more cheaply. The argument looks appealing until we recognize that it makes a generalization about the *total* demand for labor in the economy from observations and speculations concerning the demand for labor by a representative

---

1. Although U.S. military authorities observed this effect in several industries, it was not strong enough to influence the average wage in the entire Japanese economy.

employer. Actually, as we pointed out, if everyone's wages were lowered, then the total income of the workers would fall and the demand for many products would likely decline as a consequence. Employers faced with falling sales would be unwilling to hire more labor despite its reduced cost.[2]

FINANCING THE WAR

Another example of the fallacy of composition can be found in an argument used against government borrowing during World War II. In order to finance the heavy wartime expenditures the federal government borrowed money by selling government bonds to the public. Opponents of this policy claimed that it would shift the burden of the war to future generations who would have to pay back the loans when they came due. They reasoned that when an individual borrows money, he or she must promise to repay the loan in the future. Thus the borrower's *current* expenditures could be increased, but his or her *future* expenditures would be reduced as a consequence. This logic, which is valid for an individual borrower, cannot be applied to the economy as a whole. Society cannot borrow from its future, since society as a whole cannot consume goods that have yet to be produced.[3] As a matter of fact, every piece of military equipment, every bomb and bullet, supplied to the armed forces during World War II was either already on hand or produced from current resources at the time. Only the generation alive at the time of a war shoulders the economic burden of reduced consumption necessary to support the war effort. When the bonds come due the generation alive at that time will have to tax itself to pay bondholders or sell new bonds to "roll over" the debt.

2. The famous economist John Maynard Keynes brought the unemployment issue into sharp focus with *The General Theory of Employment, Interest, and Money* (1936), which is certainly one of the most influential books of the twentieth century. A good introduction to this thinking in a historical context is Temin 1976, particularly chap. 5.

3. Strictly speaking, we are talking of society as a whole: the *world* economy cannot borrow from its future. A single country, however, could and often does borrow from lenders in other countries. Israel has sold many bonds to U.S. citizens to help finance its military activities and building programs since its founding as an independent nation and has thus managed to consume more than it has produced. In this case, the analogy with individual borrowing is more apt. When the Israeli bonds are redeemed, Israel will have to transfer some of its output to Americans to settle the debt and will then experience a period in which the country consumes less than it produces. In the case of U.S. government borrowing during World War II, few government bonds were sold to foreigners. Here we have a "closed economy" and thus a "whole" economy in which the macroeconomic principle applies.

The insights gained in the study of microeconomics cannot safely be transferred to macroeconomics. To understand the economy we must know both how its institutions function and how they interact and behave as a coherent system.

THE EXISTENCE OF MACROECONOMIC CONSTRAINTS

A third way to express the necessity of a macroeconomic approach is to recognize that the system as a whole is often constrained in ways that its component parts are not. The topic just discussed, financing wartime expenditures, is an example. The individual is not constrained to hold consumption below current production and inventory withdrawals; the economy is. Since such macroeconomic constraints are an important part of the economic system, they must be incorporated into any sensible model of the economy. Macroeconomics is, then, the branch of economic logic that looks for and incorporates such constraints into our thinking. Two more examples are relevant:

FOREIGN EXCHANGE MARKETS

In a microeconomic market for foreign exchange the value of the English pound in terms of American dollars can be thought of as determined. There is a demand for pounds and a supply of pounds. Both are functions of the dollar price of pounds. When market forces are allowed to reach an equilibrium in this market, the resulting price sets the value of the pound. In precisely the same way the value of the Japanese yen in terms of dollars can be thought of as determined by the supply and the demand for yen and, generalizing further, the value of any currency in terms of any other can be modeled as the outcome of market forces in a market that links the two currencies. If there are n currencies in the world, it might seem that there must be $(n)(n-1)/2$ such markets, each independent of the others. In a sense, this is true but to put it that way is to ignore an important macroeconomic constraint.

Notice that when we know the value of the pound (in dollars) and the value of the yen (also in dollars) we simultaneously know the value of the pound in terms of yen. To see this, we start with a certain amount of Japanese yen, use them to buy dollars, then use the dollars to buy pounds. We can determine the yen value of the pound without reference to the underlying supply of and demand for pounds in terms of yen.

Many of the $(n)(n-1)/2$ markets are made superfluous by the presence of a macroeconomic constraint. As a matter of fact, there are only $n-1$ independent prices for foreign exchange.

This point is more than a matter of algebraic pedantry. It is easy to be misled by the fact that the pound sterling became a world currency in the late nineteenth and early twentieth century and the fact that the U.S. dollar took over that role after the Second World War. Forgetting that it is merely a matter of some convenience to consider the $n-1$ world currency markets in terms of a single uniform denominator currency, we might be tempted to read into the fact that every currency was quoted, first, in pounds and then in dollars as evidence of a more ominous economic hegemony than it truly indicated. The pound's unique role simply reflected England's prominence in world trade and finance coupled with the relative stability of its currency and trade policy. When this role shifted to the United States as a consequence of the depression, the war, and England's economic decline, it did not do so because Washington or Wall Street had moved against England or had decided to stamp out the competing exchange markets. Simple efficiency considerations eliminated the unnecessary.

SAVINGS AND INVESTMENT

For an individual, saving and investment are two distinct types of behavior that are motivated by different impulses. Saving, often undertaken as a precaution, consists of setting aside some proportion of income for use at a later time. In other words, saving is the act of not consuming. Investment, however, consists of purchasing capital goods or financial assets with the prospect of earning a return in the future. An investment usually entails the assumption of risk. Saving and investment often take place simultaneously when, for example, the individual's savings are invested in an asset, but they need not be. The peasant who hoards money or gold is saving but not investing. The family that borrows money to start a hardware store is investing but not saving. There is no individual-level constraint to ensure that saving will equal investment.

For the economy as a whole, however, saving and investment must always be exactly equal, down to the penny. At the macroeconomic level a constraint exists that does not apply at the individual level. It is not hard to see why. Everything that is produced must be either consumed (destroyed) or added to the stock of capital collectively owned by society. That is to say that everything produced is allocated either to consumption or to investment. So aggregate output equals aggregate consumption plus aggregate investment. From a macroeconomic perspective, the only source of income is production. So national income and aggregate output are the same thing. Those who receive income have only two choices: they can consume it or they can save it. Remember, saving means not consuming. So aggregate output also equals aggregate con sumption plus aggregate saving. It follows that aggregate investment equals aggregate saving.[4]

AGGREGATION AND QUANTIFICATION

With its concern for the whole economy, macroeconomics deals with aggregates. Macroeconomists frequently make reference to aggregate output (or gross national product), aggregate employment (the total number of people employed), and to the general (or average) price level. As concepts, these aggregates are easy enough to visualize, but to measure them is another task. Aggregates must be built up from extensive data bases.[5] The task is often beyond that of a lone researcher. For recent years, fortunately, such numbers can usually be obtained from standard sources. Their calculation is the task of government statistical bureaus and the results are usually published in great detail. The United Nations publishes macroeconomic statistics for most countries for the post–World War II period. For many countries, particularly the industrial economies of Europe and North America, the official aggregate data series have been

---

4. Here again, we are speaking of the economy as a whole—either the entire world economy or a national economy that is closed. Of course, most national economies are open to foreign trade and citizens of one country can invest in another country; these extranational investments are a second outlet for domestic saving. Thus aggregate domestic saving must exactly equal aggregate domestic investment plus *net* foreign investment. In today's world of multinational corporations, extensive foreign trade, and historically low transportation costs the net foreign investment outlet may be quite significant. It was not always so. Even the open American economy of the nineteenth century was sufficiently isolated by high transportation costs and imperfect communications that net foreign investment played only a minor role in its development. Throughout much of the century the investments by foreigners (chiefly the English) in American enterprise exceeded the volume of investments by Americans abroad, though the net flow of foreign investment rarely amounted to more than a percentage or two of gross domestic product. Near the end of the century, the relative flows reversed and net foreign investment became positive as more and more American corporations invested abroad, though the percentage of outflow was not great. As a rough generalization then, we can say that nineteenth-century American growth was endogenous and American capital stock was largely financed and owned by Americans. For data on these flows see U.S. Bureau of the Census 1975, part 2, series U15, U16, and U17.

5. Rawski's chapter describes macroeconomic data series and the methods used by historians to calculate or estimate these series.

pushed back to earlier years of this century by economic historians or by the historical division of the state statistical bureaus.

Historians of earlier periods and of second- and third-world countries, however, will not find the situation so amenable to calculation. Typically, aggregate data have yet to be computed. Moreover, a sufficient amount of basic data is simply not available to permit even approximations of the trends in output, prices, and employment. Even when the raw data exist in abundance, their collection, collation, and aggregation become a daunting task for the lone researcher. The fallacy of composition, moreover, makes any attempt to infer the movements of the aggregates from local studies, partial data, or qualitative impressions of contemporaries extremely dangerous. The use of "proxy" measures to mimic the movement of unobserved aggregates is more promising, perhaps. For example, the movements in the flow of imports from abroad (data that are sometimes available from customhouse records) might be used to indicate periods of growth, depression, and decline in an economy. The acceptance of the proxy method, however, requires that the researcher be willing to assume the validity of an economic model that connects the proxy-variable to the unobserved variable of interest. For the example just given, we might suggest that import demand was a function of the level of per capita income. The difficulty with this approach appears when the supporting hypothesis cannot be tested and alternative hypotheses are often difficult to rule out with any confidence. For example, changes in the costs and productivity of transportation would also affect the volume of imports.

This state of affairs, I fear, has left many historians with the view that to write macroeconomic history is simply not possible for the time period or region of their interest and thus they feel free to ignore the macroeconomic perspective. But this is a big mistake. The logic of macroeconomic theory is inescapable. The lack of reliable data, of course, will make the task of writing macroeconomic history more difficult and may, perhaps, limit our knowledge of the past. But, as I argue, macroeconomics is neither an alternative to microeconomics nor an optional topic in the discussion of economic history. Rather, a macroeconomic approach is necessary if we are to talk sensibly about the functioning of any economic system, past or present. No matter how weak the statistical record or how limited the time and money for research, every historian must come to grips with the macroeconomic issues of the time and period under study.

Consider the standard of living controversy as an example. The issue is whether the laboring classes benefited from the economic changes that swept England in the late eighteenth and the first half of the nineteenth century. The debate, which is still unresolved, has produced many microeconomic studies of living conditions, real wages, and the quality of life with conflicting and confusing results.[6] Yet the problem is fundamentally a macroeconomic problem, whether posed in its empirical or in its logical form. Take the empirical question first.

The question is not about an individual worker or a small group of workers (the handloom weavers of Lancashire, say) but about all workers. The lack of reliable aggregate data has of course led to a number of microcosmic studies. This is fully appropriate; all would agree that economic history is the richer for an effort that has helped us better understand the social and economic consequences of the industrialization of Britain. Yet unless each individual researcher pays close attention to the macroeconomic nature of the problem she or he is tackling with microeconomic surgery, it is easy to be misled. Beware the fallacy of composition.

The declining wages of handloom weavers do not prove that the standard of living of all workers declined nor do they prove that the average wage declined. This point is obvious, but less so is the fact that even if we found declining real wages in study after study, in occupation after occupation, in town after town, in county after county, they would not allow us to conclude that the standard of living of the laboring class fell. Remember the postwar Japanese labor market!

In industrializing Britain, it would not be surprising to find that some occupations and industrial technologies were declining while other sectors were expanding. Over time workers could be shifting from the declining sectors to the expanding ones. If this process were motivated—as both economic theory and common sense suggest—by higher wages in the expanding sectors, then even if wages in all sectors had declined the *average* laborer could be enjoying a higher standard of living as a consequence of these changes.

The alert reader will notice my use of the subjunctive mood in the preceding argument: "workers *could be* shifting", "*If* this process," "*then* . . . the average laborer *could be* enjoying a higher standard of living." The point is not that we know these things (yet) or that theory tells us that they must be true. The point is that these are researchable issues. They are amenable to the standard research techniques of traditional eco-

6. O'Brien and Engerman 1981 provide a good introduction. Also see Harley 1993.

nomic historians and require neither aggregates nor the attention of government statisticians before they can be tackled. Such issues will not even be addressed, however, unless we are alert to the macroeconomic nature of the question under consideration. John Lyons wrote about the handloom weavers of Lancashire:

> By the 1820s, children of urban weavers were able to earn higher wages outside the handloom sector than within it. In later years, rural weaving families moved to urban areas to gain access to better employment for their children. In both cases, however, adults tended to remain in handloom weaving, despite their falling wage level. Alternative occupations for the weavers' children were provided by the new and rapidly-growing industries of the region; a paucity of alternatives for the adult weavers was related to the heavy bias of these same industries in favor of hiring very young entrants to the unskilled labor force. (Lyons 1978, 283–284)

In this case, the high and rising earnings of the children "buffered the falling earnings of their parents." In another case, it might have been someone else's children.

Notice, too, that the relative expansion and contraction of the various occupations, industries, and population centers—events that make so much difference to the aggregate picture of the standard of living—could (in principle) take place without affecting a single individual. It is possible for each worker to remain for life in a single occupation, never to "gain access to better employment," and yet for that organic whole we call society to change occupations and to move. Every individual could be getting worse off, while society is getting better off! The *average* computer programmer is growing younger each year, even though indisputably the actual age of each and every person at work writing computer programs is increasing daily.

Next I turn to the logic of the standard of living controversy. It is good to ask of such questions, what is at stake? Here I think historians want to know whether changes like the introduction of industrial technology, the factory system, and capitalism benefited society at large or only one class (the capitalist factory owners). It should be obvious that this is a macroeconomic question. Here the *ceteris paribus* assumption is unrealistic: we cannot change the technology and the mode of production for a whole economy and leave other things (like political organizations and output prices) unchanged. Disentangling all the changes brought about by industrialization on the level and distribution of income involves us in an extremely complex general equilibrium question, not just something we can handle with simple comparative static microeconomic modeling. We need to ask not just what happened to real wages, but what happened to the whole economy and the whole society. Was the political power of capitalists (or workers) enhanced? Was the availability of education for the children of workers expanded? If so, did they make use of this education to increase their geographical, occupational, or social mobility? Did they use it to increase their political influence and effectiveness? Did parents' attitudes about child labor shift? Did child labor increase or decline as a result? There is much left to animate our research and enliven the debate.

WRITING MACROECONOMIC HISTORY

To write macroeconomic history—or, at least, an economic history sensitive to macroeconomic issues—is, I suggest, possible even without aggregate data. On one level it is not only possible, but easy. It merely requires that we think *systemically,* whether we are economic historians (where systemic thinking has been elevated to a separate methodology), social historians (where systemic thinking often involves talking about social "forces" and "movements"), intellectual historians (where "paradigm shifts" are an organizing principle), or simply tellers of tales (where the "big picture" is as interesting and important as the narrative).

At a deeper, and ultimately more important, level good macroeconomic history requires knowledge of and skill with a wide range of macroeconomic concepts and theories. This is neither the time nor the appropriate forum to offer a treatise on macroeconomic theory. What I can do is provide one more illustration of macroeconomic concepts that have been historically insightful—even in the absence of macroeconomic data. There are three things to watch for as we explore this example.[7] First, notice how the macroeconomic perspective produced a sharply different interpretation of a historical event than would have been true of a history written entirely from the perspective of "those who lived at the time." Then notice how this altered view led to a research effort that focused on sources and evidence and used standard historical methods. Finally, note the use of price data as a vehicle for historical research. Their

7. This example draws on my earlier account of the destructive impact of the American Civil War written in collaboration with Roger Ransom; see Ransom and Sutch 1977, 40–55, 324–329. Also see Ransom and Sutch 1975.

use reflects the centrality of prices in economic theory as well as the fact that it is most often the case that price data are abundant, comprehensive, and the most accurate data surviving the passage of time. Price data are the potsherds of economic theory.

WARTIME DESTRUCTION AND POSTWAR RECOVERY

The American Civil War has been called the first modern war. There may be several reasons for this, but not the least of them is that it was a war waged as much on civilians, the capital stock, and the economy as on the opposing armies. The North won this war; the South was devastated. Several major cities of the South—Atlanta, Richmond, Charleston, and Columbia—were burned. Throughout the South the loss of human life, work animals, and other livestock was enormous. Many farms and plantations lost barns, fences, and cotton gins. The transportation system of railroads, wharves, steamships, and levees was completely destroyed.

Historians of this period who relied primarily on the firsthand accounts of witnesses, diaries, and other microlevel evidence painted a bleak picture. Many of the great families were ruined, the capital they had accumulated through several generations had been wiped out, and often their energy and spirit had been crushed by the defeat of the Southern cause.[8] Even when these families were traced in the years following the war, it was discovered that many never recovered their fortunes. A microeconomic perspective thus led many historians to conclude that the Civil War had dealt the Southern states a blow from which it took them generations to recover.[9] A macroeconomic perspective shows they were misled.

If we look, not at family fortunes, but at various sectors of the Southern economy we find that a remarkable recovery took place in the immediate postwar period. The railroads were restored within a year or two, manufacturing activity in 1869 exceeded the prewar levels, the plantations were back in operation within a year, and the predominately black labor force had returned to work. Judging from the frequent com-

8. Warfare did not cause all the loss of capital. Most of the wealthy landowners in the South had a considerable fraction of their assets invested in the ownership of enslaved African Americans. These people were emancipated following the war without compensation to their former owners. Moreover, many Southerners had invested in paper currency and bonds issued by the rebel government. Both assets became worthless with the Confederate collapse.

9. For an explicit argument along these lines see Sellers 1927.

plaints by landowners of a labor shortage and high wages, there was no widespread unemployment.

How can we reconcile this macroeconomic view of rapid recovery with the microeconomic perspective that emerged from the diaries and family histories?

In the first place the macroeconomic view focuses attention not on people but on the factors of production: land, labor, capital, and natural resources. Family fortunes may have been destroyed, but the factors of production remained, though often in the hands of *new* owners. Certainly the land and natural resources of the South remained productive. Although not wishing to minimize the terrible loss of life, we also note that the laboring population was larger after the war than before. Moreover, its skills, knowledge, and aptitudes were intact. The only factor of production that suffered significant destruction was capital. But the capital that was lost was rapidly replaced. In this regard, the experience of the American South presaged the post–World War II recoveries of the Japanese and West German economies.

Macroeconomic theory can help explain why. The aggregate volume of output can be thought of as determined by an "aggregate production function"—a statistical recipe that associates the inputs of land, labor, and capital with output. It is a formula in which the aggregate volume of land, the aggregate supply of labor, and the aggregate capital stock enter as the determinants of total output (GNP). The precise specification of this production function will determine the relative rates of return to the owners of the factors. In a market economy these rates of return (wages for labor, rents for land, and profits for capital) are set in the factor markets at a level related to the factors' marginal productivity.[10] The war reduces the capital stock relative to the inputs of land and labor. After the war each surviving worker has less capital to work with and, as a result, is less productive than before the war. At the same time, however, more labor is available to work with each remaining unit of capital and the productivity of capital rises. Machines are run around the clock rather than shut down each night, offices are crowded with office workers, roads and communication facilities are congested. Potential investors observe the abnormally high rate of return to capital that in turn stimulates a strong demand to increase the capital stock.[11]

10. For discussion of marginal productivity see the chapters by Carter and Cullenberg and by Rawski.

11. Those who wish to explore this topic may consult Gordon and Walton 1982.

But where will the potential investors get the money to invest? As we observed, it must come from saving.[12] Fortunately, saving too responded to the crisis. The purpose of saving, after all, is to build up a store of wealth. For any individual there is a desired level of wealth holding that is determined primarily by that person's income and his or her particular point in the life course. Individuals try to build up their wealth when they are young and their earning capacity is high before they draw it down in old age. Economists would say that for society as a whole, given the existing mix of young and old individuals, there is an equilibrium ratio of wealth to income—a balance between wealth and income that the population is content to maintain. If wealth is too low relative to income, saving will be stimulated as people struggle to build up wealth. If wealth is too high, it will be drawn down. In the case of a temporary setback in income, say when bad weather or floods ruin the crops of an agricultural economy, people will dip into their accumulated savings to maintain consumption. As they do so, wealth will fall. When incomes return to normal, wealth will then be out of balance with income and saving will be stimulated until the wealth-income balance is restored.

The destruction of Southern capital during the Civil War reduced the aggregate amount of wealth owned by individuals (capital is wealth) relative to their income-generating potential. According to the theory, this temporarily stimulates a high rate of saving as individuals work to restore the balance between their wealth and their income. Thus, a rapid replacement of capital takes place since the reward to investment is high and the flow of savings to finance the investment is also high. The equilibrium recurs when the stock of capital once again comes into balance with the stock of labor and land. After that, investment and saving rates then fall to normal levels.

Can we test this theory? The direct method involves examining a time series on the aggregate capital stock. If the theory derived from the model of the aggregate production function is correct, the data should clearly show the rebound effect predicted for the capital stock. An alternative approach is to examine the aggregate levels of investment (or, equiva-

12. Or from abroad. After World War II, of course, a considerable flow of foreign capital poured into Germany and Japan to assist in the rebuilding of the capital stock of those countries—through the Marshall plan to Germany and by the U.S. occupation forces to Japan—by government rather than private investors. Very little foreign capital flowed into the post–Civil War South, and we have few details about what probably was a significant flow of capital from the North.

lently, the aggregate levels of saving—remember, saving is always equal to investment). If the theory is applicable, investment should be abnormally high during the regenerative period following the wartime destruction of capital. Unfortunately, we do not have reliable series on either the capital stock or investment. An alternative is to look at price data.[13]

If capital had been in short supply relative to other factors of production immediately following the war, its price should be temporarily high relative to the rents on land. After the capital stock has been restored, its price should fall relative to rent on land. Although data on capital stocks and investment flows are not available, there are abundant data on land rents, land prices, and capital prices that we can use to test for the presence of the predicted movements. The results of these tests have been reported elsewhere;[14] to summarize, we note that land rents were unusually low immediately following the war but rose within a few years. The prices of mules (an essential form of capital for cotton and corn production at the time) actually fell to below their prewar level by 1870, suggesting that the recovery of the capital stock had been completed by that date.[15]

Taking a macroeconomic perspective on the impact of the Civil War on the economy of the American South gives us an understanding sharply divergent from the old picture derived from a microeconomic view. The old view rested heavily on the wartime devastation for an explanation of the economic backwardness of the South during the century that followed the war. The macroeconomic view undercuts the credibility of this explanation and clears the ground for a new research effort to explain the failure of the Southern economy to grow rapidly between 1870 and 1970. That research indicates that flawed institutions, racism, and factor immobilities—not General Sherman's march through the Confederacy—are the likely explanations.[16]

---

13. Another possibility would be to calculate the rates of return to capital, but to do so we need accurate information on the cost of capital and the flow of income it would generate, data that are scarce in the postwar South. Research into the financial records of enterprises might yield precisely the data required.

14. Ransom and Sutch 1977, 47–51. The situation in the American South was somewhat more complicated than suggested here because of the effect of emancipation on the supply of black labor (for a full account see Ransom and Sutch 1977, chap. 3 and app. C).

15. For a test of the model using the case of West Germany see Gordon and Walton 1982.

16. For more discussion of these issues see Ransom and Sutch 1977 and Wright 1986.

CONCLUDING REMARKS

The point of this chapter is to insist that macroeconomics offers a separate but essential viewpoint to inform historical studies, whether or not they are based on aggregate economic statistics. It encourages the historian to take macroeconomics more seriously rather than concentrate on the microeconomic approach or make the opposite error of focusing on the macroeconomic side of affairs to the neglect of the microeconomic side—a fault more often found in economists than in historians. The best advice is to balance our thinking when tackling a problem and then to write the history that emerges from that careful and explicitly analytical approach. How much of the macro thinking and how much of the micro should appear in the final product will depend on the case at hand. We cannot be content to finish, however, without thinking through both sides of the question. No one said that writing good history is easy.

Money, Banking, and Inflation

An Introduction for Historians

HUGH ROCKOFF

Most of us like a good story. This is one reason we became historians of one sort or another. What follows is a story about the development of the monetary system in an imaginary economy, tracing the evolution from a pure gold standard to a modern system complete with central bank. The story is intended simply to illustrate some of the important ideas in monetary theory and how working historians might apply them. It does not correspond exactly to the history of any one economy but combines historical features from many. The purpose of the story is to introduce the language of monetary economics to historians. Once they master that language, fruitful dialogue with monetary economists can begin.[1]

A PURE GOLD STANDARD

I begin not at the very beginning, when a commodity such as cattle or salt served as money;[2] nor even at some fairly advanced stage when merchants measured prices by weights of gold.[3] Instead I pick up the thread

1. I want to thank Michael Bordo, Stanley Engerman, Susan Mann, and Eugene White for a number of very useful comments on an earlier draft. Of course, they are not responsible for any remaining errors.

2. Quiggin 1949 is a fascinating worldwide survey of these early forms of money.

3. The historian working on such early material should not assume that economists are uninterested in these topics. The basic functions of money are still a matter of controversy

in medieval times. There already exists a dominant form of money: gold coins minted by the king.[4] This system, of course, adds greatly to the wealth of the kingdom for reasons that economists have talked about for generations. Money "separates the act of purchase from the act of sale." An artisan who makes furniture and needs shoes does not have to search the kingdom for someone who makes shoes and needs a chair. Instead, our furnituremaker can sell chairs for money to anyone who needs a chair and then later use the money to buy shoes.

The king produces coins at his mint setting the *mint price* of gold at $50.00 per ounce.[5] For each ounce of gold bullion brought to the mint the king will return fifty coins each stamped $1.00. The king could perform this service free of charge, paying the expenses of the mint out of some sort of general tax. In this case each coin would contain exactly $1/50$ of an ounce of gold. But he need not do so, and like most shrewd monarchs our king does not. Instead, the king makes fifty-five coins labeled one dollar out of each ounce of gold brought to the mint, each coin containing $1/55$ of an ounce of gold, and keeps five of these coins for himself. This surplus is the *seigniorage*. He uses it to pay the expenses of the mint and to finance other activities. This important concept, which is very easy to grasp when the monetary system is so simple, is one of the major tools of the monetary historian. There is always a seigniorage, even in complex modern systems. As in any case where there is a profit to be made the historian asks the usual questions. How much seigniorage is being created? Who is getting it? Did the participants in a particular historical episode accurately perceive the answers to these questions? Is that what they were really fighting about?

For a time the amount of money in our kingdom grew slowly. Each year the demand for money grew as the kingdom expanded, but balancing it was the gold brought to the mint to be minted into new coins. Prices changed little. But then other, richer, gold mines were discovered, and soon the mints were working overtime converting the new gold into new dollars. The result, which seems obvious in the simplified world we have constructed, was an increase in the price level and for a time economic activity.

There have been a number of important historical cases in which dis-

---

among monetary theorists. Information about how economies moved from barter to money would be of considerable relevance to these controversies.

4. Feavearyear 1931 is a good general history of English money that illustrates many of the points we will touch on in this section.

5. The classic history of the English mint is Craig 1953.

coveries of gold and silver have produced inflation. One of the most famous followed the Spanish conquest of the new world. The basic account
is still Hamilton 1934. Another example followed the discovery of gold
in California and Australia in the late 1840s and early 1850s; Cairnes
1873 and Jevons 1884 (1863) review these episodes. Bordo 1975 finds
Cairnes's analysis surprisingly up to date.

But new gold mines, for all the excitement of the gold rushes, were
not the main source of inflation in our kingdom. For a time our king kept
his seigniorage to the modest 10 percent mentioned above. But then the
drain on his coffers caused by an inconclusive war with a neighboring
kingdom, not to mention the increasingly lavish affairs at the palace,
forced him to look to an increase in the seigniorage for additional revenue. The remedy was simple: raise the mint price of gold from $50.00
to $60.00 per ounce (to give merchants an incentive to bring bullion to
the mint) and raise the seigniorage from $5.00 to $10.00 per ounce.

Consider first the consequences of this policy for the currency. Before,
each ounce of gold was minted into fifty-five coins each labeled one dollar—fifty for the merchant and five for the king—and so each contained
1/55 ounce of gold. Now each ounce of gold is to be minted into seventy
coins—sixty for the merchant and ten for the king—and so each coin contains only 1/70 ounce of gold. To keep the new coins similar in size and
heft to the old coins, the king was forced to add more lead, a base metal,
to the alloy used for making the coins. Thus, the term for this policy: *debasement* of the currency. Perhaps the most famous debasements were
those undertaken by Henry VIII; the best account is Gould 1970. Con-
tinental debasements are described in Miskimin 1984 and Spufford 1988.
Debasement, like seigniorage, is a concept that has its analogue in far
more complex economies.

But what were the consequences of debasement for the economy as a
whole? First, there was a strong incentive to melt down old coins and
bring them to the mint. If a merchant collected fifty-five old dollars and
melted them down, they yielded an ounce of gold. Taken to the mint that
ounce would be reminted into sixty new dollars. The collision between
the old dollars and the new ones is frequently analyzed with *Gresham's
law*—Bad (cheap) money drives out good (dear)—a concept as useful,
perhaps, to moralists as to economic historians. If law and convenience
force the exchange of old dollars and new dollars on a one-for-one basis
then the new dollars (bad money) will tend to drive the old dollars (good
money) out of circulation. Notice, however, the qualifying phrase. It
sometimes happens that merchants start to quote prices in both kinds of

dollars, or what amounts to the same thing, that a fluctuating price develops between the two currencies. In this case Gresham's law no longer
holds. Old dollars and new dollars circulate side by side. The circumstances that determine the outcome of a collision between bad and good
money are still being debated (Rolnick and Weber 1986).

But the more important consequence for the economy was the rise in
prices. The new coins produced through debasement of the currency produced inflation in much the same way as the new coins minted when new
gold mines were discovered produced inflation. This is the basic intuition
that underlies the quantity theory of money, which I see as the fundamental working model for the monetary historian.

THE QUANTITY THEORY OF MONEY

We may write the quantity theory as

$$(1)\ P = (M{\cdot}V)/y$$

where P is the price level, M is the stock of money (here the number of
gold coins), V is velocity (the rate at which people spend money), and y
is the real output of the economy. In this form we view the equation as
a simple translation of the old adage that inflation is caused by "too much
money chasing too few goods." If M rises (too much money) or y falls
(too few goods) then other things equal, P must rise (inflation). The
adage, however, does not allow for V rising. Inflation could also result
if people simply spent the existing stock of money faster, or the inflationary effects of additional money could be offset if people decided to spend
it less rapidly or to hoard some of it.

On one level we can regard the equation as a simple tautology. Given
any values for prices, money, and real income we can always compute a
value for velocity that makes the equation true. But for many monetary
economists the equation is more than a tautology. If velocity is some sort
of natural constant, or if at least it bears a stable relationship to other
economic variables, the equation becomes a powerful tool for explaining the relationship among the variables. The old adage about too much
money explains inflation because it implicitly assumes that velocity
doesn't change to offset the increase in money.

We can also write the quantity theory in certain other ways that may
be of use to the historian. A slightly different form of equation (1) is

$$(2)\ M = k{\cdot}P{\cdot}y$$

The k term is simply the inverse of V.[6] The advantage of writing the equation this way is that it asks a slightly different question: what determines the amount of money that people want to hold?[7] It leads us to focus on k, the fraction of income that people hold as money, and the variables that might affect k. For example, this equation leads us more directly to the role of interest rates. When looking at this equation we recognize that if interest rates are higher then, other things equal, people would want to hold a smaller fraction of their income (k) in the form of money.

It is also useful at times to express equation (1) in rate of change form.

$$(3) \quad \%P = \%M + \%V - \%y$$

Here the % sign in front of a variable refers to the percentage increase or decrease. Thus, if the stock of money was rising at 10 percent per year, if velocity was stable (percent change = 0), and if real income was rising at 3 percent per year, we would know that prices were rising at 7 percent per year. This form of the equation helps us to focus on what is often of most interest: how the system is changing over time. It also happens that on some occasions a historian will be more comfortable with an estimate, or simple guess about the rate of change of the variable than with an estimate of the level. For example, the historian might be unwilling to try to estimate the level of real GNP in a country at the beginning of some period. But he may feel comfortable—after looking at the trends in industrial production, labor force, exports, and so on—in arguing that the growth rate over a particular period falls within a certain range.

The suggestion that monetary historians use the quantity theory of money immediately puts some historians on guard; they have heard bad things about the quantity theory. So it is well to consider explicitly the case for its use. First and most important, it provides a relevant and parsimonious language for dealing with the key variables. Each term of the equation refers to a variable that the historian is interested in and would like to measure. More complex models are likely to leave the historian searching for an intuitive understanding of the mathematical relations and searching for data that are not readily available. Second, there is a long and distinguished tradition of monetary history that uses the quantity theory. Fledgling monetary historians have a wide range of models

6. This is the form used in Lindert's paper, 232–234.
7. Friedman 1956 has become the classic modern statement of the quantity theory. See Friedman 1989 for an update.

to choose from. Using a model that has already been applied in a wide range of circumstances has many advantages.

But how should the quantity theory be used? In most cases the historian should not try, I believe, to prove or disprove the quantity theory! At first blush some variation of the following plan seems natural. Measure each of the variables: money, prices, and real income. Compare the increase in prices with the increase in money per unit of real output. If prices follow exactly the same path as money per unit of real output, conclude that the quantity theory has been confirmed; if prices do not follow the same path, conclude that the quantity theory has been disproved. Submit the article to a journal for publication. The problem here is that the chance is remote that in any one particular case the quantity theory will fit exactly; in many cases the results are likely to diverge substantially from the simple velocity-is-constant version of the quantity theory. For one thing, measurement of the variables, especially real income, may contain error. Perhaps even more important, numerous variables are likely to affect velocity and thus produce a significant divergence between prices and money per unit of real output. The obvious plan encourages the monetary historian to stop where the real intellectual work begins.

A better plan, it seems to me, is to allow the quantity theory to suggest relationships among the variables that might not be obvious at first. Measure each of the variables: money, prices, and real income, and compute velocity. Stare at the result and ask why velocity changed in such a peculiar way.

An example of this approach comes from Milton Friedman and Anna Schwartz's (1963, 306–307) analysis of monetary behavior in the United States following the stock market crash of 1929. Friedman and Schwartz could have looked at their data, observed that velocity was not stable (it fell substantially between 1929 and 1930) and concluded that the quantity theory didn't "work." But quitting at that point would have left them without much insight or much of a story. Instead they chose a more satisfying approach. They asked, what would be the effect of a stock market crash on the willingness of people to spend, on velocity? Their answer, derived to be sure with an eye on the numbers, was that the crash would increase uncertainty about the future. People and business firms would rather hold their money for a rainy day. Velocity in other words would fall. In the end they had achieved some insight into the actual course of events.

Schwartz 1973 gives a masterful series of illustrations showing how to apply the quantity theory to cases with relatively few data. Her examples include the contrast between Greek and Roman monetary systems, the debasements of the currency under Henry VIII and Edward VI, the restoration of the currency under Edward VI and Elizabeth, the price revolution based on new world supplies of gold and silver, and numerous recent events.

But does this mean that we can never reject the quantity theory, or that no other models are useful in monetary history? The response to both these extremist positions is clearly, no. Economists and monetary historians may eventually conclude that other models are more fruitful and other languages offer a better way to talk about monetary history. But as a starting point to organize and think about the data, the quantity theory still provides one of the simplest and most flexible tools available.

The reaction of many historians to the idea of using the quantity theory, of course, results from a political concern. The quantity theory has been associated closely with a series of distinguished conservative economists, in recent years Milton Friedman in particular. Is there something inherently conservative about the quantity theory? If I use the quantity theory will I somehow support Milton Friedman's views on education, drug legalization, or welfare expenditures? To state the concern as simply as this helps, I hope, to dismiss it.

The close historical association between conservative politics and the quantity theory is, however, understandable. If velocity is stable, or predictable from a few economic variables that change in a regular fashion, then the implication is that providing a stable monetary system will go a long way toward providing a stable economy. Further oversight and intervention by the central government may not be necessary. But this point is probably not the full explanation, which must await the work of historians of economic thought.

What is clear is that as a language for organizing experience, and as an intellectual machine for suggesting hypotheses, the quantity theory carries no political associations that should discourage any historian from using it.

THE INTRODUCTION OF FOREIGN TRADE

In time trade developed between our kingdom and a neighbor. The neighboring kingdom also relied on a gold standard but used a different unit of account, pounds rather than dollars. A crucial monetary relation then was the *mint par* between the two currencies. In our kingdom $70.00 contained an ounce of gold. But in the neighboring kingdom, it was £35.00 that contained an ounce of gold, so the mint par was $2.00 = £1.00. For practical purposes this was the exchange rate between the two currencies. For imported goods worth £50 in the neighboring community, traders had to pay $100 [= £50·($2/£1,]. For exported goods worth $150, traders in the neighboring kingdom paid £75 [= $150·(£1/$2)].

Why couldn't the exchange rate be, say, $3.00 = £1.00? Why, to put it in the language of the market, was such an extreme *depreciation* of the dollar impossible? The answer is simply that when the price of the pound had risen sufficiently above $2.00 = £1.00, rather than pay a still higher price for pounds importers could simply melt down dollars, ship them abroad, and have them reminted into pounds. The price at which this process became economic was known as the *gold export point*. The importers of goods and services did not have to constantly watch all of the costs affecting the gold export point. Specialists, known as *arbitragers* entered the market, and they made it their business to take quick advantage of an increase in the price of the pound to the gold export point. If the price of pounds fell sufficiently below $2.00 = £1.00, the opposite process started. Arbitragers found they could buy pounds at the lower price, melt them down, import the gold, and remint it into dollars at a profit. The price at which this process became economic was known as the *gold import point*.

Some time after trade had been opened up a gold mine was discovered in the land of dollars: it could produce gold at an average cost far below the mint price. There was, of course, considerable fear in the land of pounds that the land of dollars would retain all of its new gold and therefore become "richer" than the land of pounds. But this did not happen. Instead, prices rose for a time in the land of dollars as considerable amounts of bullion were brought to the mint and coined into new dollars. But rising prices in the land of dollars affected the trade between the kingdoms. Prices of exports from the land of dollars rose.

To be more explicit, makers of candles, the chief export of the land of dollars, now paid more dollars for the labor and wax used to make export goods. So candlemakers raised their price and people in the land of pounds bought fewer candles. At the same time, because the price of clothes made in the land of dollars was rising, people tended to import more clothes from the land of pounds. Imports exceeded exports and the land of dollars was said to run a *balance-of-payments deficit*. More gold flowed out to buy imports than flowed in to buy exports.

But the flow of gold set in motion forces that tended to bring trade back into equilibrium. The rates of increase of money and prices in the land of dollars slowed down because the increase in the stock of money from newly mined gold was offset by the loss through the balance-of-payments deficit. And prices in the land of pounds began to rise as gold acquired in foreign trade was brought to the mint and coined into pounds. All this made exports of the land of dollars seem more attractive than before; their prices were no longer so high compared with the prices of similar items produced in the land of pounds. And imports to the land of dollars no longer seemed like such a bargain. The balance-of-payments deficit gradually disappeared.

This story is what economists know as *Hume's price-specie flow mechanism*. A temporary increase in the *price* level in one country produces a balance-of-payments deficit, an outflow of *specie* (gold or silver), and a return of prices and the balance of payments to equilibrium. Bordo 1984 provides a good summary of the price-specie-flow approach, and a guide to the important papers.

As with most of the stories economists tell, subsequent writers have challenged the traditional view. The critics wonder how the prices of internationally traded goods could remain out of equilibrium for so long. Instead, they suggest that prices should remain fairly stable while the balance of payments deficit redistributes the temporary excess of money in the land of dollars. This view has come to be called the *monetary theory of the balance of payments*. McCloskey and Zecher 1976 provide a good summary of the monetary approach together with an application to the classical gold standard era (1879–1914).

As in the case of the quantity theory, I would suggest that the historian should not view these ideas primarily as theories of invariable accuracy, but as sources of useful insights. One should, of course, try to measure the variables involved in these stories—money, prices, exports and imports, and so forth. But suppose that the historian found that the balance-of-payments deficit actually decreased when the supply of money rose. The wrong thing to do, in my view, would be to declare these theories invalid, and the work completed. Instead, these stories should serve as starting points: the real task is to explain, in a convincing way, the inevitable departures from the simple models. Here, the historian's special talents for working with nonquantitative documents can be put to good use. How did traders react to changes in prices, interest rates, and other variables? Account books, diaries, and other business records can yield considerable information. What the models can do is sharpen the questions that historians ask and create a basis for discussing their findings with economists and economic historians.

SOME ALTERNATIVE SYSTEMS

Monetary historians will recognize that in some respects the foregoing story of an isolated kingdom opening trade after perfecting its gold standard is largely apocryphal. The actual evolution of most monetary systems was more complex and more interesting. Let us consider some possible alternative paths. For one thing, it is not at all necessary that only one metal serve as the basic medium of exchange. Suppose that the mint was willing to coin not only one ounce of gold into $50.00, but also one ounce of silver into $5.00. Then we would have a *bimetallic* standard. Neglecting seigniorage, we note that a silver dollar would have ten times as much metal in it as a gold dollar—the silver dollar has 1/5 of an ounce of silver, and the gold dollar 1/50 of an ounce of gold. The *bimetallic ratio,* in this case, is 10:1. Ten ounces of silver would buy one ounce of gold. Could the two coins circulate alongside each other? They could. It might be the case, for example, that smaller transactions would be carried out with silver coins and larger ones with gold coins.

But problems could develop in a bimetallic system. Suppose that on world markets, owing to nonmonetary demands or the mint practices of other countries, the bimetallic ratio rose above 10:1, say to 11:1. One ounce of gold would exchange for more silver in other countries than it would at home. Then we would say that silver was overvalued at home and gold undervalued at home. Then the possibility for successful arbitrage would be at hand. A merchant who converted fifty silver dollars into fifty gold dollars would, in our example, have one ounce of gold. By shipping that gold abroad and converting it into silver on the world market (the details would depend on the foreign monetary systems), our merchant would now have eleven ounces of silver. Brought home and taken to the mint those eleven ounces of silver could be converted into fifty-five dollars. Of course, that $5.00 earned on the transaction would have to cover various costs of shipping and insuring gold, and so on. So the foreign bimetallic ratio would have to be sufficiently high to make this process profitable. But the result could be to drain the economy of gold and convert the currency from a mixture of gold and silver to pure silver.

A key assumption of this story, we should stress, is that the mint is open to anyone to convert silver or gold into money. This need not be the case. The mint could simply buy gold or silver in amounts of its own choosing from time to time and mint the bullion into coins. In this case the face value of the coins could greatly exceed their bullion value; they would be *subsidiary* coins. This is how our current system of coinage works. We don't know how much metal is contained in our coins or how much it is worth, except on those rare occasions when the bullion value of the coins rises above their face value and the coins are withdrawn from circulation.

The outflow of the undervalued metal in a bimetallic system is another instance of Gresham's law. In this case the bad money (silver) drove the good money (gold) out of circulation. Was this a bad thing? In one respect it may have been. Silver might not be as convenient in large transactions as gold. It might be possible to use gold in large transactions by paying a premium to compensate the owner of gold for not converting it into silver on the world market, but this makeshift would also make transacting less convenient. But we also have to ask why the value of gold was rising relative to silver on world markets. Suppose it was because the supply of silver was rising rapidly while the supply of gold was not. Then we might have been better off under the bimetallic standard than either a pure silver standard or a pure gold standard. Under the former we might experience inflation, and under the latter deflation, while the bimetallic standard might serve to keep prices relatively stable.

For many years the standard view was that the difficulty of maintaining both metals in circulation made a bimetallic system unworkable. But Friedman (1990a, 1990b) argues forcefully that in some cases the benefits are likely to outweigh the costs.

The United States had a bimetallic standard before the Civil War and many of the costs and benefits of this system emerged during this period. Laughlin 1892 analyzed this experience in his classic work, *The History of Bimetallism in the United States*. In the early eighteenth century Isaac Newton, it is interesting to note, revealed a sophisticated understanding of the problems of a bimetallic standard that he had to deal with during his tenure as master of the mint. We should also add that while gold and silver bimetallism is the most familiar case, it is not the only one. Many other metals have served as media of exchange. China, for example, used a system based on silver and copper until recent times (Chen 1975; Rawski 1989, 125–180).

Our apocryphal story also assumes a degree of monetary hegemony that is far from universal. It asserts throughout that the dollar is the *unit of account*, the basic quantity that prices are denominated in, and that merchants use to keep their books. And it posits that dollar-denominated coins minted by the king are the sole *medium of exchange*, the asset that actually changes hands when goods are bought and sold, and debts repaid. This is a state of affairs obviously attractive to the king since the wide circulation of his money maximizes his seigniorage. It is also highly satisfactory to the public since having one unit of account and one medium of exchange denominated in that unit of account is highly convenient. The king has some powerful tools for assuring that this state of affairs prevails. First of all he can require that taxes be paid in his money, and he can use his money to pay wages, salaries, and other expenses of government. In addition, he can make contracts specifying payment in his money enforceable in the courts, and, if he chooses, make contracts specifying other monies unenforceable. In other words he can make his money, and if he chooses, his money alone, a *legal tender*—the coin of the realm.

But in some circumstances, through weakness or choice or because of the constant debasement of his money, the king might not establish the hegemony of his own money. The monies of neighboring kingdoms might circulate in the land of dollars simply because merchants find them more convenient to use. The law could even recognize the arrangement by making foreign coins legal tender. If these currencies are made of the same metal the process is relatively straightforward. In our example the law could simply recognize both dollars and pounds as legal tender at the ratio of two dollars equal one pound. Before the Civil War, numerous foreign coins circulated in the United States and many of them were legal tenders (Schilke and Solomon 1964). Today the dollar serves as a parallel money in a number of smaller countries. Nor is it necessary that the unit of account in which the king's money is denominated serve as the public's common unit of account. The unit of account derived from a defunct monetary system, or the unit of account used in other perhaps larger economies might serve as well. After the Revolutionary War, many American merchants continued to keep their books in colonial systems based on pounds, shillings, and pence.

But let us return to our story. Years passed. Except for the occasional inflation when more gold mines were discovered, or when kings found it necessary to debase the currency, the economy enjoyed growth in real income, price stability, and balanced trade with her neighbors.

THE INTRODUCTION OF BANKING

People found that a money supply consisting simply of gold coins was increasingly inconvenient. Some relatively wealthy individuals began the practice of depositing surplus coins with the local goldsmith. The goldsmith in turn would issue a certificate showing that the coins had been left, and entitling the depositor to retrieve them when he needed the actual coins. At first, this arrangement was not much different from the warehousing of any other commodity.

But in time two developments occurred that significantly altered the monetary system. First, the recognition that if the receipts for deposit were made out to the bearer (the coins to be delivered to whoever was in legal possession of the receipt) then those receipts functioned as money almost like coins. Instead of coins circulating from hand to hand, receipts that could be redeemed at the goldsmith for coin, also circulated from hand to hand.

Second, the goldsmiths noted that not all individuals wanted to redeem their notes at the same time. On many days, there were no redemptions, and on others, the amount of redemptions would about balance new deposits. The goldsmiths recognized that they could lend out part of their gold at interest and still redeem any notes for anyone who actually needed coin. Thus was born *fractional reserve banking*. For a detailed discussion of the origins of banking in England see Richards 1929; for an interesting contemporary discussion of the goldsmith bankers see "The Mystery" 1974.

Was there an element of fraud in this? No. The customers of the goldsmiths knew that the goldsmiths no longer kept one dollar in gold for each dollar in notes. What depositors cared about was the goldsmiths' promise to redeem the notes, and customers, like the goldsmiths, knew that the promise could be met because not all persons would want their coins at once. The customer benefited, moreover, because the goldsmiths no longer charged explicitly for the service they performed. In the early days when they kept 100 percent reserves they charged a fee for storing gold, as ordinary warehouses did for storing furniture or tobacco. But now the goldsmiths could pay their expenses and make a profit out of the interest earned on the loans they made. One could store one's gold for "free."

For the economy as a whole fractional reserve banking proved to be a mixed blessing. On the positive side, fractional reserve banking increased the amount of loanable funds available in the economy and so encouraged economic growth and development. Only in the unlikely case that all the additional funds were wasted would the result have been different. It is important to be clear about this point, since so many critics of the goldsmith bankers miss it. Previously, to meet an increased demand for money it was necessary to dig up gold or bring it from abroad. Now only a fraction of any given increase in the stock of money needed to be created in this way. Instead the goldsmith bankers could create money by printing pieces of paper. The resources saved in the gold mining industry or in foreign trade could be employed elsewhere in the economy to increase real income.

Initially, competition among the goldsmiths forced them to pass much of the benefits of fractional reserve banking to borrowers in the form of lower interest rates on loans, and on to depositors in the form of interest payments to depositors. But later, after several goldsmiths failed, the government began the practice of requiring special royal charters to operate a bank. By limiting competition these charters greatly increased the profitability of banking. The fight for these charters led to many unseemly battles. The king frequently required a payment in cash for a charter, but even so the issue of a charter was not automatic. Often investors seeking a charter would attempt to bribe members of the royal household to get the cash payment reduced, or to overcome the opposition of the existing banks to the issue of a new charter.

Economic historians have recently begun to pay close attention to the issue of competition in banking. In the past, historians usually argued that unregulated banking was a failure. But recent investigations reject this judgment. Most of the recent research focuses on so-called free banking, a term whose meaning varies from time to time, and is sometimes applied to systems that were a far cry from laissez-faire. In the United States during the free-banking era (1838–1863), a number of states passed laws that permitted anyone to start a bank provided the new bank could meet certain minimum standards and that the notes the bank issued were backed by government bonds. A large literature has grown up around this episode, and about related episodes in Scotland and other countries (for the United States see Rockoff 1974; Rolnick and Weber 1983, 1984; and Kahn 1985; for Scotland see White 1984). While the stability of a competitive banking system is the focus of most recent research, there are other important questions, such as the one addressed by Schwartz 1947 in her illuminating study of early banking in Philadelphia: how many banks does it take to establish workable competition?

A more concrete description of what happened to the economy when the banking system switched from 100 percent reserves to fractional reserves will bring home the nature of the benefits of fractional reserve banking. In the first stage of goldsmith banking the stock of money consisted of one thousand dollars: $500 in gold coins that circulated from hand to hand and $500 in goldsmith notes. Behind the $500 in notes there stood $500 in coins in the vaults of the goldsmiths. But after a time the goldsmiths discovered that they could get by with $100 worth of coins in reserve. The system had gone from 100 percent reserves to a fractional system with a reserve ratio of 20 percent. The surplus $400 that had been locked up in the vaults of the goldsmiths was lent to cotton textile manufacturers who used it to import machines from abroad. The economy was better off, because gold locked up in the vaults of goldsmiths had been converted into machines that could produce textiles at lower cost than before.

Adam Smith believed that fractional reserve banking had greatly enhanced the real income of Scotland in his lifetime. He argued that

> The gold and silver money which circulates in any country may very properly be compared to a highway, which while it circulates and carries to market all the grass and corn of the country, produces itself not a single pile of either. The judicious operations of banking, by providing . . . a sort of waggon-way through the air, enable the country to convert . . . a great part of its highways into good pastures and cornfields, and thereby to increase very considerably the annual produce of its land and labour. (1937 [1776], 305)

With paper money, no costly construction of mines or mints was needed to facilitate the exchange of goods.

But Smith also recognized the dangers in fractional reserve banking: "commerce and industry . . . though they may be somewhat augmented, cannot be altogether so secure, when they are . . . suspended on the Daedalian wings of paper money, as when they travel about on the solid ground of gold and silver" (ibid.). If people become concerned about the safety of the banks, and many people start demanding their coins at once, the system might collapse. There would be, as we will discuss below, a panic and a run on the banks.

How the banks invested their money was of extreme importance to the economy. Long-term high-yield investments might contribute to rapid capital formation, but if the banking system's portfolio did not yield a sufficient flow of revenue to permit it to redeem easily any notes that were presented, the seeds of a failure might be planted.

But what constitutes a good or bad investment for a bank? One particularly influential doctrine, one whose reputation has had its ups and downs, is the *real-bills doctrine*. This principle, also known as the *com-*

mercial loan theory, holds that the ideal bank loan should be made to a business, secured by a real commodity, extended for only a short term, and be self-liquidating (the money to repay the loan should arise naturally from the activity financed by the loan). Thus, a ninety-day loan to a clothing store might be consistent with this doctrine. It could be secured by the clothes themselves and could be paid off (liquidated) when the clothes were sold. Notice that in the case described above, the purchase of textile machinery would violate the real-bills doctrine by funding a long-term investment. Mints 1945 offers a critical history of this doctrine, along with a scathing attack on its usefulness as a guide to monetary policy. The basic problem with the doctrine in Mints's view is that the value of the bills being offered to the banks will increase with the price level, so that the real-bills approach provides no effective check on the stock of money. Sargent and Wallace 1982 attempted to rehabilitate the real-bills doctrine. Their study is quite technical, but Laidler's (1984) comment on this paper lays out some of the questions at issue.

There is much work to be done on the investment policies of banks, work that historians are especially well equipped to do. The real-bills doctrine suggests some of the key variables. What sectors were favored by banks? Were bank loans secured by real commodities or by the general reputation of the borrowers? What was the typical duration of a bank loan? Did bankers attempt to conceal long-term investments by rolling over a series of short-term loans? Why did the banks follow certain policies? What were the influences of cultural factors, ideas such as the real-bills doctrine, and the legal framework of banking?

The real-bills doctrine also suggests some of the trade-offs that must be kept in mind. Following the doctrine to the letter may reduce the probability of bank failures but may also reduce the banking system's contribution to economic development. Long-term investments, prohibited by the real-bills doctrine, might be just what the economy needs. The contrast is often drawn, with respect to this issue, between banking in English-speaking countries, where the real-bills doctrine has been most influential, and banking in Japan, Germany, and other European countries where long-term lending has won greater acceptance. Two papers by Neuberger and Stokes (1974, 1975) explore this issue.

In considering the real-bills doctrine, we need to keep in mind that what is true for the individual institution or sector may not be true for the system as a whole.[8] For example, suppose we compare two banking

---

8. See the extended discussion of fallacies of composition in Sutch's essay, 162–163.

systems and find that one was willing to lend long-term to heavy industry, while the other, bound by the real-bills doctrine, was not. We cannot jump to the conclusion that the first economy had a much greater supply of long-term capital. The primary effect may have been simply that in the first economy retailers unable to find accommodation at the banks turned to their partners, private investors, or trade credit for short-term working capital, while in the economy where this need was met by the banking system, private investors supplied a larger proportion of long-term capital. The role of institutions is very different in the two economies, but not the supplies of different types of capital. Or take the problem of bank safety. It would make any one bank safer if it followed the real-bills doctrine while other banks were making risky long-term investments. But if all banks in the system adhered to the real-bills doctrine, the system as a whole might become riskier because it would be tied to a relatively narrow range of investments.

The process of financial innovation did not cease with the issue of the goldsmith bank notes. Rather than take a large supply of notes each time they deposited some gold, some merchants preferred an agreement that the bank would hold the gold until ordered to transfer it by the merchant, and so deposit banking was created. Deposits, like bank notes, were liabilities of the banks, backed only partly by gold.[9]

This innovation raised one of the time-honored questions in monetary history: were bank deposits (or other financial assets) money? Today it seems obvious that bank deposits are money, and controversy surrounds only more exotic financial instruments.[10] But such was not always the case. In the early days of banking some observers argued that only gold coins or only gold coins and bank notes were really money. Here again there is much work that can be done by the historian in exploring how financial assets were used, and in particular which ones served as a medium of exchange. But in this case, perhaps even more than some of the others, the simplest plan may not be the best. The historian could settle on one particular definition of money, examine how a particular asset was used, and declare it to be (or not to be) money. Then, perhaps, the bottom line would be that an eminent authority who had declared this particular asset to be money was right or (more likely) wrong. But

9. This sequence, first note issues and then deposits, is by no means the only path that has been followed. For the classic history of a powerful early bank that relied on deposits see DeRoover 1963.

10. In 1992 currency was about 8 percent of the United States money supply as most frequently defined (M2).

even now economists are far from agreeing that any one definition of money is best. And the definition that is best for one purpose, say for explaining the rate of inflation, may not be best for other purposes, say for explaining why certain kinds of financial regulations were adopted.

A more fruitful plan is to recognize the diversity of underlying concerns that give rise to the debate over the definition of money, and to allow these concerns to suggest a set of questions for research. Did increases in the volume of a particular asset place an upward pressure on prices? Should this asset be counted as money when using the quantity theory of money? Did the creation of a particular type of financial instrument facilitate trade? Was it for some purposes, in other words, a medium of exchange?

A BANKING PANIC

By far the most exciting problem associated with fractional reserve banking in our kingdom, and perhaps the most important, was the occurrence of banking panics. One could fall from Smith's wagon road in the sky. It happened that several of our goldsmith bankers were rumored to have been speculating heavily in real estate. They had long since left the real-bills doctrine behind. When real estate prices fell there were runs on those banks. The other goldsmith banks were sound and should not have been attacked. But they were. People who had heard about the speculations were not overly cautious in generalizing. The observation that some of the banks were weak quickly ignited the less accurate and dangerous thought that all the banks were weak. Lines formed outside the banks as people demanded gold for their notes and deposits. But with fractional reserve banks, not all depositors could get their money at once.

It is important to distinguish here between *illiquid* banks and *insolvent* banks. At the height of the panic many banks were solvent (the value of their assets exceeded their liabilities) but illiquid (they didn't have enough gold to meet immediate demands for withdrawals). But the panic set in motion forces that undermined the solvency of the banks. As banks sold assets to raise cash, the value of those assets declined. As banks tried to build up their gold holdings by refusing to make new loans, the supplies of money and credit shrank, and what had been a spirit of optimism and enterprise became one of pessimism and hoarding. The economy sank into a long depression. The conclusion that people drew was that fractional reserve banking system seemed to work well during good times but was subject to the risk of a cataclysmic implosion.

The literature on banking panics is enormous. And every feature of the story we have so confidently sketched above has been examined and, for certain panics, challenged. Our sketch of a standardized panic naturally raises a number of questions. How exactly do rumors spread during banking panics? Are sound banks really brought down with unsound banks? Most important, what institutions exist or could be created that might ameliorate panics? Part of the problem in our example is the hidden assumption that by law or custom people expect to be able to convert their notes or deposits into gold instantly on demand. What if this connection were broken so that banks could temporarily suspend immediate payment and pay later with interest? More frequently, attention focuses on institutions omitted from our simplified model, such as a government agency that could act as an emergency *lender of last resort*, government underwritten note and deposit insurance, or clearinghouses that could help banks cooperate in emergencies.

The most famous panic and collapse was that of the American banking system from 1929 to 1933. Friedman and Schwartz (1963, chap. 7) argue that collapse was an independent factor that produced a decline in the stock of money, thus turning a recession into a depression. The collapse of the banking system, in their view, was the result of a panic operating on a relatively weak banking system and could have been avoided. White 1983 discusses the role of banking legislation in increasing the vulnerability of the system. Temin 1976 argues the opposite—that the bank failures were merely a by-product of the depression. The true cause of the depression, in his view, was a collapse of consumption spending.

The ensuing debate over the roles of money and the banking panic in the depression that followed has been long and acrimonious. Extensive references to both sides appear in Schwartz 1981, which answers many of the objections to the interpretations of Friedman and Schwartz. Christina Romer 1992 strengthens the Friedman-Schwartz "historical" approach by using a model that emphasizes the stock of money to analyze the slide into the abyss from 1929 to 1933 as well as the recovery between 1933 and 1942. In a related paper, Christina Romer and David Romer 1989 shows that the Friedman-Schwartz approach fits well with several monetary episodes after World War II. These studies cover issues outside the scope of Friedman and Schwartz's *Monetary History* (1963), especially the 1979 decision by the Federal Reserve to launch a fight against inflation, even at the cost of increased unemployment.

The emphasis on banking and financial aspects of the crisis takes a different turn in Bernanke 1983, who distinguishes between the effects of the banking crisis on the stock of money, emphasized by Friedman and Schwartz, and the effects on the supply of credit. Bernanke's point is that the decline in commodity prices, land values, and security values reduced the collateral available to borrowers which in turn made it hard for banks to lend to borrowers who otherwise appeared credit-worthy. In addition, the bank failures disrupted long-term relations between banks and their customers, further eroding the ability of banks to negotiate with otherwise credit-worthy buyers.

There are, of course, many other panics in financial history—including for the United States major crises in 1837, 1857, 1873, 1893, and 1907—that have been studied by financial historians and are good candidates for more work. Indeed, the savings and loan crisis in the mid-1980s proves that banking crises are by no means an extinct species. Nevertheless the working historian can gain a great deal of insight into the crucial issues by reading through the debate over the relationship between the banking crisis and the Great Depression in the United States because it has been studied so intensively.

THE INTRODUCTION OF FIAT MONEY

Although banking panics occurred frequently in our apocryphal kingdom, this was not the feature of the banking system that caught the eye of the king's finance minister. What interested the minister the most was the thought that if banks could create money simply by printing "one dollar" on a piece of paper, the government could do so as well. And when a government deficit dictated the need for more revenue, the government decided to meet part of that need by printing paper money. Initially, the government promised to redeem the paper money in gold as did the banks. But soon this provision was dropped. The government was now issuing a pure *fiat money*. To encourage its acceptance the government made this paper money a legal tender and repealed the laws that had made the coins of other countries legal tenders.

The issue of paper money raised the government's seigniorage. Unlike the case of the pure gold standard, where most of the resources people gave up to increase their holdings of money went into mining or foreign trade, and unlike the case of fractional reserve banking, where a small but necessary fraction of these resources had to be used in this way, the fiat standard made all the resources traded for money balances available to the government.

The truth, it is sad to say, is that the initial issues of paper money did not prove to be the temporary expedient the finance minister had claimed they would be. The king subsidized the price of bread and won the love of his people (for a time). But the increase in the stock of money led to inflation and still larger bread subsidies were required. Soldiers and bureaucrats were paid with the fiat money. But when prices rose it was necessary to raise their wages and salaries as well. The result was a vicious circle of inflation.

One result was that the country was forced to abandon the gold standard. As prices and incomes rose the demand for gold coins to use in foreign trade rose as well. There was a run on the banks, and they soon stopped paying gold for their notes, paying instead with the paper money printed by the government. This state of affairs was ratified quickly by legislation. The result was that the ancient fixed rate of exchange between the dollar and the pound fell by the wayside. The dollar price of the pound was determined by supply and demand in the private market. Steadily the price of the pound rose from the old fixed rate of $2.00 per pound, to $2.49 and then to $3.11. The dollar was depreciating, and the pound appreciating rapidly.[11]

INFLATION

When inflation increases to very high rates it is known as *hyperinflation*. In his classic study of this experience, Cagan 1956 defines the onset of hyperinflation by a rate of inflation of 50 percent per month. His study covers seven European cases of hyperinflation including the most famous and most studied case, Germany after World War I. It also discusses what may be the champion hyperinflation, Hungary after World War II, during which prices rose on average 19,800 percent per month for twelve months. A number of other hyperinflations have been studied, and advances have been made in the statistical methods applied to the study of hyperinflations. Cagan 1989 is a good, brief, and accessible survey of the current state of the literature. There are obviously numerous questions raised by the experience of hyperinflation that the skills of traditional historians are particularly suited to answering. What were the social and political circumstances that led to hyperinflation? What was the state of expert opinion on monetary affairs during the hyperinflation? What

---

11. This sequence describes very much what happened in the United States during the Civil War. See Mitchell (1968 [1903], 1–43).

were the long-term political and social consequences? Dornbusch and Edwards 1991 is a good collection of papers that discuss the linkages between inflation and politics in Latin America.

Inflation is often but not always the major effect of issuing more money. An increase in output may result from an increase in money as well. The older view on whether an increase in money produced mostly inflation or increased output was simply that it depended on the degree of unemployment of labor and capital. If there were lots of unemployed resources about, increased spending that resulted from increased supplies of money brought more real output and little inflation. If the economy was at full employment, increased spending brought inflation. Lester 1939 made this point by giving numerous historical examples, ranging from the "playing card" money of Canada to depression-era experiments in Scandinavia, all showing that fiat money issued during periods of high unemployment increased real economic activity.

This view was formalized and generalized in the *Phillips curve,* which posits a negative relation between the rate of unemployment and the rate of inflation.[12] This analysis implies that there was a permanent tradeoff between inflation and unemployment. Policymakers could choose an economy characterized by rapid money growth, high inflation, and low unemployment. Or they could choose one characterized by slow money growth, stable prices, and high unemployment. The choice then depended on how policymakers weighed the costs of high inflation and the benefits of low unemployment. This interpretation of the Phillips curve, however, lost supporters in the 1960s and 1970s when many countries discovered that maintaining a low rate of unemployment meant adopting policies that accelerated inflation.

Recent analyses have stressed the role of expectations in shaping the relationship between inflation and employment. An increase in inflation might produce greater employment and output, but only if the inflation was unexpected. If prices rose and wages and other costs lagged behind, then for a time employers would find their real profits higher, and they would have an incentive to hire additional workers and increase output. But once workers and other suppliers of resources adjusted their demands to reflect the inflation, the incentive to increase output over what it had been at lower rates of inflation would disappear. This implies that increasing the money stock produces at best only a temporary increase in

---

12. There is an enormous literature on the Phillips curve, but the original paper, Phillips 1958, can still be read with profit.

real output. In the long run the economy returns to its *natural rate of unemployment,* as determined by the real conditions in labor markets.[13]

Recognizing the key role of expectations in determining the effect of a policy action, economists began to explore the determinants of expectations, and a large and lively literature has grown up in this area during the last two decades.[14] The main debate is over the type of errors people might make in forming their expectations of the future. A simple but powerful argument runs as follows: it is implausible to assume that people would continually over- or underestimate the rate of inflation or that they would continually ignore an important determinant of inflation such as money. On average we would expect their estimates to be accurate, although there might be many errors. What is plausible to assume, to use the standard term with which most of us are now familiar, are *rational expectations.* To assume rational expectations does not force us to assume that no one makes mistakes. Rather, it forces us to analyze why a smart, motivated individual might have made a mistake in a particular circumstance. We need not assume, for example, that everyone correctly predicted the course of prices and wages during the Great Depression. What the theory asks us to do is focus on why people may have over- or underestimated the extent of the deflation.

Think of an archer. We do not expect all of his arrows to fall on the bullseye. But we expect them to be scattered about the bullseye. If arrow after arrow falls to the left because the wind is blowing across the target, we expect the archer to adjust, to aim a little to the right so that the arrows will again fall in the middle. The concept of rational expectations reinforced skepticism about the power of increases in the money supply to propel the real economy. If most people form rational expectations, then an increase in money might lead to parallel increases in prices and wages—the economy might move from low inflation to high inflation with little change in real economic activity. The argument is symmetrical: a rapid decrease in the rate of growth of the money supply, if fully anticipated, should lead to a reduction in the rate of inflation, with lit-

---

13. Friedman 1968 introduced the idea of a "natural rate of unemployment" in his presidential address to the American Economic Association. Phelps 1967 presented similar arguments. Both articles are well worth reading (Friedman's employs no mathematics). McCallum 1988 and Mankiw 1988 survey recent developments in this field.

14. The literature on rational expectations is immense and controversial. One of the most influential early papers is Lucas 1973. Barro 1977 helps to clarify this approach by distinguishing between anticipated and unanticipated changes in the stock of money. Sargent 1986 and Miller 1994 provide accessible accounts that reflect more recent developments.

tle increase in unemployment. Sargent 1982 tests the theory with several European historical examples, finding that little unemployment resulted when people understood that inflation had been halted. Wicker 1986 provides a counterexample.

Whether a deflation runs smoothly, to look at the matter from a different perspective, depends on the *credibility* of the monetary authority. If the government promises to reduce the growth rate of the money supply, if people believe the government, and if it then follows through on its promise, expectations will prove correct, and the impact on the real economy will be limited.

The idea of everyone anticipating inflation and every wage and price rising in exactly the same proportion is a good starting point for analysis of the effects of inflation on various sectors of the economy. For in this extreme case there would be no real effects at all. Suppose workers' income rose 10 percent and the price of everything they bought rose exactly 10 percent as well. Then what really mattered, their standard of living in terms of their consumption of food, clothing, and shelter, would be exactly the same as before. Inflation can create real effects on the economy, as we have seen in our discussion of the Phillips curve, when one price or group of prices fails to adjust to the inflation.

Relative prices—the price of good X compared with the average price of all goods—are always adjusting in response to supply and demand. But inflation may distort this process. In some inflationary periods wages, for whatever reason, do not rise as fast as prices; there is a *wage lag*. At times the effect on the living standards of the working classes is severe.

The formula for computing the *real wage rate* is

$$(4)\ w = W/P$$

where w is the real wage rate measured in dollars of constant purchasing power. If the *nominal* (market) wage rate (W) is \$3.00 per hour and the price level stands at 2.00 relative to 1959 then we can say that the real wage in 1959 dollars is \$3.00/2 or \$1.50. Looking at the formula, it is easy to see that if W and P rise by the same percentage, the real wage will remain constant. But if P rises while W lags behind, the real wage will fall.

Why wages lag can be hard to explain, particularly if we adopt a rational expectations approach. During the American Civil War, for example, wages did not rise as much as prices. Some historians argue that workers simply delayed in pushing for higher wages (an error that we would not expect them to repeat indefinitely), while others see the lag as a reflection of declining productivity. The difference is important. If wages lagged simply because workers were slow to appreciate the extent of the inflation or because they refrained from pressing their demands for patriotic reasons, employers gained what workers lost. If wages lagged because productivity declined, real profits need not have been higher.[15]

Any contract written in nominal dollars will be affected by inflation. Thus a fixed rate mortgage, because it is a contract to pay fixed amounts of dollars at fixed intervals, is affected by inflation. The general rule here is that *net monetary debtors*—those who owe more dollars to others than others owe to them—tend to gain from an inflation. In nineteenth-century America farmers tended to be net monetary debtors, and their spokesmen argued that inflation would be good for the farmers because it would allow them to repay their debts with dollars worth less in goods and services.

Much depends, again, on whether inflation is anticipated. If inflation comes as a surprise, net monetary debtors benefit. But if lenders have time to adjust interest rates to reflect the expected inflation, any gain for net monetary debtors may prove to be illusory. John B. Clark and Irving Fisher, two of the pioneers in the study of the effects of inflation on interest rates, made precisely this point to those who advocated monetizing silver in the 1890s—introducing silver would not help farmers who generally relied on short-term mortgages, because mortgage interest rates would rise.

In a frictionless world where inflation was fully anticipated, we would expect the interest rate to rise by the amount of inflation. If the rate of interest would be 5 percent in a world of stable prices, we would expect the interest rate to increase to 15 percent in a world in which prices are rising at 10 percent per year. Here we distinguish between the *real rate of interest* and the *nominal* rate. The real rate is the percentage paid measured in goods and services, the nominal rate is the rate measured in money terms. The real rate is computed by subtracting the rate of inflation from the nominal rate. The formula is

$$(5)\ r = n-p$$

where r is the real rate of interest, n is the nominal (observed market) rate, and p is the rate of inflation. In the world of stable prices, the nom-

15. The classic study of wages in the Civil War is Mitchell (1960 [1903], 280–351). Mitchell's view that labor's losses were capital's gain was challenged by Kessel and Alchian 1959. Later Mitchell's view was reinforced by DeCanio and Mokyr 1977. They argue that the real income sacrificed by labor was a major source of funding for the union war effort.

inal (n) rate was 5, and the rate of inflation (p) was 0, so the real rate (r) was 5 percent. When prices were rising at 10 percent per year, n was 15 and p was 10, so the real rate was still 5 percent. What we have described is generally known as the realized or ex post real rate. When the loan is made, what matters is the ex ante real rate, the nominal rate less the expected rate of inflation.

The idea that the real rate should be relatively stable and that the nominal rate should incorporate the rate of inflation, is often referred to as the *Fisher effect*. Fisher's (1896) view was that the real rate of interest would be determined in the long run by the stocks of real resources (labor, land, and capital) and the fundamental time preferences of borrowers and lenders.[16] So changes in the rate of inflation should be matched in the long run by changes in nominal interest rates leaving real rates unchanged.

This argument is elegant and persuasive. But again, the historian's task is not limited to calculating the real rate of interest for an inflationary period and discovering that, far from being stationary, the real interest rate may actually have declined. Indeed, we almost never find stable real rates of interest during inflations and almost always face the problem of explaining the divergence from the simple model. Fisher found that the simplest and crudest applications of his model did not work. And he himself suggested the reason: people changed their expectations of inflation only after a long lag.

We sometimes forget that money itself is an asset that suffers capital depreciation during an inflation. If prices rise 5 percent, then the currency in my wallet has lost 5 percent of its real value. A similar argument applies to my bank deposits if the interest rate they pay does not rise. It is as if the government has levied a tax on money—an analogy that monetary economists frequently find useful. For one thing the notion of an *inflation tax on money* reminds us that the government cannot acquire real resources unless someone in the private sector gives them up. The government may find it less convenient to tax houses, incomes, or imports than to levy an inflation tax on current holdings of cash and deposits by printing new money. But someone must get less if the government gets more.

---

16. Economists use the term "time preference" to describe the relative valuation of present and future consumption on the part of individuals or businesses. We can imagine two individuals with identical income, wealth, and career prospects, of whom one borrows money, displaying high time preference; the other, with lower time preference, saves for the future.

Because inflation is primarily a monetary phenomenon, whether the increase in the money supply comes from a gold discovery, currency debasement, or a new issue of paper money, the ultimate effect is similar. Many historians I know are fond of the notion that an increase in a single strategic price—the price of steel, the price of oil, the wages of autoworkers, the rate of interest, the price of wheat, whatever—could send the whole price level upward. They should be aware, at least, that most economists find this idea doubtful. The reason is that absent any increase in the stock of money, or any increase in the rate of spending, an increase in prices in one sector leaves people with less to spend in other sectors and reduces inflationary pressures in them.[17] The overall price level should not rise. Like all generalizations this one has its limits. A shortage of some crucial raw material at current prices that influenced the whole productive machinery of the economy might reduce real incomes sufficiently to affect the general price level. But to reiterate our warning, the historian should be wary of strategic price arguments when trying to explain movements in the aggregate price level.

INTRODUCTION OF CENTRAL BANKING

After a time certain banks in our kingdom, the Imperial Bank in particular, grew to relatively large size and came to play what some claimed was a dominant role in the banking system.[18] Why this was so is not entirely clear. There may have been *economies of scale* in banking. The cost per dollar of administering loans may have been lower for a large bank than for a small one, because it could spread overhead costs, because more experience in making loans reduced its chance of making bad loans, or for other reasons. Perhaps the Imperial Bank's special relationship with the crown was a factor. It held the crown's deposits, probably paying less than the market interest on them, and was the sole underwriter of government bond issues.

In any case, the dominant position of the Imperial Bank eventually led the market to think of the Imperial as the banks' bank. Rather than

17. The example of Japanese and U.S. response to the oil price shock of 1978 offers a perfect illustration. The shock was greater for Japan, which imports 100 percent of its oil requirements. Firm monetary restraint, however, caused the inflationary consequences of higher oil prices to be smaller in Japan than in the United States. See page 8.

18. The Bank of England has been favored with three brilliant official histories that are models for historians: Clapham 1958, Sayers 1976, which uses new documents to carry Clapham's story forward, and Fforde 1992.

hold all of their reserves in the form of government issued paper money, some banks began to think of their deposits at the Imperial, or notes issued by the Imperial, as another form of reserves. The Imperial, some observers claimed, had become a central bank.[19]

But what is the essence of a central bank? How do we know if and when the Imperial ceased to be simply the largest private bank, and when it became a central bank? One of the classic characteristics of a central bank is its willingness to act as a *lender of last resort*. This term, which is often associated with the English economist Walter Bagehot (1924 [1873]), refers to the idea that a central bank should supply credit to the market during a banking panic.

In a panic, as we noted above, banks tend to clamp down on their lending to protect their reserves. But what makes sense for each bank separately does not make sense in the aggregate; it only aggravates the panic. If one bank, the central bank, boldly supplies credit to the market, the panic might end. Once the mob sees that there is money to be had it may cease to be a mob. In any particular case the motives behind a large private bank's decision to take on the role of lender of last resort may be difficult to untangle. Even at the height of a panic a strong bank might lend to weaker institutions for purely commercial reasons, if the interest rate is high enough. Or the lending bank may simply feel that the risks it takes in the short run will be balanced by larger profits in the long run if it can nip a panic in the bud. But other considerations, say preserving its special relationship with the government, may also play a role.[20]

Doubts about the motives of the Imperial Bank during times of crisis (and the king's incessant search for revenues) led eventually to the nationalization of the Imperial Bank. Like other modern state-owned central banks, it was expected to bail out weak banks in times of crisis and to do what it could to keep the economy on an even keel in normal times.

One tool for influencing the economy is the rate at which a central bank lends to other institutions, generally known as the *rate of discount*. The term derives from the days when loans were made by buying a

---

19. I have been describing the development of central banking much along the lines of what happened in Britain and a number of other countries—as related in Goodhart 1988. In the United States a much more deliberate path was followed; see Timberlake 1978.

20. The Scottish banking system survived for quite a long time without a formal central bank. For the implications of the Scottish experience for monetary theory and policy see White 1984. But it may be true that the Scottish banks were relying on the largest Scottish banks, and ultimately on the Bank of England. For the history of the Scottish system see Checkland 1975.

promise to pay a certain sum at a future date for an amount less than that sum, by "discounting" the promise. A central bank could set the discount rate simply to maximize its profits. But it will normally be influenced more by concerns about the effect of discount rate changes on the economy as a whole. By lowering the discount rate and lending more to other banks, or other institutions, a central bank would encourage an expansion of money and credit—an expansion of economic activity. There might, however, be negative consequences such as inflation, or a capital outflow. We must guard against the view that the discount rate set by the bank completely determines the rate of interest in the economy as a whole.[21] Other variables—the level of economic activity, the rate of inflation, the savings rate, and so on—may well be more important.

The central bank's actions, moreover, may have different consequences in the long run than in the short run. In the short run the central bank might be able to lower interest rates by lowering the discount rate. But in the long run the increase in economic activity set in motion by the bank's expansionary policy might encourage businesses to borrow more and so push the rate of interest back up. If the expansionary policy continued to the point where inflation emerged, lenders might incorporate an inflation premium in interest rates, the Fisher effect. Thus, the long-run effect on the interest rate could turn out to be the exact opposite of the short-run effect.

Perhaps more important than the central bank's discount rate policy is its effect on bank reserves. Suppose that the central bank acquires an asset by simply printing up more notes or by writing a check (and thus increasing its deposit liabilities). The notes that it prints or the deposits that it creates will flow into the ordinary banks as recipients of checks written by the central bank deposit these funds in their own accounts. Reserves of the ordinary banks will rise, providing the basis for an expansion of lending, which increases the money supply (currency plus deposits). A decision by the central bank to sell an asset will lead to the re-

21. Reference to "the" rate of interest is, of course, merely a useful simplification that refers to the central tendency of the vast array of interest rates that exists at any one time. Classification of this array begins with a distinction between term structure and risk structure. The term structure describes the pattern of interest rates on assets with similar risk of default but different terms to maturity; long-term government bonds, for example, generally pay a higher rate than short-term government bonds, but the difference varies through time (Malkiel 1966 provides a good introduction to this concept). The risk structure describes the pattern of rates on assets with similar terms to maturity but different risks of default.

verse: a reduction of the reserves of the banking system, and a contraction of money and credit. Typically, the central bank might buy or sell a government bond in an *open-market operation*. Government bonds are not the only asset a central bank could buy or sell. But they are a frequent choice, for many reasons. For one thing, the purchase of government bonds channels the purchasing power created by the central bank into the hands of the government. Thus, the central bank through its open-market operations exercises a major influence over the total supply of money and credit.

This influence is expressed through the language used to describe the central bank's liabilities. Its notes and deposits (the latter typically held by banks or foreign financial institutions) constitute the *monetary base*, also known as *high-powered money*.

The impact of a central bank's open-market operations can be seen most clearly in wars or other periods when the government has heavy expenditures and typically cannot or will not raise taxes to finance all of its expenditures: it must try to sell bonds. But if it sold all the bonds to the public, bond prices would fall and interest rates would rise dramatically. If this result, like higher taxes, is also unacceptable, the government is likely to ask (require) the central bank to purchase some portion of the newly issued bonds. Adding the demand from the central bank to the demand from the public will keep bond prices up and nominal interest rates down.[22] But as the central bank purchases bonds, it increases bank reserves (the government spends the new money and the recipients deposit it in their banks), the stock of money, and inflation.

In this case the ultimate result is similar to that achieved in days before central banks when governments resorted to simply printing paper money to finance wars, or to still earlier days when our king debased his currency. Indeed, many economists refer to a decision by the central bank to purchase government bonds as *monetizing the debt*.

But in cases less extreme than war it is often hard to determine the impact of a particular operation by the central bank on the economy as a whole. The textbook sequence is that an increase in the monetary base will lead to an increase in the money supply, which in turn leads to an increase in spending and hence in real output or prices. But it is clear from our discussion that the professional literature contains intense contro-

---

22. Bond prices and interest rates are always inversely related. The interest rate is a measure of the income from an investment relative to the amount invested. Since bonds pay out fixed annual sums, the interest rate must fall as the cost of the investment, the price of the bond, rises.

versy about each link in the chain. Can the central bank really alter the stock of money, or are its actions often offset by the behavior of the banks, other financial institutions, or international capital flows? Does an increase in the stock of money really quicken the pace of spending? And does increased spending typically lead to inflation or to increased output?

Just as it is difficult to know how a particular action by the central bank affected the economy, it is also difficult to know why the central bank undertook a particular policy. A complex task awaits historians who would study the actual actions undertaken by the bank, and the various memoranda, diaries, and memoirs that may illuminate the motives of those deciding on the bank's course of action. Among monetary historians the liveliest debate has been over the motives of the Federal Reserve system in the Great Depression—for example, Friedman and Schwartz (1963, 411–419), Wicker 1965, Meltzer 1976, and Epstein and Ferguson 1984. But there are many other episodes for which it would be useful to know the motives of policymakers.

CONCLUSIONS

Most of the ideas presented here seigniorage, debasement, the quantity theory of money, the Fisher effect are subject to intense debate by monetary theorists. The ideas, so simple on first hearing, contain numerous subtleties and paradoxes. Friedman (1969, v) compares monetary theory to a Japanese garden. "It has aesthetic unity born of variety; an apparent simplicity that conceals a sophisticated reality; a surface view that dissolves in ever deeper perspectives." Historians specializing in another area might be tempted to conclude that it is useless to learn any monetary economics. Wouldn't it be better, they might think, to just wait fifty or one hundred years until monetary theorists reach a consensus on the major issues?

Nevertheless, I believe that historians have much to gain merely from becoming familiar with monetary economics. First, once historians master its basic terminology and understand the key quantitative relationships, they can discuss their work with specialists. In my experience there are few monetary economists who cannot be drawn into a discussion of a particular episode by someone who is familiar with the central concerns of the discipline. And discussion is often the catalyst for fruitful exchange of ideas.

Second, by learning about the major controversies in monetary economics, historians can avoid the danger of making confident and simplistic judgments in areas where expert opinion is divided. Such assertions are likely to tarnish their work in the eyes of economists and thus detract, perhaps unfairly, from the attention that might be paid to other parts of the story. A historian who writes that "the central bank raised the discount rate, thus pushing up interest rates and with them the rate of inflation" should at least be aware that what seems simple and obvious to him would seem dead wrong to most economists.

Finally, a modest investment in the study of monetary economics, of the type provided here, can give historians a sense of where best their professional skills can be put to use. The apocryphal story we have spun provides a clear example. Economists have much to say about the effects of monetary change within one set of institutional arrangements. They have much less to say about why and when one set of arrangements is replaced by another. Here the economist has much to learn from the historian.

International Economics
and the Historian

PETER H. LINDERT

The international side of economics often looks like unpromising reading for the historian. Jargon, diagrams, and math abound, obscuring any
clear view of issues worth debating. It need not be so. International economics is no more imposing a discipline than the rest of economics. In
fact, it offers a particular advantage to those historians who are excited
by, and versed in, international history. They have the comparative perspective, the sense of political forces, and the long view that elude many
international economists imprisoned by offer curves and sterile theorems.
The opportunity to combine international economics and history is still
rarely tapped by young scholars at the threshold of specialization. For
those who venture to merge the fields, a wide audience is guaranteed by
the recurring storms and crises in international economic history.

The special advantage awaiting historians willing to work with international economics is one of the three keynotes of this chapter. The
second is also optimistic: of the various tools available in international
economics, the most powerful ones are the simplest to grasp. The third
keynote is that the field contains common pitfalls, ones historians can
avoid with a mixture of common sense, facts, and the simple tools at
hand. These notes guide the following survey of some basic issues in international economic history.

THE IMPACT OF TRADE ON GROWTH

The economic historiography of every country raises the question of how
foreign trade has affected the growth of national income. The question

follows naturally from our interest in the effects of national sovereignty, or lack of it, on national well-being. How dependent were nations on their foreign trade? Was exporting specialty goods in exchange for other products the "engine" of economic growth? Or did it subvert growth, as asserted by so many partisans of emerging or threatened countries, from import-threatened mercantilists through Friedrich List and the *dependencia* school of Latin American history to today's American protectionists? Did their inability to prevent trade stunt the growth of colonial economies?

The impact of foreign trade is a particularly live issue among early modernists and historians of less developed countries, for good historical reasons.[1] Trade occupies a larger share of the least developed economies, just as it was larger in colonial America than in the United States today. Trade is also a more popular object for taxation in these settings, since an underdeveloped state apparatus in a semiliterate nation could more easily run customhouses at ports and borders than it could generate the same revenue with less enforceable taxes on overall income, sales, or wealth. Foreign trade has also been associated with socially disruptive processes, making observers wonder whether its economic benefits to some were worth its social side effects.

Another source of the popularity of trade-related issues for less developed countries and for the distant past is the uneven pattern of data availability. For a new nation, or a newly developing nation, or the early history of now developed nations, data on exports and imports are among the few decent time series available. Typically, the historian shopping for quantitative data from the early stages of a nation's modern economic growth has time series on exports, imports, population, prices, government budgets, and little else. Small wonder that so much early modern, or third-world, economic historiography ponders the economic impact of foreign trade—and of population, prices, and government budgets. Our hypotheses naturally take shape around the data available.[2]

---

1. There is not sufficient space to cite the literature on trade's early impact in dozens of countries. For clear summaries of the issue in modern British and American history, see the chapters on foreign trade in Floud and McCloskey 1981 (by Thomas in vol. 1 and by McCloskey and Harley in vol. 2) and Davis et al. 1971 (chap. 14). There is a richer tradition of charting the impact of foreign trade in Latin American history. For strong national case studies, see Diaz-Alejandro 1970 on Argentina and Thorp and Betram 1978 on Peru. Influential presentations of dependency theories doubting the benefits of trade for Latin America include Frank 1969; Furtado 1976; and Cardoso and Faletto 1979.

2. An illustration of the shaping of hypotheses to data in a third-world setting is the stimulating analysis of Birnberg and Resnick 1975 on colonial economies, which assigns

TRADE RELATIVE TO WHAT?

Curiosity about the past impact of trade on a nation's overall national income tends to prompt three different kinds of question: what was the overall effect of trade? and what effects did shifts in trade conditions have on the nation? And finally what effect did changes in trade policies have on national income?

Many inquiries start with the first question. This is unfortunate, because asking about the effects of trade is usually too vague. Trade relative to what? The obvious answer is relative to no trade, a hypothetical history in which the nation or colony did not trade at all. But for the actually trading majority of nations, this counterfactual conditional is seldom of great interest. Very little of our historical curiosity relates to comparisons of autarky with trade. The relative autarky of Maoist China and the Soviet Union is of considerable interest, but both countries have since moved away from autarky themselves into a managed intermediate level of foreign trade, with little debate about the merits of trading at all.

History has sometimes moved in the other direction, however, with the sudden opening of trade in countries that had been virtually sealed off. Data permitting, the net effect on national income could be quantified through the use of conventional tools of economic analysis. In fact, such work has already been done in a case where foreign trade was first opened up. A sound and readable study by J. Richard Huber 1971 made frugal use of trade and price figures to quantify the likely effect on Japan of her being forced to open trade after 1858. All he needed were figures on Japan's export and import volumes soon after trade was opened plus data on the domestic Japanese prices of export goods and import goods both before and after the opening of trade (1846–1855 versus 1871–1879).

Opening trade allowed Japanese merchants to sell exports like silk and tea at a much higher price, relative to the prices of cotton, iron, sugar, and other importable goods, than they could before the opening of overseas trade. The ratio of export prices to import prices, Japan's terms of trade, rose 3.5-fold. The net gain to the merchants and to Japan started

---

major roles to trade, government budgets, and foreign government pressure. To find the available aggregate time series on trade, population, prices and government budgets, along with some other macroeconomic series, see the volumes of historical statistics (Britain, Europe since 1750, Americas and Australasia, Asia and Africa) edited by Brian Mitchell and his collaborators for the Cambridge University Press (1982, 1988, 1992, 1993). Be sure, however, to go beyond these handy series to their sources to find the necessary caveats about the data.

out equaling the price gap between the foreign and domestic prices of exports. As trade expanded, the net gain on each extra unit of exports or imports dropped toward zero. It took lower and lower prices of cotton and other imports to interest extra buyers, and higher and higher prices for Japanese silk to evoke further production at rising costs. The net gain to Japan from the whole process was therefore a fraction of the large initial price gaps times the volume of exports (or of imports) generated by the opening of trade.[3] We shall see an exact diagrammatic representation of this net national gain in a Chinese example. Measures of the price effects of opening trade (Huber 1971) and the net national gains caused by those price changes (see 218–226) could also be derived, data permitting, for some other countries around the opening of their foreign trade: Southeast Asia, Polynesia, sub-Saharan Africa, pre-Columbian America, and Eastern Europe since 1989.

THE EFFECT OF SHIFTING TRADE WINDS

Let us begin with our second question, the one on conditions of trade: what difference did shifts in the willingness of foreigners to trade with this country make to the growth of its national product?

A light-footed historian knows better than to trudge straight into the full causal complexity of such an issue. Before grappling with the total explanation of event B (national economic growth), and the quantitative role of A (shift of foreign trade currents) in causing B, the historian wisely asks first, did A happen? and did B happen? If one or the other didn't happen, documenting the nonevent takes logical precedence over any difficult causal accounting. Documenting an absence is also a fine way to short-circuit a bad debate.[4]

The first step in debating what effect an imagined shift of foreign will-

3. At this point, in the final calculation of the percentage of national income gain to Japan, Huber departs from the kind of calculation referred to in the present text. Instead of the conventional triangular measure of trade gains, Huber made a rough argument that national income, which he proxied by an urban real-wage rate, might have gone up by 65 percent, and probably less. Probably less indeed, since the opening of trade favored Japanese producers of labor-intensive products like silk, tea, and rice, probably raising wage rates faster than average incomes throughout Japan.

4. An excellent recent example of debate preemption by disproving the premised event is one not relating to foreign trade. In 1962 Habakkuk's famous book set off two decades of debate over why American industry, and the whole American economy, was more mechanized and capital-intensive than Britain's. The American mechanization and capital-intensity became Event B, with scholars debating just how Event A, America's land abundance, could have shaped B. After a dozen fine articles with alternative theories, it

ingness to trade might have is to decide whether there were any great shifts in foreign willingness to buy this country's exports or to supply its imports. The basic economics of demand and supply of a commodity gives a simple test:

if we can see that from one period to another:	we can infer that:
price rose and quantity rose,	demand rose for any given price
price rose and quantity fell,	supply fell for any given price
price fell and quantity rose,	supply rose for any given price
price fell and quantity fell,	demand fell for any given price[5]

To decide whether demand or supply shifted, gather data on the movements in quantities and relative prices, and apply these rules of thumb. The procedure is useful for analyzing either export markets or import markets, as long as they are as competitive in the later period as they were earlier.

A good example of how such simple rules of thumb can prevent bad hypotheses is their use by Deane and Cole (1967, 85) in their treatment of British growth in the eighteenth century. Previous scholars had occasionally mused that a rise in foreign demand for Britain's manufactures might have played a crucial role in triggering the acceleration of growth in the Industrial Revolution era. Deane and Cole noted, however, that the decades of rapidly rising export quantities were also decades in which the relative price of Britain's exports were falling fastest. Given the fall in relative price along with the rise in volumes, they reasoned, it was hard to see how a rise in foreign demand (for any given price) could have been the dominant shift in Britain's export markets. More likely the prime shift was a dramatic rise in productivity within the textile sector and other export lines of the British economy. Thus Deane and Cole finessed the need to come up with a quantitative account of the role of rising foreign demand.[6]

---

fell to Alex Field 1983 to show that American production was *less* capital-intensive and mechanized than British (B didn't happen), and to James and Skinner (1985, 517) to note that Habakkuk had not really asserted otherwise!

5. Other variants are implied for cases when either price or quantity did not change significantly. For example, if we see that price stayed the same while quantity fell, as in some crises, we infer that both demand and supply must have fallen for any given price (unless we believe that either demand or supply was infinitely "elastic" without shifting).

6. Further arguments against a large role for foreign demand in Britain's Industrial Revolution are given in Mokyr 1977 and in Floud and McCloskey 1981 (vol. 1, chap. 5, by Thomas).

THE TERMS OF TRADE

In interpretations of the role of trade in economic growth, a key measure is one noted above as the "relative price of exports," alias the "terms of trade." The terms of trade are the ratio of export prices over import prices, where each price measure is an index comparing prices in the year in question to those in a base year. We construct both the export-price index and the import-price index from the prices of as many traded goods and services as possible, using the quantities traded in the base period as weights.[7] The idea of dividing export prices by import prices is to express the price of a unit of exports in terms of a unit of imports, the goods and services that exports are used to buy sooner or later. Dividing the one by the other has the virtue of eliminating any deceiving effects of general inflation, since if all prices are rising together the ratio will be unaffected.

The terms of trade are a key exhibit in any history of the role of foreign trade. They are the appropriate measure of prices in the rules of thumb given above. And for most countries they can be measured farther back in history than most other economic variables. Developing better indices of the terms of trade for more countries and for earlier eras remains high on the research agenda in international economic history.

At least three pitfalls await the user of terms-of-trade measures, however. First, remember not to use them as solitary measures of how well trade currents are treating a country. As in the rules of thumb above, we cannot just look at whether prices (the terms of trade) rose or fell and then decide whether it was foreign or domestic conditions that were changing faster. Instead, we must weigh both price changes and quantity changes. Scholars have often made the mistake of arguing that a country was being harmed because its terms of trade were declining (export prices falling relative to import prices). But a decline in the terms of trade can be a healthy reflection of improved ability to produce and export—a rise in export *supply*—just as in the British Industrial Revolution. To be sure, it would have been better for the country if foreign demand bought up all of its burgeoning export supply at the same price instead of letting the price drop, but the moving force was the shift in supply, not a new limitation on demand.

A second pitfall is the natural belief that one country's terms of trade

---

7. For a further introduction to how terms of trade are calculated and how they have changed for primary products since 1900, see Lindert 1991b, 256–262.

are the mirror image of the terms of trade faced by the country's trading partners. In the case of nineteenth-century Britain, for example, the assumption would be that Britain's export prices/import prices moved in direct proportion to prices of the rest of the world's imports from Britain/exports to Britain. So when finding that Britain's terms of trade rose by 30 percent from 1860 to 1900 (McCloskey and Harley, in Floud and McCloskey, 2:55, citing Imlah), an observer might assume that Britain's trading partners—North America, for example—had their terms of trade drop 30 percent on the average. Not so. In fact the United States, Canada, and other countries trading with Britain also had their terms of trade rise over the same forty years. How could that be? Each country's terms of trade are measured at that country's ports and borders. Between 1860 and 1900, as Douglass North and others have often pointed out, the cost of transportation fell greatly. In the case of wheat, for example, the American farmers got higher prices at their farm gates while the British importers got lower prices in Liverpool. Similarly for other goods and services flowing in both directions. (And similarly within countries, thanks to reduction in the domestic freight costs.)

Finally, we must be wary of any facile generalizations about long-term trends in the terms of trade for any class of goods. In particular, we must avoid frequent generalizations about the relative prices of primary products (agricultural and extractive products). The long historical record is nuanced, and the available measures need great care (again, see Lindert 1991b, 256–262).

HISTORICAL DEBATES ABOUT
THE GROWTH EFFECTS OF TRADE POLICIES

Perhaps the most common variant on the issue of how trade affects a nation's growth, however, makes a different comparison: what difference would it make to have policies restricting trade? The debate usually revolves around restrictions on imports, ones that reduce imports without eliminating them altogether. The free-trade orthodoxy of Adam Smith and others has been challenged repeatedly, by scholars and policymakers alike. The case for protection against imports is usually traced from Alexander Hamilton and Friedrich List, though its roots extend much further into the past.

The issue can be handled well enough with conventional demand-and-supply analysis, making suitable adaptations for cases where the standard assumption of a competitive market is inappropriate. This particular policy issue is well mapped by international economists, though there is still an unsettled research frontier in this as in most areas. The basic analytics for quantifying the effects of trade-restricting policies can be followed in examples based on Chinese economic history. Here, however, we can conveniently summarize where the existing literature draws the border between the pros and cons of import barriers:

1.   An import barrier lowers world well-being. The exceptions here are few and strained and are a subset of cases imagined under (4c) below.

2.   In most real-world cases, an import barrier lowers the well-being of the nation imposing it, as well as the well-being of foreigners.

3.   As a general rule, whatever social goal an import barrier can achieve, some other policy can achieve better. Most cases of import barriers reflect poor institutional imagination or a particular political juncture preventing an economically superior way of achieving a particular social goal.

4.   There are three kinds of exceptions to the rule in favor of free trade (and against an import barrier):

4a.   The national optimal tariff: when a nation can affect the world prices at which it trades with foreigners, it can gain from policies restricting trade. There are limits to its ability to manipulate world prices, however. Even a dominant economy like the United States between the 1920s and the 1960s had only limited power over world prices. And the national optimal trade barrier, being just an exploitation of market power, could not raise world income.

4b.   There are a host of what the economist calls "second-best" arguments for a trade barrier. When other incurable distortions exist in an economy, restricting imports *may* be a better remedy than doing nothing.

4c.   In a narrow range of cases with distortions specific to international trade itself, imposing a trade barrier can be better than any other policy, and not just better than doing nothing. The most common case is the infant-government case, in which a weak state apparatus must tax foreign trade because it has no other way to generate revenues for essential public services.

5.   A trade barrier absolutely *helps* groups whose incomes are closely tied to producing import substitutes, even when the tariff is likely to lower national income.

These rules, elaborated elsewhere (Lindert 1991b, chaps. 6–8, 12), represent a surprising consensus—surprising, to the extent that *any* clear consensus among economists is surprising. They are subject to two major caveats, however. First, their facile assertions about national and world well-being contain value judgments about opposing material interests that we must weigh. The implicit value judgment is "one dollar, one vote"—or, for a broader historical reference, "one loaf of bread, one vote." Any material stake weighs the same as any other, regardless of who the gainers and losers are. This judgment is sweeping, of course. It sweeps the issue of the desirability of the distribution of those gains and losses into the discussion below.

Second, the now-codified consensus view of the pros and cons of policies restricting trade is not particularly empirical. It makes good sense, but it is not based on any convincing empirical test from history. Testing is hard in this area, and for now the economists' consensus on trade policy remains a vulnerable target for the well-trained historian. The closest thing to supporting evidence comes from comparative studies of third-world economies in the 1970s (Lindert 1991b, 267–272).

THE IMPACT OF TRADE ON THE INCOME DISTRIBUTION

The other issue about the effects of trade in history is concerned not with its impact on the growth of overall national income but with its effects on how that income is distributed within a nation. The distributional consequences turn out to be strong.

As we grow more familiar with economics, with its tendency to describe market compromises, we might expect that national gains from trade are distributed across the whole economy, with only minor changes in the distribution of income among different sectors or different social strata. No such tale is told here. Theory makes a very different prediction, and the facts remain to be gathered. The established theory of international trade predicts that, under a broad range of plausible conditions, the growth of foreign trade, or any other shift in trade currents, has strong effects on the distribution of income within a country.

The most applicable parts of established trade theory are, fortunately, very simple. The economics of trade and the income distribution sounds one of the keynotes of this chapter, one that is muffled all too well by the economist's diagrams and equations: The practical historian can reap the main fruits of economic theory without making unrealistic assumptions. We survey the applicable parts of trade theory in three stages.

STAGE ONE: INITIAL DISEQUILIBRIUM

When foreign trade in a new good first opens up, a large share of the gains is likely to go to the traders themselves, with the remainder being split between their customers and their suppliers. This is true whether the new good in question is an import or an export good (implicitly, it is always the trading of one for the other, as elaborated below). The traders gain by buying cheap and selling dear, at a price differential more than wide enough to cover their costs of dealing in this good. Their net gains continue as long as it takes for market competition to bid down the price differential to the marginal costs of trading.

To illustrate, we take an example from Chinese economic history in the late nineteenth century. A hypothetical case (Figure 12) sets out the traders' revenues and the likely gains to their customers and suppliers, approximating the early phase of China's importing of cotton yarn, as of 1870.[8] The issue is, who gained and who lost from the penetration of the China market by foreign cotton yarn after the mid-nineteenth century? Though the diagram imposes the economist's traditional curves of demand and supply, historians need not follow the curves very far to establish the distribution of gains and losses among the relevant groups.

The gains to the traders themselves are easy to estimate. All we need to know is the volume of trade and the prices at which the traders buy and sell. In the example here, we observe that the traders acquired 70,000 piculs of foreign cotton yarn delivered at Canton and other treaty ports at a cost of 30 taels per picul and sold them at an average price of 40 taels per picul. Their markup revenue of 700,000 taels, the shaded area in Figure 12, is an upper-bound estimate of their gain. It would exactly equal their net gain if we knew that the price of 30 taels covered all their costs on these particular trades. If they had additional costs (including opportunity costs of the use of their time and money), these would be subtracted from the 700,000 taels. In judging the historical meaning of the gain of 700,000 taels or less, we naturally want to know the identities of the traders. Historical data should allow us to divide the overall gain among foreign merchants, compradors, and other traders.

---

8. I avoid the special case of opium imports, the adverse effects of which presumably extended beyond those on the users themselves.

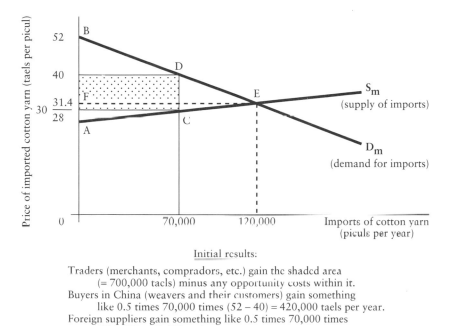

Traders (merchants, compradors, etc.) gain the shaded area
   (= 700,000 taels) minus any opportunity costs within it.
Buyers in China (weavers and their customers) gain something
   like 0.5 times 70,000 times (52 – 40) = 420,000 taels per year.
Foreign suppliers gain something like 0.5 times 70,000 times
   (30 – 28) = 70,000 taels per year.

FIGURE 12.   Initial disequilibrium effects of the opening of trade: China's cotton
yarn imports as of 1870.

How much did the Chinese customers and the foreign suppliers gain?
All we need to add are estimates of the prices that would have prevailed
if trade had not opened. Suppose we judge from historical data that without trade in 1870 the domestic price of fine-count cotton yarn would have
been 52 taels per picul and the foreign price (delivered at Canton, say)
would have been 28 taels per picul. We might know this from the ratio
of domestic to foreign prices just before trade opened, or from the 1870
domestic price in a market unreached by competition with foreign yarn
and the likely small effect of trade with China on the foreign price. Note
that I pick prices that reflect a presumed reality of China's trade with the
outside world: as a small market whose imports never reached 3 percent
of world trade (Dernberger in Perkins 1975b, 27), China's willingness
to trade had no great effect on the world-market prices of goods.

The gains for China's buyers of imported cotton yarn—her weavers
and the customers they served—were tied to the drop in price from 52
to 40 taels per picul, and to the annual volume they chose to buy (70,000
piculs). Their gains must have been greater than zero but less than
840,000 taels (70,000 times the full drop of 12 taels per picul). To see

why, and to see the most likely gain, consider the dual meaning of the demand curve in Figure 12.

Its direct behavioral meaning, of course, shows the different amounts that somebody in China would be willing to buy at different domestic prices of yarn. It also has a practical welfare meaning, however. The demand curve ranks purchases by the maximum amount that somebody in China would willingly pay for that yarn, given incomes and tastes. Starting with no imported yarn at point B, the most somebody was willing to pay for the first picul of foreign yarn was the observed (or estimated) no-trade price of 52 taels for yarn of that quality.[9] Each extra unit of imports would be worth progressively less to marginal buyers, because the market price sorts people out by their willingness to pay (based on their tastes and ability to pay). The observed trade of 70,000 piculs at a market price of 40 taels means that the traders found those buyers willing to pay amounts descending from 52 taels down to 40 taels. The value of the imported cotton yarn to its buyers is the area under the demand curve from point B down to point D. But the buyers paid only 40 taels per picul to the traders.[10] They therefore experienced a net gain (a "consumer surplus") equal to the triangular area to the left of BD, or $0.5 \times 70{,}000 \times 12 = 420{,}000$ taels.[11] Here is a measure of net gain that can be usefully compared with the traders' gains, or with likely national product, or with other magnitudes.

Similar reasoning could be applied to the gains accruing to the foreign suppliers of the China traders. Presumably their gains were small, since without the chance to sell to traders at China ports, they could have sold elsewhere (e.g., in Japan) at similar prices. If they sold elsewhere at the resource equivalent of 28 taels, the value of their gain from selling to China traders (their producer surplus net of costs to any foreign competing buyers) would work out to something like $0.5 \times 70{,}000 \times (30 - 28) =$ only 70,000 taels, a smaller figure than the gain to buyers simply

9. The value of the first imported unit could conceivably be below 52, but only in the unrealistic case of a perfectly vertical demand curve at the very edge of opening imports.

10. If the traders completely exploited maximum market power over individual buyers and exacted discriminatory prices descending from 52 taels down to 40, they would capture all of the buyers' gains described here. If the existence of such rare extra market power were documented, what are described as buyers' gains would have to be added to the 700,000 of traders' gains described above.

11. The use of a straight-line demand curve might or might not be historically justified. Whatever curvature we deem most realistic between no trade and trade at B, it would imply a net gain between zero and 840,000 taels. I use the midpoint estimate for illustration here.

because the foreign sellers experienced less change in price from the same trade. These welfare effects follow from the observed prices and quantities and the nature of market exchange, with little in the way of extra theoretical assumptions.

We should next reflect on the resource meaning of the taels. What real resources do they represent? Such reflection allows us to deal with three other troublesome questions that will arise sooner or later: if the taels are really silver money, what about the monetary implications of the extra imports? What about the fact that China's overall trade seldom balanced? And are there other gains to consider on China's exports?

In expressing import prices and values in the monetary unit, the trade economist usually means that they are the other real goods and services given up in exchange for the imported good. Taels here are not silver but the bundle of exports (net of other imports). We should ask whether this simplification does not oversimplify and miss serious macroeconomic side effects of international trade. It may, though in fewer cases than commonly feared. The mere fact that commodity trade does not balance, as it usually did not under the Ch'ing dynasty, does not invalidate the implicit view that the imports were balanced by exports of other goods and services. Things not usually called exports weigh into the balance of payments in a similar offsetting fashion. For example, China's capital imports, which were often heavy until the 1930s, represent an export of sorts: China was paying for her apparent import surplus by exporting paper—the promise to repay—as a real resource cost to be borne at repayment time (except to the extent that China defaulted on her foreign borrowings in the 1930s). When she paid debt service to foreign creditors, that too was a net resource flow in goods and services, most directly in the form of payment for the lending services received. The trade models are not far off the mark by assuming that the value of imports is balanced by a net export outflow, even when the data seem to show a trade deficit or surplus.

The trade economist's mirror-image view of imports and exports carries another implication. Once the buyers' gains have been calculated on the whole range of China's imports, it is not necessary to make a separate calculation of the gains of Chinese sellers on exports. They are already implicit in the net import gains like the 420,000 taels on cotton yarn, which refer to the purchase of imports with resources that eventually become net exports. The export gain (producer-surplus gain) on exports of silk, tea, soybeans, and other exports is already implicit in the gains from buying imports. Alternatively, gains from importing cotton yarn, machinery, and other goods and services would be implicit in an exercise measuring China's gains from all exports.

STAGE TWO: TRADE EQUILIBRIUM

With time and competition, trade would tend to expand further than the disequilibrium import volume illustrated in Figure 12. If the traders are not sheltered from competition by government or other forces, their trading margin will be squeezed. The economist portrays the result as a tendency toward point E in Figure 12. Had trade competition been in full bloom in 1870, one would expect results like those at E, with the price paid by buyers bid down to something just above 30 taels—say the 31.4 taels implied by the straight-line demand and supply curves D_m and S_m. At this lower price they would be willing and able to buy 120,000 piculs a year. The price received by the merchants' foreign suppliers, plus the competitive marginal cost of the merchants' own operations, would rise slightly, to that 31.4 taels at E.

The gains and losses to buyers and sellers could be quantified with the same consumer-surplus and producer-surplus measures as before. Buyers would gain the full area BEF, or $(0.5) \times (120,000) \times (52-31.4) = 1,236,000$ taels a year. Foreign sellers would gain area $AEF = (0.5) \times (120,000) \times (31.4-28) = 204,000$ taels a year. Under this competitive extreme, the traders themselves might gain nothing.

Is the cotton yarn example too optimistic in implying that Ch'ing China got more gains than the foreigners from her trade in the late nineteenth century? No, the example correctly picks up a welfare implication of the fact that China was a "small country" in the economic sense. The very fact that expanding trade affected her prices more than foreign prices means that the opportunity to trade at a new set of prices made more difference to the Chinese residents than to others. As we have seen, Huber 1971 got the same result for the entry of tiny Japan into the world market after the arrival of Perry's ships. In general, the gains from trade are split in direct proportion to the absolute price changes that trade brings to the respective sides. The ratio of China's gains to foreign gains, or $(1,236,000/204,000) = 6.06$ equals the ratio of the price movements caused by expanding trade: $(52-31.4)/(31.4-28) = 6.06$ again.

It may seem counterintuitive that the side that has its economy more "disrupted" with a price change gets the greater net gain. There are indeed disruptive distributional consequences to be explored further, and one should remember that in many cases the "Chinese" buyers gaining from trade were foreign merchants or Japanese subsidiaries resident in China. But each side's gains from trade are undeniably tied to the opportunities that come with changing prices.

The basic theorem that the gains from trade are proportional to price changes carries an important implication for the historical literature on the integration of regional markets within a country. The analysis is in fact the same: the regions that experience the greater price change, the greater price disruption, are the ones that make the greater net gain. In the case of Ch'ing China, the spread of the trade network caused bigger changes in price in remote areas than in the coastal port cities. The economist infers that the gains from interregional market integration in China accrued mainly to the hinterland regions and not to the major coastal cities. This follows from the fact that prices in the major coastal cities were already fixed into proportion with world market prices outside China. For example, Brandt's study of market integration (1985) shows that Shanghai rice prices moved largely in sympathy with those in the larger British-sphere markets of Southeast Asia. Therefore, the observed convergence of rice prices within the Yangtze provinces must have brought more gains from trade expansion to the less developed hinterland than to Shanghai. The growing literature on market integration within China should incorporate this egalitarian implication of the spread of market contacts.

STAGE THREE:
THE WHOLE INCOME DISTRIBUTION IS AFFECTED

So far, our trade example has confined itself to the division of gains between buyers and sellers of a particular product. This is a bit removed from the usual interest in the division between social economic groups within each region. We have already been able to say that the initial gains from trade accrue to China's merchants, presumably an affluent (and partly foreign) group. We have also noted that the ultimate division of gains from interregional trade is likely to favor somebody in the lower-income hinterland more than parties in the richer coastal cities. But who within each region gains most, and does anybody lose?

The effects of trade on the intraregional distributions of income vary between the shorter and longer runs. In the short run, before relative "factor" prices (wages, rents, profits, interest) are affected by movements between sectors, anybody deriving income mainly from producing the import-competing (i.e., import-threatened) goods is hurt by general trade expansion, and anybody deriving income mainly from producing exportable goods is helped. Later on, when the import-competing sectors have contracted their hirings of factors and the exporting sectors have expanded their hirings, things work out differently. The final distributional effects will depend on which sectors use which factors most intensively. A point to be stressed, though, is that as long as there is a domestic sector displaced by trade, *somebody* loses from trade. The trade theorist has little patience for the extravagant claim of extreme free traders that "everybody" gains from freer trade. That cannot be true unless the trade brings only imports that do not compete with domestic sellers and exports that do not bid away resources from domestic buyers—a rare case indeed.

To follow the distributional effects of trade more closely, we could return to our example of cotton yarn imports around 1870. In that case, we would find that the group most hurt in the short run by the importing of foreign yarn were the domestic spinners, both capitalists and workers, while the rest of society gained enough more to make the net national[12] gain equal to the consumer-surplus gain on imports shown above. Later on, with the migration of labor and capital out of cotton spinning and into the expanding sectors (e.g., tea, cotton, silk), the pattern would depend on the strength of association of different factor groups (e.g., unskilled labor) with the cotton spinning sector versus other sectors. Let us leave this example, however, because it happens to be one with undramatic implications for the overall distribution of income between rich and poor in China. In the long run, the relative demands for unskilled labor and for property would not be much affected by a displacement of yarn production with extra tea, cotton, and silk production, since both sets of goods had about the same average labor intensity. The kinds of workers displaced from spinning (especially women and children) could also find employment in the expanding export sectors. In all likelihood, the rise of foreign trade late in the Ch'ing dynasty (1644–1911) had relatively mild effects on the overall distribution of income once the initial merchant gains were bid away. Let us turn to the

---

12. This phrase implies that every tael of gain or loss is worth the same to the nation regardless of who within China captures it. Alternatively, we could insist on weighing the interests of different groups less equally (Sen 1980). Even with such unequal weighing of economic stakes, the same analysis applies, though it gives a different view of net national gains or losses.

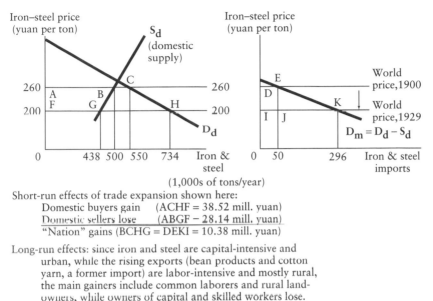

Short-run effects of trade expansion shown here:
  Domestic buyers gain   (ACHF = 38.52 mill. yuan)
  Domestic sellers lose   (ABGF = 28.14 mill. yuan)
  "Nation" gains (BCHG = DEKI = 10.38 mill. yuan)

Long-run effects: since iron and steel are capital-intensive and
  urban, while the rising exports (bean products and cotton
  yarn, a former import) are labor-intensive and mostly rural,
  the main gainers include common laborers and rural landowners, while owners of capital and skilled workers lose.

FIGURE 13.   Distributional effects of iron and steel imports into China,
1900–1929.

probably stronger implications of expanding trade in the Republican era
(1912–1949).

Between the turn of the century and the 1930s, China's industrial trade
pattern was transformed. Cotton products, especially yarn, switched
from being China's largest net import item to being a net export. The
new top import was the broad category of machinery and metals. Meanwhile, bean products rose as a share of exports, while silks and tea
declined (Yeh 1979, 116).

The short-run distributional effects of this new pattern of trade expansion can be discussed most conveniently with the help of a semi-
hypothetical example of iron and steel imports, Figure 13. The world
price of iron and steel products (here viewed as a single product) fell relative to the prices of China's exports, let us say, from 260 to 200 yuan
per ton between 1900 and 1925–29. To simplify, we also assume that actions in China had no effect on the world price, making the world's supply curve to China perfectly horizontal.[13] The lower price brought gains

13. This assumption is not necessary to any major point here. If it seems more realistic to posit that China could have some effect on the world price, the same diagram can
be given the extra complication of a sloped foreign-supply curve, like that in Figure 12.

to firms using ferrous metals, and to their employees and customers, while bringing losses to China's makers of iron and steel.[14] Their gains and losses are quantified in the caption to Figure 13, following the logic of consumer and producer surplus illustrated for cotton yarn imports above. If we give any yuan of gain or loss the same weight regardless of who experienced it, then China as a whole gained from the cheaper foreign supply of iron and steel.

Over the long run, as workers, capital and materials are withdrawn from the ferrous-metals sector and as the exports use more of the same inputs in different proportions, input prices will adjust. The adjustment is necessary because the rising and declining sectors do not use inputs in the same proportions. By the 1920s, China's rising exports, noted in Figure 13, caused generally intensive use of unskilled labor and, to a lesser extent, rural land. In contrast the iron and steel sector released more capital and skilled labor relative to land or common labor. The unskilled wage rate would therefore be bid up, other things equal, in all sectors of the economy (even iron and steel) in the long run. The rate of return on capital, and the wage rates of urban skilled workers, would be bid down, other things equal. The comparative advantage of Republican China in world trade was such that the expansion of foreign trade in the Republican era probably had an egalitarian effect on the distribution of income within China.

At this point in the description of the effects of trade expansion on the distribution of rewards, the economic theorist tends to wade off into incoherence, leaving the practical historian with a host of legitimate doubts. The theorist often heaps on special assumptions that allow a tractable solution for the effects of changes in foreign trade conditions on every factor reward in a simplified world of perfect competition, full employment, and the like, as in the classic Stolper-Samuelson theorem.[15] This is a shame. The extra assumptions are absolutely unnecessary. The historian's main suspicions can be addressed without them.

The historian has good reasons to doubt that changes in world mar-

14. To simplify further, I assume that the demand and supply curves show what quantities would have been demanded and supplied in 1929 if only the world price had changed. Other forces affecting China's production and consumption of iron and steel between 1900 and 1929 would have to be factored out to yield the present diagram. Such factoring would have to be done in rough and ready fashion, given the paucity of data for this sector of the Chinese economy. For more on the realities of the iron and steel sector in Republican China, see Rawski 1975. For more on the theory of trade's impact on the distribution of income, see Lindert 1991b, chap. 4.

15. On Stolper-Samuelson and related theorems, see Lindert 1986, chap. 4 and app. C.

ket conditions would have any dramatic effect on relative rewards within China. These reasons could best be summarized as follows[16]

> A *hunch*: Surely changing foreign trade conditions could not have had any great effect on such relative rewards as local wage, interest, rent, and profit rates. Both exports and imports remained below 7 percent of China's gross domestic product. Besides, China's economy was so diverse and so far from being integrated that rewards from trade in the major coastal ports could not have diffused very far into the hinterland. Granted, trade probably affected relative commodity prices at the ports, but surely the percentage effects on, say, average unskilled wage rates in agriculture or the average rate of profit were smaller, and probably negligible. Trade expansion has little to do with the income distribution.

This hunch is incorrect, by virtue of basic accounting that requires no strained assumptions about perfect competition, full employment, and the like. The first step toward a clearer perspective is to translate the phrases "trade" or "changing foreign trade conditions" into a truly exogenous shift, a causal force. China's terms of trade—the ratio of her export prices to her import prices—were virtually exogenous, dictated on world markets with China in the small-country price-taking role. From World War I until the 1930s, as it happened, China's terms of trade "improved," rising 28 percent from 1913 to 1932–36 after little trend between 1870 and 1913 (Mah 1979, 286–287).

A rise in the terms of trade by, say, 28 percent must have bid up some group's wage rate or profit rate or other earnings rate by more than 28 percent, while absolutely cutting some other group's ability to purchase either exports or imports. Such a strong effect on the distribution of incomes is what the theorist Ronald W. Jones calls the "magnification effect," meaning that the percentage effect of the ratio of the first group's income to the second group's income must be a magnification of the percentage price shift that caused it, contrary to the historian's hunch.

The magnification effect says that there must be two extreme distributional results of a 28 percent rise in the nation's terms of trade:

a.   Some group's reward must be rising faster than the relative price of exports—in fact even faster than the fastest-rising export price for an individual good or service.

---

16. Note that economists as well as historians have such hunches. Thus Perkins writes that "the net impact of all foreign trade on Chinese agriculture" prior to 1910 "was not great . . . whatever its direction" (1969, 133); Rawski suggests that the small scale of China's international trade prior to World War II "makes it difficult to avoid the view that key economic forces originate in the domestic rather than the international sphere" (1989, 4).

b.   At the other extreme, some group's reward must be falling relative to the price of the import item that experiences the largest price decline.

So merely changing the terms of trade must leave some group absolutely less able to buy any traded product, while raising others' rewards
faster than any traded-good price.

How do we know that? To avoid algebra here, let us simply reflect
on the accounting for the price of any one product. Its total price must
equal the returns to all the inputs (labor, capital, raw materials, merchant
knowledge, land, pure profit, etc.) per unit of output. When the price of
an export good changes by, say, 28 percent, the returns to the inputs must
rise by 28 percent. They could rise by having input prices rise or by having inputs become less productive on the average. Lacking any reason
why a price increase should bring a net drop in the productivity
of all inputs, we can plausibly suppose that productivity does not change
because of the change in price. This means that the 28 percent change in
price must be matched by a change in input prices that averages 28 percent. But unless every input happened by luck to change exactly 28
percent (implausible), some input group must be gaining more than
28 percent in its return on this product. Hence the first result above.

Meanwhile, on the import side, there must again be a dispersion in
the changes in input rewards that average out to the same relative fall in
the import price, whether we are talking about one good or the whole
set of them. For the import good with the largest fall in price, not all input
rewards can fall at exactly the same rate as that import price. Some must
therefore be falling less, and—as in the first result above—some must be
falling even faster. Basic accounting (plus the assumption of no induced
productivity changes) drives both of these seemingly extreme results.

Which groups are likely to be the winners and losers from a change
in the world-market prices? The winners will tend to be those groups
whose incomes are tied most closely to the rising-price goods (in this case,
Republican China's exports), while the losers will tend to be those whose
incomes are most closely tied to the goods whose prices are falling. We
might suspect that initially the greatest winners would be the merchants
and capitalists collecting residual economic rents on the rising-price
goods. But we must take care not to assume that they can avoid passing
these gains on. If their gains were initially only a 10 percent share of the
value of the export good, and we thought nobody else gained, then a 28

percent rise in the price of an export good would imply that their earn-ings rose 28/(0.10), or 280 percent. Such fortunes would yield to com-petition sooner or later.[17] The greatest gains would eventually be passed on to some group whose services were heavily used in the rising-price sector and the greatest losses would go to those whose services were heav-ily used in the falling-price sector.

To this inescapable conclusion, we could add softer conjectures. In the long run, a type of income will be favored or harmed in all of the sec-tors it can move into or out of, and not just in the initial foreign-trade sectors. Given that China's comparative advantage by the 1930s was in goods that used unskilled labor, especially rural labor, intensively, I con-jecture that common folk were among the greatest gainers from the rise in China's terms of trade, and her volume of trade, between the 1910s and the 1930s. Similar analysis can be applied to other periods. The same reasoning can be applied to interregional trade within China. Forces in-tegrating the regions more would favor unskilled laborers in regions ex-porting unskilled-labor-intensive products but would favor capitalists and the highly skilled in regions that ended up exporting capital- or skill-intensive products.

EXPLAINING THE HISTORY OF TRADE POLICIES

International economics needs to import materials and ideas from his-torians as well as export tools to them. Like the rest of economics, it has a comparative disadvantage in explaining the policies that economics often takes as given (exogenous). In the case of policies toward interna-tional trade, a particular opportunity presents itself for historical re-search. Economists have come up with real-world puzzles that they have had no particular success in explaining, puzzles awaiting historians able to distill powerful generalizations from a broad range of experience.

For industrial products, the history of tariffs and other trade barriers is not too puzzling. Free trade made its greatest gains in the two eras in which the main industrial power had political as well as economic hege-mony: the Pax Britannica of the nineteenth century and the postwar trade liberalization backed by the United States. It is not surprising that in-dustrial protectionism revived in the interwar period, especially in the

17. See the parallel discussion of entry and of passing on the effects of taxes in Mc-Closkey's chapter, 126–130.

worldwide depression of the 1930s. Economists have also come up with fair explanations of the details of the industrial protectionist pattern, using statistical regressions to link differences in legislated protection to economic variables.[18]

Agriculture is different. The real puzzle of trade-related policy relates to the different way in which agricultural producers have been insulated from the world marketplace. Surveying agricultural policies in dozens of countries in the 1970s and 1980s, economists have found two curious patterns, the developmental pattern: as a country develops, it switches from a trade policy that taxes the agricultural sector to one that generously protects farm incomes; and the anti-trade bias: for any given level of income per capita, producers of exportable agricultural products are more taxed or less subsidized than producers of importable farm products, so that trade is discouraged in both kinds of products.

These two policy patterns emerge with statistical significance from multicountry studies in the 1950s through 1980s (e.g., Bale and Lutz 1981; World Bank 1982; Binswanger and Scandizzo 1983; Anderson and Hayami 1986; Tyers and Anderson 1992). They both reappear in the historical experience of now industrialized countries since 1860, though perhaps not earlier (Lindert 1991a). In most cases trade barriers such as tariffs, quotas, and government marketing monopolies are key tools, though other taxes and subsidies are also used.

Several "obvious" explanations of the developmental pattern prove inadequate. First, there is no point in just noting the rise in urban sympathy for supporting declining agriculture. If we have no way of predicting when and where it arises, the argument is circular: there was growing support for agriculture because there was growing support for agriculture. Second, official concern over food security plays much less role in fact than in rhetoric. Many developing countries are discouraging their own food supplies with taxes on farmers. Even the government of Japan, where the fear of food insecurity is a rhetorical tradition, pays farmers to leave rice land fallow and subsidizes rice exports. Third, farm aid in the industrialized countries is not aid to a population poorer than the average: the support programs bring disproportionate gains to landowners and farm operators with above-average incomes.

18. For a survey of most of the empirical literature on the political economy of industrial protectionism, see Baldwin 1984 and Krueger 1984. Most of the studies relate to the postwar era.

One explanation developed by economists seems appealing at a glance but not on a closer look. This is the small-is-powerful argument: the more a country develops, the smaller its farm sector, and small groups are politically powerful. True, small groups are often able to inflict greater losses on the rest of society than they gain from the policies they lobby for. But of the innumerable small-group lobbies that could emerge, only a very few win great lobbying power in most industrial countries. Why is agriculture so frequently among the handful of winners? Why not other declining sectors? Why is the textile industry protected so much less? Or the buggy makers, the fisheries, or timber producers? The explanation of the developmental pattern in agricultural trade policy remains an open issue.

Historians can work this field profitably. First, of course, they can craft detailed studies of individual cases. But beware the uniqueness trap. The policy patterns are global and persistent. A scholar who says that a persistent global pattern is just the result of thousands of unique historical junctures has chosen to remain impotent. Comparative studies are crucial to our search for the most reliable general forces. A few historians have taken a lead in writing a comparative history of policies toward agricultural trade, focusing on the European reactions to the American grain invasion that started in the late 1870s (e.g., Gerschenkron 1943; Kindleberger 1951; Gourevitch 1977). Now we need a truly global view.

THE ECONOMICS OF EXCHANGE RATES: HUMBLE PIE AND A HELPFUL GUIDE

Exchange rates between currencies are a frequent nuisance to the historian. They seem to affect the whole economy, and they complicate the comparison of economic values expressed in different currencies. Unfortunately, their movements are often hard to explain. Here the economists offer some help, but with a heavy dose of humility. We have models that help explain exchange rates over the very long run and in the special case of hyperinflation, even though all models fail miserably to predict short-run movements. Let us look first at a limited consensus model, then at its limits, and finally at some helpful guidelines for comparing economic values between currencies.

Economists can identify the main forces that should explain movements in exchange rates. With only slight injustice to factional views, a relatively monetarist approach can summarize the modest consensus of exchange-rate economics.[19] We begin with the equation of purchasing power parity (PPP). In competitive international markets, prices and exchange rates will tend toward levels that make a traded good cost the same in any one currency regardless of where it is purchased. This means that between, say, the United States and Britain

$$P = r \text{ times } P_f, \text{ so that } r = P / P_f$$

more or less, where P is the American price of a traded good (e.g., $300 per Schwinn mountain bike), r is the exchange rate defined as the price of the foreign (British) currency (e.g., $2.00 per pound), and P_f is the foreign price of the same kind of bike (e.g., £150 per bike). Does it really work out that way? The degree of error in this equation depends on the kind of price data being used. The equation works best when the price pairs P and P_f refer to homogeneous goods heavily traded between nations (e.g., number 2 red durum wheat or sweet light Saudi crude oil). This is the case closest to the law of one price mentioned in other chapters of this book. The PPP equation works less well when the prices are aggregate price indexes for all traded goods. It does quite poorly using the overall national-product or cost-of-living price indexes.[20]

By itself, PPP is not a very satisfying theory of the exchange rate. It says only that an exchange rate between two currencies (r) should tend to equal the ratio of price levels in the two currencies. We would be more satisfied with a sense of what determined those price levels simultaneously with the exchange rate. The handiest device here is the quantity theory of the demand for money. It is a partisan model, championed by one side of a perennial debate, though one with enough flexibility (or "fudge factor," or "wiggle room") to placate some critics. The quantity theory says that the money supply (M) over which the central bank has rough control tends to be related to nominal national product (P times y) by a constant k, or, in our two-nation case,

	in the United States	in Britain
money supply = money demand	$M = k P y$	$M_f = k_f P_f y_f$

---

19. The arguments that follow can be reapplied to fixed-exchange-rate settings, such as the great gold standard era 1870–1914 or the nearly fixed exchange rates of the Bretton Woods era (1944–1971). In these settings, the same forces discussed as determinants of fixed exchange rates serve as pressures on fixed rates, ones compelling official policy response. Also, the text's later points about purchasing-power comparisons between countries still apply in the fixed-rate case.

20. For tests and conflicting interpretations of PPP, and the quantity theory of money, see the literature surveyed in Lindert 1991b, chap. 16.

so that

price depends on M, k, and y: $P = M / ky$ $P_f = M_f / k_f y_f$

where the y's are real (constant-price, inflation-adjusted) values of national product, and k and k_f are fudge-factor "constants," assumed not to vary much.

Taken together, the purchasing power parity hypothesis and the quantity theory of money yield the prediction that the exchange rate between two currencies is determined by money supplies and by real national product:

$$r = P / P_f = (M / M_f) \text{ times } (k_f / k) \text{ times } (y_f / y)$$

Here is a plausible and testable prediction: the exchange rate should be determined by the ratio of the two countries' money supplies, the ratio of their real national products, and a miscellany wrapped up in the k's.

A more sophisticated and flexible version of this model has been put to the test. As a short-run forecaster, it is a dismal failure. Richard Meese and Kenneth Rogoff 1983 gave the model a fighting chance by replacing its mystery constants with interest rates and trade balances, which are also popular as imagined determinants of exchange rates. When forced to predict exchange rates outside the sample period to which it was fitted, the economists' consensus model failed to predict one month ahead any better than a crude "naive" model, one that just predicted no change in the exchange rate from one month to the next.[21] A humbling result, given all that has been invested in forecasting exchange rates.

The basic model of exchange rates does better, however, in the long run and for extreme cases of countries experiencing hyperinflation. Over such a broad reach of time or inflation, the model makes smaller percentage errors than it makes in its one-month forecasts of the exchange rate. It also outperforms the naive model predicting no change in the exchange rate. It has greater accuracy in the long haul for the right reasons: money supplies and national product levels are indeed key influences on price levels, and price levels do eventually relate to exchange rates, as PPP would have forecast.

What we have, then, is a basic economic model that makes sense and

---

21. For that matter, even the predictions of market traders themselves, summarized in the forward exchange rate, failed to outperform the naive model that just predicted no change in the spot exchange rate.

is useful if it is not pressed too hard. The historian can safely view month-to-month movements in an exchange rate as exogenous surprises, knowing that they surprised the experts as well. Yet the historian can with equal confidence write that money supplies and national productivities are key partial determinants of exchange rates in the long run. Indeed, it would be very hard to explain the declining exchange-rate value of the Brazilian cruzeiro or the Israeli shekel without reference to the money supply or to production trends. Using M's and y's is also essential in explaining why the dollar sank relative to the yen and Swiss franc since 1970 yet rose relative to the Italian lira and the pound sterling.

If purchasing-power-parity works only very roughly and sluggishly, there is a corollary that historians need to know and use. The fact that PPP is far from perfect means that we cannot compare real purchasing powers between two countries using the exchange rate. To see why, suppose that we were trying to decide whether Japan had a higher or lower income per capita than the United States in 1986. What we have at hand are Japan's income (or GNP) per capita measured in current yen, and America's income per capita measured in current dollars. We would like to know whether the average Japanese income can buy more of a representative bundle of goods and services than the average American income. The right comparison is between two purchasing powers over the same bundle of goods, or Japanese income in yen / yen price of the bundle versus American income in dollars / dollar price of the bundle. Those two prices are our P_f and P above, using Japan as the foreign country. A major measurement problem arises: it takes a lot of work to estimate P_f and P in truly comparable ways.[22]

To avoid that work, scholars and journalists opt for a cheap and dangerous substitute: the exchange rate, r. Since PPP fails to work, r is a poor proxy for P / P_f. Just how poor was dramatized by that 1986 comparison of incomes in Japan and the United States. A splashy cover article in the *Economist* in October 1986 announced that Japan was 12 percent richer than the United States, confirming popular American fears. The source of the revelation was their conversion of yen incomes into dollars using the current exchange rate (r). Overlooked was the fact that a similar conversion by the World Bank in 1984 found Japanese incomes only 69 percent of the U.S. level—yet separate calculations found no dif-

22. See the discussion of index-number problems in Rawski's essay on trends, 30–32.

ference between American and Japanese growth rates between 1984 and 1986. How could Japan switch from trailing badly to leading by 12 percent within two years, without growing faster? The exchange-rate conversion was the culprit: the dollar fell in yen value by 33 percent between 1984 and 1986, while the two countries had similar rates of inflation (P / P_f changed little). Let the user of exchange-rate conversions beware.

The needed calculation of international purchasing power, with comparable P's and P_f's (the right method), has been performed, and is still being performed, by a research project historians need to read about. For the last quarter century Alan Heston, Irving Kravis, and Robert Summers have labored on the International Comparisons Project (ICP) at the University of Pennsylvania, with funding from the United Nations, the World Bank, and the U.S. National Science Foundation. They have developed internationally comparable prices of basic bundles of goods and services in 130 countries from the 1950s to the present.[23] Current work is extending their series on prices and real national product back to 1920 for as many countries as possible. Economic historians have already begun to use the ICP estimates as the anchor for all their international comparisons of prices and real incomes, to judge such issues as the tendencies toward international income convergence and divergence. To reach back into the nineteenth century, the same historians have spliced conventional national data series onto the ICP estimates for the 1950s, assuming tentatively that international differences in relative prices did not change before that decade.

The International Comparisons Project has revealed a reliable—"robust," the economists like to say—pattern that historians can put to good use in earlier settings for which ICP estimates are unavailable. They have found that the exchange rate is biased as a measure of the desired price ratio P / P_f in this way:

> In any two settings with different nominal incomes per capita, the readily available traded-good prices that are closely tied to the exchange rate *understate* the relative cheapness (dearness) of overall prices in the lower-income (higher-income) setting. The reason is that the demands and prices for nontraded services are much more elastic with respect to income than are those

---

23. A spate of books and articles by the Penn team has elaborated their procedures and estimates. For an overview and a criticism, see Kravis 1984 and Marris 1984. For the full set of estimates for 130 countries, 1950s through 1985, including a floppy-disk copy, see Summers and Heston 1988.

for the traded goods on which we have the best data. *Implication:* If you compare the two settings by using the exchange rate or the usual price series to deflate nominal-price values, you will *overstate* the real income difference, while getting the direction of inequality correct.[24]

Note that the result speaks simultaneously of two biases, a bias caused by using exchange rates and a bias caused by using the kinds of price data that are usually more available. The former bias is the one revealed over and over by the Penn project. The latter is one typically confronted by economic historians: we have access to price data on traded goods like wheat and cloth and iron yet lack data on the prices of nontraded services, such as house rents and servants' wages. The common-traded-good price indexes behave much like exchange rates, that is, they differ less across countries and over time than true overall price indexes that include prices of nontraded services. So the bias in using exchange rates also turns out to be a bias in the price data historians find more readily.

As an application, consider the question of international differences in living standards before and during the Industrial Revolution.[25] We want to know, for example, whether Gregory King was right in guessing that England's income per capita was slightly below that of Holland and above that of France in 1688. Scholarly research surveyed by Jan De Vries 1984 suggests that the nominal incomes of England and Holland were indeed comparable around 1688. The difference between English and French nominal income per capita, however, is tentatively upheld by the available indirect evidence. The above result suggests that the advantage of English-Dutch incomes over French incomes was real but was overstated by the available figures, which used exchange rates and tradable-goods prices instead of the unavailable true price comparisons between currencies.[26] In this way, what might be an economist's problem—the departure of prices from the purchasing power parity principle—becomes a tool useful to the historian because the departure has a reliable pattern.

---

24. The only exception to the rule that exchange-rate comparisons overstate real income gaps arises when the higher-income country has much cheaper space rents, as in the comparison between the North America and Japan-plus-Europe up to 1990. In this situation, getting the right comparison of P and P_f actually raises the relative income advantage of North America. In general, though, higher-income countries have much more expensive space for living and working.

25. For more on this topic, see Sutch's chapter, 168–171.

26. For more on how to use systematic biases in historical data in comparing real incomes between regions and over time, see Lindert 1988.

CONCLUSION

Historians have an opportunity to be smart shoppers in the economists'
supermarket, in the international aisle as in others. Much of the technical literature is sterile and of little use. Two kinds of bargains should
tempt historians. In some cases the economists have established reliable
tools, and these are worth learning. An example from this chapter is the
measurement of the gains from trade and its magnified effect on the distribution of income within any region. Another is the simple observation of contemporaneous movements in prices and quantities to infer
whether demand shifts or supply shifts dominated movements in international markets. Another is the crude monetary theory of the determination of exchange rates.

The other kind of bargain involves patterns in the failures of conventional economic explanations, patterns that can guide the historian toward good research topics and good conclusions. For example, the fact
that economists do a poorer job of charting the cause of policies (and institutions) than in charting their economic consequences leaves the explanation of the policies themselves to the historian and to other social
scientists. So it is with the two current puzzles of how policies disrupt
international agricultural trade: the shift from taxing agriculture to pro
tecting it as a country develops, and the anti-trade bias that favors
import-competing farmers over those producing exportable products.
Another example is the systematic failure of purchasing power parity to
hold between regions and countries. This failure has a systematic relationship to income levels. Knowing that systematic bias allows the historian to use the failure of PPP as a tool for comparing living standards
from long ago, instead of discarding the whole notion.

Suggestions for Readings
and How to Approach Them

The readings are useful for initial excursions into the literature of economics. Economics texts and the *New Palgrave Dictionary of Economics* (Eatwell, Milgate, and Newman 1987) can serve as helpful sources of information on specific topics. Hawke 1980 is directed specifically toward historians. You might usefully refer to a standard introductory volume like Samuelson and Nordhaus 1985 or Stiglitz 1993 and to intermediate level texts in microeconomics (e.g., McCloskey 1985a; Milgrom and Roberts 1992) and macroeconomics (e.g., Parkin 1992, which devotes considerable effort to applying theory concepts to Canadian economic history).

A. GENERAL

R. A. Radford, "The Economic Organization of a P.O.W. Camp," (1945). Economics in 12 fascinating pages. Reprinted in Samuelson 1970.

Robert W. Fogel, *Railroads and American Economic Growth* (1964), 1–37, offers seminal treatment of opportunity cost. For more along these lines see G. R. Hawke, "Transport and Social Overhead Cost" (1981).

Donald N. McCloskey, *The Applied Theory of Price* (2d ed.). Allegedly a text, this book is filled with simple questions that even economists have difficulty answering. Every excursion into this volume produces a different list of topics that we all "must" think about, such as chaps. 1–8, 9.2, 10.1 2, 11, 14, 15, 20, 22, 23.2, 24.1, 25.2 and 26. Browsing is recommended.

B. STATISTICS

Now that we have computers to do the work, there is little need to ingest the details of how to calculate correlation coefficients, regression lines, and t-statistics. What we do need is advice about how to scrutinize the numbers that the computer works with (to avoid the "garbage in, garbage out" syndrome) and help in interpreting what the computer results *mean.*

G. Ohlin, "No Safety in Numbers: Some Pitfalls of Historical Statistics" (1966) uses demographic examples to illustrate pitfalls. To pursue the matter, consult Oskar Morgenstern's classic monograph *On the Accuracy of Economic Observations* (1960).

Roderick Floud, *Quantitative Methods for Historians* (1973), especially chaps. 6–8 on time series, relationships between variables, and imperfect data. Also,

Byron D. Eastman, *Interpreting Mathematical Economics and Econometrics* (1984), especially 43–105.

C. TRENDS

Peter H. Lindert and Jeffrey G. Williamson, "English Workers' Living Standards during the Industrial Revolution: A New Look" (1983). How do economists put together estimates of such concepts as living standards from fragile data? To pursue questions of living standards, consult Arthur J. Taylor, ed., *The Standard of Living in Britain in the Industrial Revolution* (1975) which contains both "optimistic" and "pessimistic" accounts, of which the (nontechnical) Hartwell-Engerman paper on "Models of Immiseration: The Theoretical Basis of Pessimism" may be especially useful for specifying shadowy and poorly articulated (but influential) viewpoints about the costs of economic "progress."

C. K. Harley, "British Industrialization before 1841: Evidence of Slower Growth during the Industrial Revolution" (1982). If you have good output data for 15 industries, all growing at different rates, what is the combined growth rate for industry as a whole? Or, if you have price data for 15 important consumer products in 1920 and 1930, what is the consumer price index or overall inflation measure linking 1920 and 1930? The answer depends on how each industry (or each consumer product) is weighted. Economists spend much effort determining such weights. Here is a good example showing the significance of such index-number issues.

Kozo Yamamura, "Toward an Examination of the Economic History of Tokugawa Japan" (1973). The paper is a fine example of how to use a formal model to organize thoughts and questions about a preindustrial economy. Danger: the model may have unexpected implications. In this case, agricultural employment falls in all regions of Japan even though households enjoy higher living standards and presumably consume more farm products per person.

Donald N. McCloskey, "The Industrial Revolution 1780–1860: A Survey" (1981). Note especially the nontechnical discussions of technological change.

N. F. R. Crafts, "Income Elasticities of Demand and the Release of Labour by Agriculture during the British Industrial Revolution" (1980). Using types of data that are widely available, the author links developments in one set of markets (for consumer goods) with those in others (for farm labor) by taking advantage of common patterns of consumer behavior involving the income elasticity of demand (percentage change in quantity of X purchased when income rises by 1 percent). Basic necessities (salt, milk) tend to have low or even negative (margarine before butter was viewed as unhealthy) income elasticities; luxuries (diamonds) have high income elasticities.

D. INSTITUTIONS AND THE SOCIAL FRAMEWORK OF ECONOMIC ACTIVITY

Efforts by economists to integrate issues arising from the study of management, sociology, and law into the study of organizations make this a particularly exciting field for historians.

R. H. Coase, *The Firm, The Market, and The Law* (1988) lays out the issues in two brief essays (chaps. 1 and 3) that have a lyric quality.

Oliver E. Williamson and Sidney G. Winter, eds., *The Nature of the Firm: Origins, Evolution, and Development* (1993) maps out some of the economists' efforts to respond to these issues.

Douglass North's paper, "Government and the Cost of Exchange in History" (1984), illustrates new thinking on the contribution of institutions to economic outcomes, a theme explored at length in North's (1990) *Institutions, Institutional Change, and Economic Performance.*

Stephen A. Marglin, "What Do Bosses Do? The Origin and Functions of Hierarchy in Capitalist Production" (1974) argues that production shifted from cottage to factory to increase managerial control rather than to reduce direct production costs. Marglin's paper has stimulated further study, e.g., Kenneth L. Sokoloff, "Was the Transition from the Artisanal Shop to the Nonmechanized Factory Associated with Gains in Efficiency?" (1984) and David Landes, "What Do Bosses Really Do?" (1986).

Albert O. Hirschman, *Exit, Voice, and Loyalty* (1970). An iconoclastic economist thinks about how people behave in economic organizations from a viewpoint that reaches far beyond the assumptions of conventional economic theory.

E. LABOR

In addition to the citations in the chapter on labor, see

David W. Galenson, *White Servitude in Colonial America* (1981). Chapter 9 is a beautiful piece of supply and demand analysis of a labor market.

George A. Akerlof, *An Economic Theorist's Book of Tales* (1984)—ignore the mathematics and concentrate on the author's thoughts about aspects of the marketplace that economists often ignore.

F. CHOICE

Charles K. Harley, "The Shift from Sailing Ships to Steamships, 1850–1890: A Study in Technological Change and its Diffusion" (1971), offers clear exposition of an essential subject. See also McCloskey's survey on the Industrial Revolution (1981, mentioned above). For more, see Douglass North, "Sources of Productivity Change in Ocean Shipping, 1600–1850" (1968), and

Y. Yasuba, "Freight Rates and Productivity in Ocean Transportation for Japan, 1875–1943" (1978). For a broader treatment of technological change (no numbers), see one of many studies by Nathan Rosenberg, "Technological Change in the Machine Tool Industry" (1963), reprinted in his *Perspectives on Technology* (1976).

Scott R. Dittrich and Ramon H. Myers, "Resource Allocation in Traditional Agriculture: Republican China, 1937–1940" (1971) is tough going, but worthwhile. The authors use farm survey data (the same sources used by many historians of China) to determine how much income farmers could earn from the best possible mix of crops, then see what they actually earned. Result: the difference between actual and potential earnings was small as long as prices remained fairly stable. Conclusion: Chinese farmers seem highly efficient in responding to (moderate) economic change.

Winifred B. Rothenberg, "The Market and Massachusetts Farmers, 1750–1855" (1981), delves into the meaning of a "market system," a subject pursued in the author's book *From Market Places to a Market Economy: The Transformation of Rural Massachusetts, 1750–1850* (1992).

G. MACROECONOMICS AND MONEY

G. R. Hawke, *Economics for Historians* (1980), chap. 5, "Money," offers a solid point of departure. Further pursuit of monetary economics could begin with William Poole, *Money and the Economy: A Monetarist View* (1978), especially 1–41.

Armen A. Alchian, *Economic Forces at Work* (1977) offers a fine discussion of "Why Money?" (111–126). The chapter on "Real Wages in the North During the Civil War: Mitchell's Data Reinterpreted" is difficult but covers a lot of ground.

Winifred B. Rothenberg, "The Emergence of a Capital Market in Rural Massachusetts" (1985) illustrates how financial markets can contribute to the production and exchange of commodities and services.

Peter Lindert, "English Population, Wages, and Prices, 1541–1913" (1985) weds Malthusian issues with monetary matters.

H. INTERNATIONAL ECONOMICS

J. Richard Huber, "Effect on Prices of Japan's Entry into World Commerce after 1858" (1971) provides a neat exposition of gains from trade. The author finds that the forced opening of Japan to trade (under unequal treaties) encouraged a shift of resources from production of import goods (now obtained more cheaply from abroad) to production of exports (now much dearer because of new foreign demand). The result was a large increase in Japanese real incomes.

Stanley Lebergott, "The Returns to U.S. Imperialism, 1890–1929" (1980) views economic impact of imperialism from the side of the imperialists.

Lance Davis and Robert Huttenback, *Mammon and the Pursuit of Empire: The Political Economy of British Imperialism, 1860–1912* (1989) evaluate the economic consequences of empire for Britain.

Charles K. Harley and Donald N. McCloskey, "Foreign Trade: Competition and the Expanding International Economy" (1981, Floud and McCloskey, vol. 2) use a British case study to show how economists think about the impact of trade on the domestic economy. The new edition of Floud and McCloskey (1994) contains a revised version of the essay.

Paul R. Krugman, "Is Free Trade Passé?" (1987) and *Geography and Trade* (1991) lay out recent and, for historians, relevant developments in this field.

Some Advice to the Reader

As you deepen your acquaintance with economics, some advice about ways of approaching the "dismal science" may be useful. Economics is above all a way of thinking. It comes complete with its own assumptions and language. Indeed, learning economics has much in common with studying a foreign language. So, especially as you set out,

1. DON'T ASK TOO MANY QUESTIONS AT FIRST. CONCENTRATE ON SOAKING UP NEW IDEAS.

Just as beginning students of German smooth their progress by avoiding the puzzle of why apples are masculine and pears are feminine, the economic novice must learn to play by the rules. Even if the eventual objective is to challenge and perhaps reject the rules, it is essential to understand their structure and implications. The chief tenets of economics are not the creation of contemporary social science, but are firmly rooted in the writings of practical Englishmen: Adam Smith, who observed Britain's eighteenth-century economy from his post as a Scottish customs official; David Ricardo, a stockbroker; and John Stuart Mill, who had little patience with "purely abstract investigations." The central ideas of modern economics came not from academic treatises, but from "contributions to public debate on the burning issues of the day . . . food prices, the causes of poverty, taxation, monetary instability" (Winch 1973, 561, 529–530).

The economist's mission is to identify "the burning issues of the day," develop logical structures that permit a deep and searching analysis of trends and structures surrounding these issues, and use the resulting body of theory as a vehicle for more comprehensive investigations of the initial (and subsequent) "burning issues" than would be possible from an unstructured, purely empirical inquiry.

This approach, with its emphasis on abstract analysis, is not a contemporary innovation, but was present from the beginning. Adam Smith wrote that

> it is not from the benevolence of the butcher, the brewer, or the baker that we expect our dinner, but from their regard to their own interest. We address ourselves, not to their humanity but to their self-love, and never talk to them of our own necessities but of their advantages. (14)

Smith's observations on butchers and bakers thinly conceal an abstract conception of the economy as an arena for the pursuit of material self-interest by independent, well informed, and selfish individuals whose activities are bounded only by the laws and institutions of society and by their own preferences, abilities, and resources. His conclusion that the self-serving individual is "led by an invisible hand to promote an end which was no part of his intention," namely the wealth of nations and the general social good, is deservedly recognized as an intellectual landmark of vast historical significance (423). The ideas embodied in these passages—the logic of self-interest, the interdependence among the myriad agents in a single economy, the possibility that government intervention may be confounded by the complexity of economic arrangements, the underlying harmony of conflicting interests—retain their centrality in economic thinking to this day.

Anyone listening to discussions among economists will soon recognize that while the commentary may focus on concrete issues, for instance the consequences of cheaper ocean shipping for the nineteenth-century Atlantic economy, the participants, following the intellectual footsteps of Adam Smith, constantly draw on a shared background of abstractions about the market mechanism. One of the high points of the initial seminar that produced this book came when a historian suddenly interrupted the economists' colloquy by observing that "you seem to be talking about the Chinese rice market, but you're really talking about a model of the market mechanism!" Exactly. Economic discourse is loaded with logical deductions based on assumptions seemingly far removed from the case at hand. Therefore, the historian must

2. DECONSTRUCT THE CONVERSATION AMONG ECONOMISTS; FOLLOW THEIR MENTAL LEAPS FROM REALITY TO THEORY AND BACK.

Historians often balk at the abstraction of *homo economicus* motivated exclusively by material advantage. After all, we do not live by bread alone. True enough. But admit that most people devote a considerable proportion of their energies to seeking material gain, especially in the realm of activity that deals with producing, earning, buying, and selling, and you open the intellectual door to *homo economicus*. Let's temporarily ignore non-pecuniary motivations, construct a model featuring economic man, take it for a ride, and see whether the results (in terms of predictive power) justify such an extreme assumption. Furthermore, don't forget that economics makes no predictions about the uses to which *homo economicus* puts his wealth; grasping merchants may use their profits to support the church, to build monuments to themselves, or to endow homes for stray cats—the economist pays no heed.

Remember that economists do not insist on regarding employers, consumers, and investors as perpetual calculating machines. Calculation requires information, which is costly to collect and analyze. Even a hyper-rational agent can make impulse purchases. But real people, like *homo economicus,* are less likely to make impulsive, unconsidered decisions about changing jobs, retirement, buying a house or a car, or any transaction that may have a major impact on their total income or wealth. Let's suppose that the *homo economicus* assumption is *approximately* true for a large proportion of participants in the market. Then we should expect empirical research to *approximately* verify predictions of a model built on the rational-behavior assumption. This is the economist's reasonable plea, and in fact, it is the best that we can hope for, because empirical verification in the uncontrolled laboratory of human history can never be more than approximate. So

3. DON'T EXPECT ECONOMICS TO PERFORM MAGIC
   TRICKS EVEN IF ECONOMISTS SEEM TO THINK THAT IT
   CAN DO SO.

Economists, like practitioners of any trade, employ specialized jargon that is initially difficult for outsiders to comprehend. Economic jargon can be confusing. Worse yet, it often serves to conceal (sometimes from economists as well as historians) fundamental building blocks of economic analysis that appear again and again in all varieties of economics. The problem facing historians is to identify and comprehend these essential features of economists' abstractions. This book is designed to accomplish this very objective. Fortunately, mastery of a few key concepts can open the door for historians to make use of a wide variety of economic ideas. Furthermore, these concepts are not difficult to grasp, even though their ramifications may be tricky and deep. So

4. A FEW KEY ELEMENTS, WELL DIGESTED, WILL SUFFICE
   TO GET YOU STARTED.

The first central item, already discussed, is *self-interest.* Economists assume that people seek to achieve clearly defined objectives. Consumers seek satisfaction from accumulating things that they prefer (plush dinners, fancy clothes, money in the bank, university professorships endowed in their names) and deploy their limited resources and abilities in order to achieve the highest possible level of satisfaction. Similarly, businesses deploy their limited resources to generate the largest amount of profit. If a business is placed under the direction of hired executives, economists look for conflicts of interest among shareholders (whose main interest is higher profits) and managers (whose interests may dictate the pursuit of perquisites, growth, or self-promotion along with, or instead of profits). Similarly, the interests of civil servants may systematically diverge from those of the citizen-taxpayers who indirectly employ them. Economists typically formalize the behavior of consumers, employees, investors, and similar groups in terms of *constrained optimization,* meaning that people pursue their objectives (e.g., maximizing income or minimizing cost) within the confines of their limited capacity (income, knowledge, ability, time).

Having assigned an "objective function" that each agent seeks to maximize (satisfaction, profit, etc.), the economist then considers how agents decide whether to buy, sell, save, invest, work, loaf, and so forth. A key concept here is *opportunity cost,* which means, quite literally, the value of the road not taken. The opportunity cost of going to college includes not just the financial outlay on tuition and textbooks, but the amount of wages foregone by spending four years in the classroom rather than in the labor market. The opportunity cost of setting aside funds for a child's education consists of the value of items that could have been (but weren't) provided by spending the same funds to fulfill current needs. Participants in the economy have individual, and different purposes and may face different opportunity costs. But each agent is assumed to dispose of available resources in ways that promise the best possible outcome (measured by that individual's "objective function") given the limited availability of labor, funds, assets, and time.

Here we see the cold-blooded aspect of the discipline. Economics implicitly views people as calculating machines. It assumes quite literally that people treat one another no differently from the way they treat commodities or machines. To a university administrator, my stipend for teaching an extra course represents the incremental or marginal cost of teaching services in exactly the same sense as the price of electricity represents the marginal cost of heating or cooling my office (note the typical attribution to actual administrators of the decision processes contained in the theory; economists find it natural and unremarkable to attribute to real people the calculations that their models elicit from *homo economicus*).

Purposeful consumers, workers, merchants, and administrators interact in *markets*. Historians will be surprised to learn that economics has little to say about markets themselves. The four-volume *New Palgrave Dictionary of Economics* edited by Eatwell, Milgate, and Newman (1987), for instance, has no articles and no index entries under "markets," or "market system," or "market economy."[1]

Indeed, the best descriptions come from noneconomists—see, for example, Clifford Geertz's striking portrait of the Moroccan *suq* (1979, 123–313). This is because, to the intense dissatisfaction of Buchanan (1979) and others, economics has much to say about outcomes (selling price, volume transacted) and little to say about the process that generates these results. Indeed, as the critics emphasize, economists often assume that the process is irrelevant. Sometimes this works well: in reviewing the past half century of experience in the world food economy, Timmer, Falcon, and Pearson find that the basic economic theory of production and consumption "has withstood exposure to the real world remarkably well, and the basic assumptions about rationality and the importance of prices and income have been repeatedly confirmed" (1983, 35–36). When the neglect of process leads to analytic disaster, historians may be better situated than economists to repair the damage.

---

1. The essay on marketplaces is by Polly Hill, an anthropologist whose views of economics can be inferred from the title of her (1986) book *Development Economics on Trial: The Anthropological Case for a Prosecution.*

What interests economists most about markets is the idea of *equilibrium*, implying a balance between the opposing forces of *demand*, which arises from a combination of desire and income on the part of potential purchasers (note that unless I control sufficient resources to make a purchase, my desire to obtain the commodity has no effect on market outcomes), and *supply*, which originates in the income-seeking activities of potential sellers. The idea of equilibrium should interest historians. Although the historical record may not reveal the forces that contribute to an equilibrium position, realignments of these forces (e.g., an improvement in productivity as villagers acclimate themselves to factory discipline) generate changes (a decline in product price, increased profits, expansion of factories at the expense of cottage industry) that are visible to the historian, sometimes in quantitative as well as qualitative terms. Small deviations from equilibrium can produce dramatic results: a decline in food supplies amounting to as little as 3–5 percent of normal supplies can "frequently lead to panic buying and price increases of several *hundred* percent" (Timmer, Falcon, and Pearson 1983, 46).

This is exactly the sort of problem that economists are best able to work with. Their preferred approach is the method of *comparative statics*, in which one works out the consequences of a single event (a flood; the development of a new product; an increase in the supply of labor; large-scale import of Mexican silver to Europe) on a preexisting equilibrium position in a market or group of interlinked markets. Here again, the focus is on the outcome rather than the process. In contrast to their highly refined treatment of comparative statics, economists are typically ill-equipped to work with dynamics. Economics predicts which variables will change and in what direction they will move following the disturbance of equilibrium, and often the amounts by which they will change, but rarely tells much about such matters as the length of time required to move from the initial position to the revised equilibrium.

The method of comparative statics is typically pursued in several steps:

A. Describe a plausible sequence of circumstance and (self-interested) response that incorporates the main outlines of the problem or situation under examination. Economists typically preface their formal theorizing with "stories" intended to motivate and justify the approach embodied in their formal analysis. Richard Nelson refers to this as "appreciative theorizing," which he contrasts with formal modeling (1987, chap. 2).

B. Construct or identify a formal (often mathematical) model that rigorously pursues the consequences of key assumptions contained in the initial story and verifies the logic of the predicted outcome.

C. Collect empirical materials and use them to test the theory's predictions.

D. Refine the theory in both its appreciative and formal dimensions to incorporate new ideas that emerge from the process of data collection and hypothesis testing.

This outline of the economist's research strategy shows the historian where to look for quick and comprehensible explanations of what the economists are doing:

5. BECOME A CONNOISSEUR OF APPRECIATIVE THEORY.

Appreciative theorizing or storytelling is the mode of discourse that economists adopt to motivate their analysis. Their purpose is to convince the audience of the importance of the issues to be studied and the plausibility of the proposed analytic approach. Discussion of this sort tends to be broad and inclusive rather than narrow and precise. This sort of descriptive analysis offers the historian a golden opportunity for profitable eavesdropping on the dialogue among economists. Here is where new ideas are on display. The historian with economic leanings should pounce on books[2] and journals[3] that emphasize appreciative theorizing and pursue the works of economists (e.g., Akerlof 1984) who think broadly and take pains to explain their ideas in clear, nontechnical language.

This outline also undercuts the idea that economics is somehow a "scientific" or "hard" discipline as opposed to "soft" fields like history. Parts of economics are logical and rigorous; mathematical models lead to theorems that can be conclusively proved or rejected. But once we move to the stage of empirical verification, logic and rigor quickly give way to intuition and experience. The insufficiency of logic and rigor is equally evident when we discuss the scope of a theory or choose the initial assumptions.

Despite the unfamiliar element of formal theory, economics, like history, can be seen as an interactive dialogue between theoretical structures and empirical studies that serve to verify and validate the theory and also to motivate new waves of theorizing. The juxtaposition of high unemployment with a theory that denied the possibility of long-term joblessness inspired Keynes to design a model that permitted an underemployment equilibrium. The inability of Keynes's theory to explain the existence of "stagflation"—the simultaneous presence of substantial unemployment and inflation—led to so-called new classical models that label unemployment as voluntary and indicate that Keynesian monetary and fiscal policies (e.g., reducing tax rates or interest rates to stave off recession) may not produce the anticipated results. Neo-Keynesians, rejecting these conclusions, have used the assumptions favored by the new classical school to create models that generate involuntary unemployment and validate activist macroeconomic policies (Mankiew 1988; McCallum 1988). And so on.

This constant interchange between theoretical and empirical concerns offers a fertile hunting ground for historians in search of new ways of using existing data. An important strand in the recent literature of economic history (the so-called new economic history) consists of studies that apply theoretical principles to concrete historical issues. These writings can help to bridge the gap between abstract theory and actual research problems. Empirically oriented economists face an obstacle familiar to every historian: available data do not correspond to the original research agenda. Faced with these difficulties, economists exploit theoretical reasoning to frame tests that allow existing materials to evaluate seem-

2. Two types of books are particularly worthwhile. Several recent volumes explore the links between economics and other disciplines: see Bardhan 1989, Swedberg 1990, and Granovetter and Swedberg 1992. There are also a number of recent and classic volumes in which economists reach out to a wider audience. Examples of this genre include Arrow 1974, Bhagwati 1988, Blinder 1987, Friedman 1962, Hayek 1944, Hirschman 1970, Krugman 1990a, Olson 1965 and 1982, and Weitzman 1984.

3. Particularly the *Journal of Economic Perspectives,* the annual conference issue (published in May) of the *American Economic Review,* and the *Journal of Economic Literature.*

ingly distant hypotheses. The ingenuity of economists searching for information that can be used as a "proxy" or substitute for missing information is quite remarkable. Thus Robert Fogel, requiring information on the cost of merchandise lost in transit on nineteenth-century U.S. railways and canals, turned to insurance rates. The logic of self-interest assures us that insurance rates must approximate the required cost information: the insurers can be trusted to keep the premiums above the level of expected losses; the self-interest of their customers and rivalry among insurers will keep the premiums from moving far above the expected payout (Fogel 1964).

An interest in empirical research also leads to the treasure-house of comparative economics. Historians debating the importance of economic causes in China's communist revolution will want to measure the scale of taxation (Rawski 1989, chap. 1). Whatever the outcome, it is surely helpful to know that the infamous British imposts that ignited the Boston Tea Party and fanned the flames of revolution in the American colonies amounted to less than 1 percent of aggregate colonial output (McCloskey 1987, chap. 4). Students of agrarian decline should know that the share of agriculture in total output and employment has fallen rapidly in every industrializing economy, including those like Denmark and Australia that continue to export large amounts of farm produce (Kuznets 1966).

In conducting empirical research, economists tend to focus on people's actions rather than words. They see actions as responses to economic circumstance. Words are also affected by self-interest but often reflect the speaker's desire to change the circumstances rather than to achieve maximum benefit under existing arrangements. The constellation of circumstances includes, but need not be restricted to, monetary matters. The percentage of American high school graduates attending college has risen steadily for decades. A future historian who relied on newspaper accounts bemoaning the high cost of tuition might easily conclude that the percentage of young people attending college was declining rather than rising. The problem is that parental complaints and media accounts of these concerns have a hidden agenda—to build a consensus for creating new tax deductions for tuition payments.

The American press often compares current economic circumstances to the hard times of the 1930s. Again, there is a hidden agenda: announcements of doom sell newspapers and attract viewers. Even if these statements reflected the genuine belief of their authors, some of whom may have vivid personal recollections of the 1930s, no historian can seriously doubt that the income, wealth, and living standards of Americans have expanded considerably in the past half century, and that material deprivation is less common today than during the 1930s. Similar difficulties arise in other societies. A Chinese economist's account of the depression years, written in 1936, argues that

> Newspaper and magazine accounts of industrial development from which authors . . . generally draw their information—in fact, even the *so-called first hand information* from those engaged in these industries—are often based on impressions rather than absolute facts, especially when they refer to general conditions, and must be taken with more than a grain of salt.

> After 1925, the golden age of the Chinese cotton industry was over, but as may be seen from the spindlage statistics . . . its development continued. However, most writers and

252 Some Advice to the Reader

many businessmen consider the industry to have been in a state of continuous decline ever since. What actually happened was that windfall profits were no more realizable, and business had to be carried out on a more conservative basis. (Lieu 1936, 15–16, 29; emphasis added)

These examples help explain the economist's discomfort with assertions that rest exclusively on anecdotal materials. In these cases, and in many others, recourse to quantitative materials—about numbers of college students or unemployed workers, the size of welfare budgets, or increases in cotton spindles, textile employees, or yarn production—may offer more reliable insight than the testimony even of dispassionate observers. It is not that statistics are never misleading or that economists are not "concerned about people" (Sheridan 1985, 35), but rather that economists are properly skeptical of generalizations about large numbers of consumers, workers, business firms, or transactions that arise from the written or oral testimony of witnesses whose knowledge, even if disinterested, may not be typical or representative of the large population whom the historian intends to study.

In order to avoid the sins of "false quantification" (Fisher 1970, chap. 4), the historian is well advised to

6. DEVELOP A NOSE FOR NUMBERS.

There is no need to abandon traditional sources. But when these materials invite generalizations that have quantitative implications or suggest quantitative antecedents, the historian should ponder their plausibility whether or not relevant statistics are readily available. Before discussing the lack of "affordable housing," we need to compare household incomes with housing prices and look at changes in the rate of home-ownership and mortgage defaults. Claims of extortionate taxation invite questions about the ratio of tax collections to total output and about the benefits to taxpayers of public outlays. Economists constantly search for implications that can be verified with quantitative materials. Historians can benefit from joining in this endeavor. If available data confirm what we expect from other evidence, so much the better. If not, we must evaluate the relative merit of different types of evidence, a task familiar to all historians.

Finally, historians should seek opportunities to

7. TALK TO ECONOMISTS ABOUT ECONOMICS.

Economists love to discuss their field. Like the Italians or the Chinese, they will be delighted to learn that you speak their language and eager to help you learn more.

References

Abramovitz, Moses. 1968. "The Passing of the Kuznets Cycle." *Economica* 35, no. 140: 349–367.

———. 1989. *Thinking About Growth and Other Essays on Economic Growth and Welfare.* New York: Cambridge University Press.

Adams, Donald R. 1982. "The Standard of Living during American Industrialization: Evidence from the Brandywine Region, 1800–1860." *Journal of Economic History* 42, no. 4: 903–917.

Aharoni, Yair. 1991. *The Israeli Economy: Dreams and Realities.* London: Routledge.

Akerlof, George A. 1984. *An Economic Theorist's Book of Tales.* Cambridge: Cambridge University Press.

Akerlof, George A., and Janet L. Yellen. 1986. *Efficiency Wage Models of the Labor Market.* New York: Cambridge University Press.

———. 1990. "The Fair Wage-Effort Hypothesis and Unemployment." *Quarterly Journal of Economics* 105, no. 2: 255–283.

Alchian, Armen A. 1977. *Economic Forces at Work.* Indianapolis: Liberty Press.

Alchian, Armen A., and Harold Demsetz. 1972. "Production, Information Costs, and Economic Organization." *American Economic Review* 62, no. 5: 777–795.

Alston, Lee J., and Robert Higgs. 1982. "Contractual Mix in Southern Agriculture since the Civil War: Facts, Hypothesis, and Tests." *Journal of Economic History* 42, no. 2: 327–354.

Anderson, Kym, and Yujiro Hayami. 1986. *The Political Economy of Agricultural Protection: East Asia in International Perspective.* London: Allen and Unwin.

Aoki, Masahiko. 1990. "Toward an Economic Model of the Japanese Firm." *Journal of Economic Literature* 28, no. 1: 1–27.

Arrow, Kenneth. 1974. *The Limits of Organization*. New York: W. W. Norton.

Arthur, W. Brian. 1994. *Increasing Returns and Path Dependence in the Economy*. Ann Arbor: University of Michigan Press.

Bagehot, Walter. 1924 (1873). *Lombard Street: A Description of the Money Market*, 14th ed., revised. London: John Murray.

Bairoch, Paul. 1989. "Wages as an Indicator of Gross National Product." In *Real Wages in 19th- and 20th-Century Europe*, ed. Peter Scholliers, 51–60. Providence: Berg Publishers.

Baldwin, Robert E. 1984. "Trade Policy in Developed Countries." In *Handbook of International Economics*, eds. Ronald Jones and Peter Kenen, 1:571–619. New York: North-Holland.

Bale, Malcolm D., and Ernst Lutz. 1981. "Price Distortions in Agriculture and their Effects: An International Comparison." *American Journal of Agricultural Economics* 63, no. 1: 8–22.

Bardhan, Pranab, ed. 1989. *Conversations Between Economists and Anthropologists: Methodological Issues in Measuring Economic Change in Rural India*. Oxford: Oxford University Press.

Barro, Robert. 1977. "Unanticipated Money Growth and Unemployment in the United States." *American Economic Review* 67, no. 1: 101–115.

Bates, Robert H., V. Y. Mudimbe, and Jean O'Barr, eds. 1993. *Africa and the Disciplines*. Chicago: University of Chicago Press.

Becker, Gary S. 1981. *A Treatise on the Family*. Cambridge, Mass.: Harvard University Press.

————. 1993. *Human Capital: A Theoretical Analysis with Special Reference to Education*. 3d edition. Chicago: University of Chicago Press.

Bell, Lynda S. 1985. "Explaining China's Rural Crisis: Observations from Wuxi County in the Early Twentieth Century." *Republican China* 11, no. 1: 15–31.

————. 1992. "Farming, Sericulture, and Peasant Rationality in Wuxi County in the Early Twentieth Century." In *Chinese History in Economic Perspective*, eds. Thomas G. Rawski and Lillian M. Li, 207–242. Berkeley: University of California Press.

Berlant, Jeffrey. 1975. *Profession and Monopoly*. Berkeley: University of California Press.

Bernanke, Ben S. 1983. "Nonmonetary Effects of the Financial Crises in the Propagation of the Great Depression." *American Economic Review* 73, no. 3: 257–276.

Bernheim, B. Douglas, Andrei Schleifer, and Lawrence H. Summers. 1985. "The Strategic Bequest Motive." *Journal of Political Economy* 93, no. 6: 1045–1075.

Bhagwati, Jagdish. 1988. *Protectionism*. Cambridge, Mass.: MIT Press.

Bidwell, Percy W. 1916. "Rural Economy in New England at the Beginning of the Nineteenth Century." *Transactions of the Connecticut Academy of Arts and Sciences* 20 (April): 241–399.

Binswanger, Hans P., and Pascuale L. Scandizzo. 1983. "Patterns of Agricultural Protection." Discussion paper, World Bank.

Birnberg, Thomas B., and Stephen A. Resnick. *Colonial Development: An Econometric Study*. New Haven: Yale University Press, 1975.

Blanchard, Olivier J., and Lawrence H. Summers. 1990. "Hysteresis and the European Unemployment Problem." In *Understanding Unemployment,* ed. Lawrence H. Summers, 227–285. Cambridge, Mass.: MIT Press.

Blank, Rebecca M. 1993. "What Should Mainstream Economics Learn from Feminist Theory?" In *Beyond Economic Man: Feminist Theory and Economics,* ed. Marianne A. Ferber and Julie A. Nelson, 133–143. Chicago: University of Chicago Press.

Blinder, Alan S. 1974. "The Economics of Brushing Teeth." *Journal of Political Economy* 82, no. 4: 887–891.

———. 1987. *Hard Heads, Soft Hearts: Tough-minded Economics for a Just Society.* Reading, Mass.: Addison-Wesley.

Bogart, E. L., and C. M. Thompson, eds. 1929. *Readings in the Economic History of the United States.* New York: Longmans.

Bonke, Jens. 1992. "Distribution of Economic Resources: Implications of Including the Household Production." *Review of Income and Wealth* 38, no. 3: 281–294.

Bordo, Michael D. 1975. "John R. Cairnes on the Effects of the Australian Gold Discoveries, 1851–73: An Early Application of the Methodology of Positive Economics." *History of Political Economy* 7, no. 3: 337–359.

———. 1981. "The Classical Gold Standard: Some Lessons for Today." Federal Reserve Bank of St. Louis, *Review* 63, no. 1: 1–17.

———. 1984. "The Gold Standard: The Traditional Approach." In *A Retrospective on the Classical Gold Standard, 1821–1931,* ed. Michael D. Bordo and Anna J. Schwartz, 23–113. Chicago: University of Chicago Press.

———. 1989. "The Contribution of a Monetary History of the United States, 1867—1960 to Monetary History." In *Money, History, and International Finance: Essays in Honor of Anna J. Schwartz,* ed. Michael D. Bordo, 15–70. Chicago: University of Chicago Press.

Bordo, Michael D., and Anna J. Schwartz, eds. 1984. *A Retrospective on the Classical Gold Standard, 1821–1931.* Chicago: University of Chicago Press.

Bowles, Samuel. 1985. "The Production Process in a Competitive Economy: Walrasian, Neo-Hobbsian, and Marxian Models." *American Economic Review* 75, no. 1: 16–36.

Bowles, Samuel, and Herbert Gintis. 1976. *Schooling in Capitalist America: Educational Reform and the Contradictions of Economic Life.* New York: Basic Books.

Brandt, Loren. 1985. "Chinese Agriculture and the International Economy, 1870–1930s: A Reassessment." *Explorations in Economic History* 22, no. 2: 168–193.

———. 1987. Review of *The Peasant Economy and Social Change in North China,* by Philip C. C. Huang. *Economic Development and Cultural Change* 35, no. 3: 670–682.

———. 1989. *Commercialization and Agricultural Development: Central and Eastern China, 1870–1937.* Cambridge: Cambridge University Press.

Braudel, Fernand, and Frank Spooner. 1967. "Prices in Europe from 1450 to 1750." In *The Cambridge Economic History of Europe,* ed. E. E. Rich and C. H. Wilson, 4:378–486. Cambridge: Cambridge University Press.

Buchanan, James M. 1979. *What Should Economists Do?* Indianapolis: Liberty Press.

Buchanan, James M., Robert D. Tollison, and Gordon Tullock, eds. 1980. *Toward a Theory of the Rent-Seeking Society.* College Station: Texas A and M University Press.

Buck, John Lossing. 1930. *Chinese Farm Economy.* Chicago: University of Chicago Press.

———. 1937a. *Land Utilization in China.* Chicago: University of Chicago Press.

———. 1937b. *Land Utilization in China: Statistics.* Nanking: University of Nanking.

Butler, Richard J., James J. Heckman, and Brook Payner. 1989. "The Impact of the Economy and the State on the Economic Status of Blacks: A Study of South Carolina." In *Markets in History: Economic Studies of the Past,* ed. David W. Galenson, 231–346. Cambridge: Cambridge University Press.

Cagan, Phillip. 1956. "The Monetary Dynamics of Hyperinflation." In *Studies in the Quantity Theory of Money,* ed. Milton Friedman, 25–120. Chicago: University of Chicago Press.

———. 1989. "Hyperinflation." In *The New Palgrave Dictionary of Economics: Money,* ed. John Eatwell, Murray Milgate, and Peter Newman, 179–184. New York: W. W. Norton.

Calabresi, Guido, and Philip Bobbitt. 1978. *Tragic Choices.* New York: W. W. Norton.

Cairnes, John E. 1873. "Essays on the Gold Question." In *Essays in Political Economy.* London: Macmillan.

Cardoso, Fernando Henrique, and Enzo Faletto. 1979. *Dependency and Development in Latin America.* Berkeley: University of California Press.

Carter, Susan B. 1993. "Sticky Wages, Cheaper Living, and the Late Nineteenth-Century American Labor Market." Paper presented at the annual meeting of the Economic History Association, Tucson, Ariz. (September).

Carter, Susan B., and Peter W. Philips. 1990. "Continuous-Process Technologies and the Gender Gap in Manufacturing Wages." In *New Developments in the Labor Market: Toward a New Institutional Paradigm,* ed. Katherine Abraham and Robert McKersie, 213–238. Cambridge, Mass.: MIT Press.

Carter, Susan B., and Mark Prus. 1982. "The Labor Market and the American High School Girl, 1890–1928." *Journal of Economic History* 62, no. 1: 163–171.

Carter, Susan B., and Elizabeth Savoca. 1991. "Gender Differences in Learning and Earning in Nineteenth-Century America: The Role of Expected Job and Career Attachment." *Explorations in Economic History* 28, no. 3: 323–343.

Carter, Susan B., and Richard Sutch. 1991. "Sticky Wages, Short Weeks, and 'Fairness'; The Response of Connecticut Manufacturing Firms to the Depression of 1893–94." Working paper no. 2, Historical Labor Statistics project, Institute of Business and Economic Research, University of California, Berkeley.

Chandler, Alfred, Jr. 1962. *Strategy and Structure.* Cambridge, Mass.: MIT Press.

———. 1977. *The Visible Hand: The Managerial Revolution in American Business.* Cambridge, Mass.: Harvard University Press.

Chao, Kang. 1977. *The Development of Cotton Textile Production in China.* Cambridge, Mass.: Harvard University East Asian Research Center.

Chayanov, A. V. 1966. *A. V. Chayanov on The Theory of the Peasant Economy,* ed. Daniel Thorner, Basile Kerblay, and R. E. F. Smith. Homewood, Ill.: Richard D. Irwin.

Checkland, Sidney G. 1975. *Scottish Banking: A History, 1695–1973.* Glasgow: Collins.

Chen, Chau-nan. 1975. "Flexible Bimetallic Exchange Rates in China, 1650–1850: A Historical Example of Optimum Currency Areas." *Journal of Money, Credit, and Banking* 7, no. 3: 359–376.

Chen, Han-seng. 1939. *Industrial Capital and Chinese Peasants: A Study of the Livelihood of Chinese Tobacco Cultivators.* Shanghai: Kelly and Walsh. Reprint, New York: Garland, 1980.

Ch'en, Po-chuang. 1936. *Hsiao mai chi mien fen* (Wheat and wheat flour). Shanghai: Chiao-t'ung Ta Hsüeh Yen Chiu So.

Cheung, Steven N. S. 1969. *The Theory of Share Tenancy.* Chicago: University of Chicago Press.

China, Inspectorate General of Customs, Shanghai. 1914. *Returns of Trade and Trade Reports, 1914.* 3 vols.

———. 1933. *The Foreign Trade of China, 1933.*

Chiu Chung-kuo chi chih mien fen kung yeh t'ung chi tzu liao (Statistical materials on the flour industry in old China). 1966. Peking: Chung Hua Shu Chü.

Chūshi no minsengyō: Soshū minsen jittai chōsa hōkoku (The junk trade of central China: Survey report on junk conditions at Soochow). 1943. 2 vols. Tokyo: Hōbunkan.

Clapham, John H. 1958. *The Bank of England: A History.* 2 vols. Cambridge: Cambridge University Press.

Clark, Gregory. 1988. "The Cost of Capital and Medieval Agricultural Technique." *Explorations in Economic History* 25, no. 3: 265–294.

———. 1992. "The Economics of Exhaustion, the Postan Thesis, and the Agricultural Revolution." *Journal of Economic History* 52, no. 1: 61–84.

Clower, Robert W. 1989. "The State of Economics: Hopeless but not Serious?" In *The Spread of Economic Ideas,* ed. David Colander and A. W. Coats, 23–29. Cambridge: Cambridge University Press.

Coase, Ronald H. 1937. "The Nature of the Firm." *Economica,* n.s., 4. Reprinted in *The Nature of the Firm: Origins, Evolution, and Development,* ed. Oliver E. Williamson and Sidney G. Winter (New York: Oxford University Press, 1993), 18–33.

———. 1984. "The New Institutional Economics." *Journal of Institutional and Theoretical Economics* no. 140 (March): 229–231.

———. 1988. *The Firm, The Market, and the Law.* Chicago: University of Chicago Press.

Cohen, Jon S., and Martin L. Weitzman. 1975. "A Marxian Model of Enclosures." *Journal of Development Economics* 1, no. 4: 287–336.

Colander, David. 1989. "The Invisible Hand of Truth." In *The Spread of Economic Ideas,* ed. David Colander and A. W. Coats, 31–36. Cambridge: Cambridge University Press.

———. 1991. *Why Aren't Economists as Important as Garbagemen? Essays on the State of Economics.* Armonk, N.Y.: M. E. Sharpe.

Colander, David, and A. W. Coats, eds. 1989. *The Spread of Economic Ideas.* Cambridge: Cambridge University Press.

Collier, Paul. 1993. "Africa and the Study of Economics." In *Africa and the Disciplines,* ed. Robert H. Bates, V. Y. Mudimbe, and Jean O'Barr, 58–82. Chicago: University of Chicago Press.

Conrad, Alfred, and John R. Meyer. 1958. "The Economics of Slavery in the Antebellum South." *Journal of Political Economy* 66, no. 2: 95–130.

Crafts, N. F. R. 1980. "Income Elasticities of Demand and the Release of Labour by Agriculture during the British Industrial Revolution." *Journal of European Economic History* 9, no. 1: 153–168.

———. 1985. *British Economic Growth during the Industrial Revolution.* Oxford: Oxford University Press.

Craig, John. 1953. *The Mint: A History of the London Mint from A.D. 287 to 1948.* Cambridge: Cambridge University Press.

Craig, Lee A., and Elizabeth Field-Hendrey. 1993. "Industrialization and the Earnings Gap: Regional and Sectoral Tests of the Goldin-Sokoloff Hypothesis." *Explorations in Economic History* 30, no. 1: 60–80.

Cullenberg, Stephen. 1988. "The Rhetoric of Marxian Microfoundations." *Review of Radical Political Economics* 20, no. 2–3: 12–17.

David, Paul A. 1971. "The Landscape and the Machine: Technical Interrelatedness, Land Tenure and the Mechanization of the Corn Harvest in Victorian Britain." In *Essays on a Mature Economy: Britain after 1840,* ed. Donald N. McCloskey, 145–205. London: Methuen.

———. 1975a. *Technical Choice, Innovation and Economic Growth.* Cambridge: Cambridge University Press.

———. 1975b. "The Mechanization of Reaping in the Antebellum Midwest." In *Technical Choice, Innovation and Economic Growth,* 195–232. Cambridge: Cambridge University Press.

———. 1985. "Clio and the Economics of QWERTY." *American Economic Review* 75, no. 2: 332–337.

———. 1987. "Industrial Labor Market Adjustments in a Region of Recent Settlement: Chicago, 1848–1868." In *Quantity and Quiddity: Essays in U.S. Economic History,* ed. Peter Kilby, 47–97. Middletown, Conn.: Wesleyan University Press.

David, Paul A., and Peter Solar. 1977. "A Bicentenary Contribution to the History of the Cost of Living in America." *Research in Economic History* no. 2: 1–80.

Davis, Lance E. 1971. "Specification, Quantification, and Analysis in Economic History." In *Approaches to American Economic History,* ed. George Rogers Taylor, 106–120. Charlottesville: Eleutherian Mills–Hagley Foundation.

Davis, Lance E., and Robert A. Huttenback. 1989. *Mammon and the Pursuit of Empire: The Political Economy of British Imperialism, 1860–1912.* Cambridge: Cambridge University Press.

Davis, Lance E., Richard A. Easterlin, William N. Parker, Dorothy S. Brady, Albert Fishlow, Robert E. Gallman, Stanley Lebergott, Robert E. Lipsey, Douglass C. North, Nathan Rosenberg, Eugene Smolensky, and Peter Temin. 1971. *American Economic Growth.* New York: Harper and Row.

Deane, P., and W. A. Cole. 1967. *British Economic Growth 1688–1959: Trends and Structure.* Cambridge: Cambridge University Press.

DeCanio, Stephen J., and Joel Mokyr. 1977. "Inflation and Wage Lag during the American Civil War." *Explorations in Economic History* 14, no. 4: 311–336.

Defoe, Daniel. 1975 (1719). *Robinson Crusoe,* ed. Michael Shinagel. New York: Norton.

Demsetz, Harold. 1967. "Toward a Theory of Property Rights." *American Economic Review Papers and Proceedings* 57, no. 2: 347–359.

Dernberger, Robert F., ed. 1980. *China's Development Experience in Comparative Perspective.* Cambridge, Mass.: Harvard University Press.

DeRoover, Raymond. 1963. *The Rise and Decline of the Medici Bank.* Cambridge, Mass.: Harvard University Press.

De Vries, Jan. 1991. "How Did Pre-Industrial Labor Markets Function?" Paper presented at the McGill University Conference on the Evolution of Labour Markets, Montreal (February).

Diaz-Alejandro, Carlos F. 1970. *Essays on the Economic History of the Argentine Republic.* New Haven: Yale University Press.

———. 1975. "North-South Relations: The Economic Component." *International Organization* 29, no. 1: 213–241.

Dittrich, Scott R., and Ramon H. Myers. 1971. "Resource Allocation in Traditional Agriculture: Republican China, 1937–1940." *Journal of Political Economy* 79, no. 4: 887–896.

Doeringer, Peter, and Michael Piore. 1985. *Internal Labor Markets and Manpower Analysis.* New York: M. E. Sharpe.

Domar, Evsey. 1970. "The Causes of Slavery or Serfdom: A Hypothesis." *Journal of Economic History* 30, no. 1: 18–32.

Dore, Ronald P. 1959. *Land Reform in Japan.* London: Oxford University Press.

Dornbusch, Rudiger, and Sebastian Edwards, eds. 1991. *The Macroeconomics of Populism in Latin America.* Chicago: University of Chicago Press.

Easterlin, Richard. 1960. "Regional Growth of Income: Long Term Tendencies." In *Population Redistribution and Long Term Growth: United States, 1870–1950,* ed. Simon Kuznets, 2:141–204. Philadelphia: American Philosophical Society.

Eastman, Byron D. 1984. *Interpreting Mathematical Economics and Econometrics.* New York: St. Martins.

Eatwell, John, Murray Milgate, and Peter Newman, eds. 1987. *The New Palgrave Dictionary of Economics.* 4 vols. New York: Stockton Press.

Elvin, Mark. 1970. "The Last Thousand Years of Chinese History: Changing Patterns in Land Tenure." *Modern Asian Studies* 4, no. 2: 97–114.

Epstein, Gerald, and Thomas Ferguson. 1984. "Monetary Policy, Loan Liquidation, and Industrial Conflict: The Federal Reserve and the Great Contraction." *Journal of Economic History* 44, no. 4: 957–984.

Evans, Paul. 1982. "The Effects of General Price Controls in the United States during World War II." *Journal of Political Economy* 90, no. 5: 944–966.

Feavearyear, Albert Edgar. 1931. *The Pound Sterling: A History of English Money*. Oxford: Oxford University Press.

Feeny, David, Fikret Berkes, Bonnie J. McCay, and James M. Acheson. 1990. "The Tragedy of the Commons: Twenty-Two Years Later." *Human Ecology* 18, no. 1: 1–19.

Feinstein, Charles H. 1972. *National Income, Expenditure and Output of the United Kingdom, 1855–1965*. Cambridge: Cambridge University Press.

Ferber, Marianne A., and Julie A. Nelson. 1993. *Beyond Economic Man: Feminist Theory and Economics*. Chicago: University of Chicago Press.

Feuerwerker, Albert. 1978. "Handicraft and Manufactured Cotton Textiles in China, 1871–1910." *Journal of Economic History* 30, no. 2 (1970): 338–378.

Fforde, John. 1992. *The Bank of England and Public Policy, 1941–1958*. New York: Cambridge University Press.

Field, Alexander James. 1978. "Sectoral Shift in Antebellum Massachusetts: A Reconsideration." *Explorations in Economic History* 15, no. 1: 146–171.

———. 1980. "Industrialization and Skill Intensity: The Case of Massachusetts." *Journal of Human Resources* 15, no. 2: 149–175.

———. 1983. "Land Abundance, Interest/Profit Rates, and Nineteenth-Century American and British Technology." *Journal of Economic History* 43, no. 2: 405–432.

———. 1985. "On the Unimportance of Machinery." *Explorations in Economic History* 22, no. 4: 378–401.

Fishback, Price V. 1992. *Soft Coal, Hard Choices: The Economic Welfare of Bituminous Coal Miners, 1890–1930*. New York: Oxford University Press.

Fischer, David Hackett 1970. *Historians' Fallacies: Toward a Logic of Historical Thought*. New York: Harper and Row.

Fisher, Irving. 1896. "Appreciation and Interest." *Publications of the American Economic Association* 11: 331–342.

Floud, Roderick. 1973. *An Introduction to Quantitative Methods for Historians*. Princeton: Princeton University Press.

———, ed. 1974. *Essays in Quantitative Economic History*. Oxford: Oxford University Press.

Floud, Roderick, and Donald N. McCloskey, eds. 1981. *The Economic History of Britain since 1700*. 2 vols. Cambridge: Cambridge University Press.

Fogel, Robert W. 1964. *Railroads and American Economic Growth: Essays in Econometric History*. Baltimore: Johns Hopkins University Press.

Folbre, Nancy. 1986a. "Cleaning House: New Perspectives on Households and Economic Development." *Journal of Development Economics* 22, no. 1: 5–40.

———. 1986b. "Hearts and Spades: Paradigms of Household Economics." *World Development* 14, no. 2: 245–255.

Folbre, Nancy, and Barnet Wagman. 1993. "Counting Housework: New Estimates of Real Product in the United States, 1800–1860." *Journal of Economic History* 53, no. 2: 275–288.

Fong, H. D. 1932. *Cotton Industry and Trade in China.* 2 vols. Tientsin: Nankai Institute of Economics.

Frank, Andre Gunder. 1969. *Capitalism and Underdevelopment in Latin America.* New York: Modern Reader.

Franklin, Benjamin. 1840 (1760). "The Interest of Great Britain Considered, with Regard to her Colonies and the Acquisition of Canada and Guadelope." In *Works of Benjamin Franklin,* ed. J. Sparks, 4:1–53. Boston: Hilliard Gray and Company.

Friedman, Milton. 1956. "The Quantity Theory of Money: A Restatement." In *Studies in the Quantity Theory of Money,* ed. Milton Friedman, 3–21. Chicago: University of Chicago Press.

———. 1962. *Capitalism and Freedom.* Chicago: University of Chicago Press.

———. 1968. "The Role of Monetary Policy." *American Economic Review* 58, no. 1: 1–17.

———. 1969. *The Optimum Quantity of Money and Other Essays.* Chicago: Aldine.

———. 1989. "Quantity Theory of Money." In *The New Palgrave Dictionary of Economics: Money,* ed. John Eatwell, Murray Milgate, and Peter Newman, 1–40. New York: W. W. Norton.

———. 1990a. "Bimetallism Revisited." *Journal of Economic Perspectives* 4, no. 1: 85–104.

———. 1990b. "The Crime of 1873." *Journal of Political Economy* 98, no. 6: 1159–1194.

Friedman, Milton, and Anna Jacobson Schwartz. 1963. *A Monetary History of the United States, 1867–1960.* Princeton: Princeton University Press.

Furtado, Celso. 1976. *Economic Development of Latin America: Historical Background and Contemporary Problems.* Cambridge: Cambridge University Press.

Galbraith, John Kenneth. 1993. *A Short History of Financial Euphoria.* New York: Whittle Books.

Galenson, David. 1981. *White Servitude in Colonial America: An Economic Analysis.* Cambridge: Cambridge University Press.

———. 1986. *Traders, Planters and Slaves: Market Behavior in Early English America.* Cambridge: Cambridge University Press.

Geertz, Clifford 1979. "Suq: The Bazaar Economy in Sefrou." In *Meaning and Order in Moroccan Society: Three Essays in Cultural Analysis,* ed. Clifford Geertz, 123–313. Cambridge: Cambridge University Press.

Gemery, Henry A., and Jan S. Hogendorn. 1974. "The Atlantic Slave Trade: A Tentative Economic Model." *Journal of African History* 15: 223–246.

Gerschenkron, Alexander. 1943. *Bread and Democracy in Germany.* Berkeley: University of California Press.

———. 1951. *A Dollar Index of Soviet Machinery Output.* Santa Monica: RAND Corporation.

———. 1962. "Reflections on the Concept of 'Prerequisites' of Modern Industrialization." In *Economic Backwardness in Historical Perspective,* 31–51. Cambridge, Mass.: Harvard University Press.

————. 1968. "On the Concept of Continuity in History." In *Continuity in History and Other Essays*, 11–39. Cambridge, Mass.: Harvard University Press.

Gillis, Malcolm, Dwight H. Perkins, Michael Roemer, and Donald R. Snodgrass. 1992. *Economics of Development*. 3d ed. New York: W. W. Norton.

Gintis, Herbert. 1976. "The Nature of the Labour Exchange." *Review of Radical Political Economy* 8, no. 2: 36–54.

Goldin, Claudia. 1990. *Understanding the Gender Gap: An Economic History of American Women*. New York: Oxford University Press.

Goldin, Claudia, and Kenneth Sokoloff. 1982. "Women, Children, and Industrialization in the Early Republic: Evidence from the Early Manufacturing Censuses." *Journal of Economic History* 42, no. 4: 741–774.

————. 1984. "The Relative Productivity Hypothesis of Industrialization." *Quarterly Journal of Economics* 99, no. 3: 461–488.

Goodhart, Charles. 1988. *The Evolution of Central Banks*. Cambridge, Mass.: MIT Press.

Gordon, David M., Richard Edwards, and Michael Reich. 1982. *Segmented Work, Divided Workers*. Cambridge: Cambridge University Press.

Gordon, Donald F., and Gary M. Walton. 1982. "A Theory of Regenerative Growth and the Experience of Post–World War II West Germany." In *Explorations in the New Economic History: Essays in Honor of Douglass C. North*, ed. Roger L. Ransom, Richard Sutch, and Gary M. Walton, 169–190. New York: Academic Press.

Gottschang, Thomas R. 1987. "Structural Change, Disasters, and Migration: The Historical Case of Manchuria." *Economic Development and Cultural Change* 35, no. 3: 461–490.

Gould, J. D. 1970. *The Great Debasement*. Oxford: Oxford University Press.

Gourevitch, Peter Alexis. 1977. "International Trade, Domestic Coalitions, and Liberty: Comparative Responses to the Crisis of 1873–1896." *Journal of Interdisciplinary History* 8, no. 2: 281–313.

Granovetter, Mark, and Richard Swedberg, eds. 1992. *The Sociology of Economic Life*. Boulder: Westview.

Grantham, George W. 1978. "The Diffusion of the New Husbandry in Northern France, 1815–1840." *Journal of Economic History* 38, no. 2: 311–337.

Gutman, Herbert G. 1977. *Work, Culture, and Society in Industrializing America*. New York: Vintage Books.

Habakkuk, H. J. 1962. *American and British Technology in the Nineteenth Century: The Search for Labour Saving Inventions*. Cambridge: Cambridge University Press.

Hamilton, Earl J. 1934. *American Treasure and the Price Revolution in Spain, 1501–1650*. Cambridge, Mass.: Harvard University Press.

Hanes, Christopher. 1992. "Comparable Indices of Wholesale Prices and Manufacturing Wage Rates in the United States, 1895–1914." *Research in Economic History* no. 14: 269–292.

————. 1993. "The Development of Nominal Wage Rigidity in the Late 19th Century." *American Economic Review* 83, no. 4: 732–756.

Harley, Charles K. 1971. "The Shift from Sailing Ships to Steamships, 1850–1890: A Study in Technological Change and its Diffusion." In *Essays on a Mature Economy: Britain After 1840,* ed. Donald N. McCloskey, 215–231. Princeton: Princeton University Press.

———. 1982. "British Industrialization before 1841: Evidence of Slower Growth during the Industrial Revolution." *Journal of Economic History* 42, no. 2: 267–289.

———. 1993. "Reassessing the Industrial Revolution: A Macro View." In *The British Industrial Revolution: An Economic Perspective,* ed. Joel Mokyr, 171–226. Boulder: Westview.

Harper, Lucinda. 1994. "Commerce Department Now Measures Economy's Impact on the Environment." *Wall Street Journal,* 11 May.

Hatton, Timothy J., and Jeffrey G. Williamson. 1991. "Integrated and Segmented Labor Markets: Thinking in Two Sectors." *Journal of Economic History* 51, no. 2: 413–427.

Hawke, G. R. 1980. *Economics for Historians.* Cambridge: Cambridge University Press.

———. 1981. "Transport and Social Overhead Cost." In *The Economic History of Britain since 1700,* ed. Roderick Floud and Donald N. McCloskey, 1:227–252. Cambridge: Cambridge University Press.

Hayami, Yujiro, and Vernon W. Ruttan. 1971. *Agricultural Development: An International Perspective.* Baltimore: Johns Hopkins University Press.

Hayek, Friedrich A. 1944. *The Road to Serfdom.* Chicago: University of Chicago Press.

Helleiner, Gerald K. 1975. "Smallholder Decision Making: Tropical African Evidence." In *Agriculture in Development Theory,* ed. Lloyd G. Reynolds, 27–52. New Haven: Yale University Press.

Heywood, Colin. 1981. "The Role of the Peasantry in French Industrialization, 1815–80." *Economic History Review,* 2d s., 34, no. 3: 359–376.

Higgs, Robert. 1974. "Patterns of Farm Rental in the Georgia Cotton Belt, 1880–1900." *Journal of Economic History* 34, no. 2: 468–482.

Hill, Polly. 1986. *Development Economics on Trial: The Anthropological Case for a Prosecution.* Cambridge: Cambridge University Press.

Hirschman, Albert O. 1970. *Exit, Voice, and Loyalty: Responses to Decline in Firms, Organizations, and States.* Cambridge, Mass.: Harvard University Press.

Hoffman, Phillip. 1995. *Growth in a Traditional Society: The French Countryside, 1450–1781.* Princeton: Princeton University Press.

Honig, Emily. 1992. "Native Place Hierarchy and Labor Market Segmentation: The Case of Subei People in Shanghai." In *Chinese History in Economic Perspective,* ed. Thomas G. Rawski and Lillian M. Li, 271–294. Berkeley: University of California Press.

Hou, Chi-ming, and Tzong shian Yu, eds. 1979. *Modern Chinese Economic History.* Taipei: Institute of Economics, Academica Sinica.

Houthakker, H. S. 1957. "An International Comparison of Household Expenditure Patterns, Commemorating the Centenary of Engel's Law." *Econometrica* 25, no. 4: 532–551.

Hsiao, Liang-lin. 1974. *Chinese Foreign Trade Statistics, 1864–1949.* Cambridge, Mass.: Harvard University Press.

Hsü, Tao-fu. 1983. *Chung-kuo chin tai nung yeh sheng ch'an chi mao yi t'ung chi tzu liao* (Statistical materials on agricultural production and trade in modern China). Shanghai: Shang-hai Jen Min Ch'u Pan She.

Huang, Philip C. C. 1985. *The Peasant Economy and Social Change in North China.* Stanford: Stanford University Press.

———. 1990. *The Peasant Family and Rural Development in the Yangzi Delta, 1350–1988.* Stanford: Stanford University Press.

Huber, J. Richard. 1971. "Effects on Prices of Japan's Entry into World Commerce after 1858." *Journal of Political Economy* 79, no. 3: 614–628.

Huberman, Michael. 1986. "Invisible Handshakes in Lancashire: Cotton Spinning in the First Half of the Nineteenth Century." *Journal of Economic History* 46, no. 4: 987–998.

Hyde, Charles K. 1977. *Technological Change and the British Iron Industry, 1700–1870.* Princeton: Princeton University Press.

Hymer, Stephen, and Stephen Resnick. 1969. "A Model of an Agrarian Economy with Nonagricultural Activities." *American Economic Review* 59, no. 4, part 1: 493–506.

Innis, Harold A. 1954. *The Cod Fisheries: The History of an International Economy.* Toronto: University of Toronto Press.

———. 1962. *The Fur Trade in Canada: An Introduction to Canadian Economic History.* New Haven: Yale University Press.

Ippolito, Richard A. 1975. "The Effect of the 'Agricultural Depression' on Industrial Demand in England: 1730–1750." *Economica* 42, no. 167: 298–312.

Ito, Takatoshi. 1992. *The Japanese Economy.* Cambridge, Mass.: MIT Press.

James, John A., and Jonathan Skinner. 1985. "The Resolution of the Labor-Scarcity Paradox." *Journal of Economic History* 45, no. 3: 513–540.

Jaynes, Gerald David. 1984. "Economic Theory and Land Tenure." In *Contractual Arrangements, Employment, and Wages in Rural Labor Markets in Asia,* ed. Hans P. Binswanger and Mark R. Rosenzweig, 43–62. New Haven: Yale University Press.

Jensen, Michael, and William H. Meckling. 1976. "Theory of the Firm: Managerial Behavior, Agency Costs, and Ownership Structure." *Journal of Financial Economics* 3, no. 4: 305–360.

Jerome, Harry. 1926. *Migration and Business Cycles.* New York: National Bureau of Economic Research.

Jevons, William Stanley. 1884 (1863). "A Serious Fall in the Value of Gold Ascertained and Its Social Effects Set Forth." In *Investigations in Currency and Finance,* ed. H. S. Foxwell. London: Macmillan. Reprint, New York: Augustus Kelley, 1964.

Jones, Ronald W. 1965. "The Structure of Simple General Equilibrium Models." *Journal of Political Economy* 73, no. 4: 557–572.

Kaestle, Carl F. 1983. *Pillars of the Republic: Common Schools and American Society, 1780–1860.* New York: Hill and Wang.

Kahn, James A. 1985. "Another Look at Free Banking in the United States." *American Economic Review* 75, no. 4: 881–885.

Kahne, Hilda, and Andrew I. Kohen. 1975. "Economic Perspectives on the Roles of Women in the American Economy." *Journal of Economic Literature* 13, no. 4: 1249–1292.

Keegan, John. 1977. *The Face of Battle*. New York: Vintage.

Kessel, Reuben A., and Armen Alchian. 1959. "Real Wages in the North during the Civil War: Mitchell's Data Reinterpreted." *Journal of Law and Economics* 2, no. 1: 95–113.

Kessler-Harris, Alice. 1990. *A Woman's Wage: Historical Meanings and Social Consequences*. Lexington: University Press of Kentucky.

Kindleberger, Charles P. 1951. "Group Behavior and International Trade." *Journal of Political Economy* 59, no. 4: 30–47.

———. 1978. *Manias, Panics, and Crashes*. New York: Basic Books.

King, Robert G. 1983. "On the Economics of Private Money." *Journal of Monetary Economics* 12, no. 1: 127–158.

Klamer, Arjo. 1988. "Negotiating a New Conversation about Economics." In *The Consequences of Economic Rhetoric*, ed. Arjo Klamer, Donald N. McCloskey, and Robert Solow, 265–279. New York: Cambridge University Press.

Klamer, Arjo, and David Colander. 1990. *The Making of An Economist*. Boulder: Westview.

Klamer, Arjo, Donald N. McCloskey, and Robert Solow, eds. 1988. *The Consequences of Economic Rhetoric*. New York: Cambridge University Press.

Kotlikoff, Laurence J. 1988. "Intergenerational Transfers and Savings." *Journal of Economic Perspectives* 2, no. 2: 41–58.

Kraus, Richard A. 1980. *Cotton and Cotton Goods in China 1918–1936*. New York: Garland.

Kravis, Irving B. 1984. "Comparative Studies of National Income and Prices." *Journal of Economic Literature* 22, no. 1: 1–39.

Krueger, Alan B., and Lawrence H. Summers. 1987. "Reflections on the Inter-Industry Wage Structure." In *Unemployment and the Structure of Labor Markets*, ed. Kevin Lang and Jonathan S. Leonard, 17–47. New York: Basil Blackwell.

Krueger, Anne O. 1974. "The Political Economy of the Rent-Seeking Society." *American Economic Review* 64, no. 3: 291–303.

———. 1984. "Trade Policy in Developing Countries." In *Handbook of International Economics*, ed. Ronald Jones and Peter Kenen, 519–569. New York: North-Holland.

Krugman, Paul R. 1987. "Is Free Trade Passé?" *Journal of Economic Perspectives* 1, no. 2: 131–144.

———. 1990a. *The Age of Diminished Expectations: U.S. Economic Policy in the 1990s*. Cambridge, Mass.: MIT Press.

———. 1990b. *Rethinking International Trade*. Cambridge, Mass.: MIT Press.

———. 1991. *Geography and Trade*. Cambridge, Mass.: MIT Press.

Kuznets, Simon. 1961. *Capital in the American Economy*. Princeton: Princeton University Press.

———. 1966. *Modern Economic Growth: Rate, Structure, and Spread*. New Haven: Yale University Press.

Laidler, David. 1984. "Misconceptions about the Real-Bills Doctrine: A Comment on Sargent and Wallace." *Journal of Political Economy* 90, no. 1: 149–155.

Landes, David S. 1965. "Technological Change and Development in Western Europe, 1750–1914." In *The Cambridge Economic History of Europe,* ed. M. M. Postan and H. J. Habakkuk, vol. 6, part 1, 274–601. Cambridge: Cambridge University Press.

———. 1969. *The Unbound Prometheus: Technological Change and Industrial Development in Western Europe from 1750 to the Present.* Cambridge: Cambridge University Press.

———. 1986. "What Do Bosses Really Do?" *Journal of Economic History* 46, no. 3: 585–623.

Laughlin, James Laurence. 1892. *The History of Bimetallism in the United States.* New York: D. Appleton.

Lazonick, William. 1987. "Theory and History in Marxian Economics." In *The Future of Economic History,* ed. Alexander J. Field, 255–312. Boston: Kluwer-Nijhoff.

Lazonick, William, and Thomas Brush. 1985. "The 'Horndal Effect' in Early U.S. Manufacturing." *Explorations in Economic History* 22, no. 1: 53–96.

Lebergott, Stanley. 1964. *Manpower in Economic Growth: The American Record since 1800.* New York: McGraw-Hill.

———. 1980. "The Returns to U.S. Imperialism, 1890–1929." *Journal of Economic History* 40, no. 2: 229–252.

Lee, James. 1993. "State and Economy in Southwest China, 1250–1850." Manuscript, California Institute of Technology.

Leontief, Wassily. 1971. "Theoretical Assumptions and Non-Observed Facts." *American Economic Review* 61, no. 1: 1–7.

Lester, Richard A. 1939. *Monetary Experiments: Early American and Recent Scandinavian.* Princeton: Princeton University Press.

Lévy, Jean-Philippe. 1967 (1964). *The Economic Life of the Ancient World.* Trans. J. G. Biram. Chicago: University of Chicago Press.

Lewis, W. Arthur. 1954. "Economic Development with Unlimited Supplies of Labour." *Manchester School of Economics and Social Studies* 22. Reprinted in *The Economics of Underdevelopment,* ed. A. N. Agarwala and S. P. Singh. New York: Oxford University Press, 1963, 400–449.

———. 1976. *Growth and Fluctuations 1870–1913.* London: George Allen and Unwin.

Liang, Ernest P. 1982. *China: Railways and Agricultural Development, 1875–1935.* Chicago: University of Chicago Department of Geography.

Libecap, Gary D. 1984. "The Political Allocation of Mineral Rights: A Reevaluation of Teapot Dome." *Journal of Economic History* 44, no. 2: 381–392.

———. 1986. "Property Rights in Economic History: Implications for Research." *Explorations in Economic History* 23, no. 3: 227–252.

Libecap, Gary D., and Steven N. Wiggins. 1984. "Contractual Responses to the Common Pool: Prorationing of Crude Oil Production." *American Economic Review* 74, no. 1: 87–98.

———. 1985. "The Influence of Private Contractual Failure on Regulation: The

Case of Oil Field Unitization." *Journal of Political Economy* 93, no. 4: 690–714.

Lieu, D. K. 1936. *The Growth and Industrialization of Shanghai.* Shanghai: China Institute of Pacific Relations.

Lindbeck, Assar, and Dennis Snower. 1986. "Wage Setting, Unemployment, and Insider-Outsider Relations." *American Economic Review* 76, no. 2: 235–239.

Lindert, Peter H. 1985. "English Population, Wages, and Prices, 1541–1913." *Journal of Interdisciplinary History* 15, no. 4: 609–634.

———. 1988. "Probates, Prices, and Preindustrial Living Standards." In *Inventaires après-décès et ventes de meubles,* ed. M. Baulant, A. J. Schuurman and P. Servais, 171–180. Louvain-la-Neuve: Academia.

———. 1991a. "Historical Patterns of Agricultural Policy." In *Agriculture and the State,* ed. C. Peter Timmer, 29–83. Ithaca: Cornell University Press.

———. 1991b. *International Economics.* 9th ed. Homewood, Ill.: Richard D. Irwin.

Lindert, Peter H., and Jeffrey G. Williamson. 1983. "English Workers' Living Standards during the Industrial Revolution: A New Look." *Economic History Review* 36, no. 1: 1–25.

Lipton, Michael. 1989. *New Seeds and Poor People.* Baltimore: Johns Hopkins University Press.

Liu, Ta-chung, and Kung-chia Yeh. 1965. *The Economy of the Chinese Mainland, 1933–1959.* Princeton: Princeton University Press.

Long, Clarence. 1960. *Wages and Earnings in the United States, 1860–1890.* Princeton: National Bureau of Economic Research.

Lu, Xianxiang. 1993. "Statistical Consequences of the Underground Economy." *Zhongguo tongji* (China's statistics) 11: 29, 36.

Lucas, Robert E. 1973. "Some International Evidence on Output-Inflation Tradeoffs." *American Economic Review* 68, no. 3: 326–334.

Lyons, John S. 1978. "The Lancashire Cotton Industry and the Introduction of the Powerloom, 1815–1850." *Journal of Economic History* 38, no. 1: 238–239.

Mah, Feng-hwa. 1979. "External Influence and Chinese Economic Development: A Re-examination." In *Modern Chinese Economic History,* ed. Chiming Hou and Tzong-shian Yu, 273–302. Taipei: Institute of Economics, Academica Sinica.

Maine. Bureau of Industrial and Labor Statistics. 1895. *Eighth Annual Report 1894.* Augusta, Maine.

Malkiel, Burton G. 1966. *The Term Structure of Interest Rates: Expectations and Behavior Patterns.* Princeton: Princeton University Press.

The Manchuria Year Book 1932–33. Tokyo: Tôa keizai chôsakyoku.

Mankiw, N. Gregory. 1988. "Recent Developments in Macroeconomics: A Very Quick Refresher Course." *Journal of Money, Credit, and Banking* 20, no. 3: 436–458.

Marglin, Stephen A. 1974. "What do Bosses Do? The Origins and Functions of Hierarchy in Capitalist Production." *Review of Radical Political Economy* 6, no. 2: 33–60. Reprinted in *The Division of Labour: The Labour Process*

and Class-Struggle in Modern Capitalism, comp. André Gorz. Atlantic High-
lands, N.J.: Humanities Press, 1976, 13–54.

Margo, Robert A. 1990. *Race and Schooling in the South, 1880–1950.* Chicago:
University of Chicago Press.

Margo, Robert A., and Georgia C. Villaflor. 1987. "The Growth of Wages in
Antebellum America: New Evidence." *Journal of Economic History* 47, no.
4: 873–896.

Marris, Robin. "Comparing the Income of Nations: A Critique of the International Comparisons Project." *Journal of Economic Literature* 22, no. 1: 40–57.

Marshall, Alfred. 1959. *Principles of Economics.* London: Macmillan.

Marx, Karl. 1967 (1867). *Capital.* Trans. Samuel Moore and Edward Aveling.
Vol. 1. New York: International Publishers.

Mathias, Peter, and Patrick O'Brien. 1976. "Taxation in Britain and France,
1715–1810. A Comparison of the Social and Economic Incidence of Taxes
Collected for the Central Government." *Journal of European Economic History* 5, no. 3: 601–650.

Matthews, R. C. O. 1986. "The Economics of Institutions and the Sources of
Economic Growth." *Economic Journal* 96: 903–918.

McAlpin, Michelle Burge. 1983. *Subject to Famine: Food Crises and Economic
Change in Western India, 1860–1920.* Princeton: Princeton University Press.

McCallum, Bennett T. 1988. "Postwar Developments in Business Cycle Theory:
A Moderately Classical Perspective." *Journal of Money, Credit, and Banking* 20, no. 3, part 2: 459–478.

McCloskey, Donald N. 1972. "The Enclosure of Open Fields." *Journal of Economic History* 32, no. 1: 15–35.

———. 1975. "The Economics of Enclosures: A Market Analysis." In *European
Peasants and Their Markets,* ed. W. N. Parker and E. L. Jones, 123–160.
Princeton: Princeton University Press.

———. 1981. "The Industrial Revolution 1780–1860: A Survey." In *The Economic History of Britain since 1700,* ed. Roderick Floud and Donald N. Mc-
Closkey, 1:103–127. Cambridge: Cambridge University Press.

———. 1985a. *The Applied Theory of Price.* 2d ed. New York: Macmillan.

———. 1985b. *The Rhetoric of Economics.* Madison: University of Wisconsin
Press.

———. 1987a. "Continuity in Economic History." In *The New Palgrave Dictionary of Economics,* ed. John Eatwell, Murray Milgate, and Peter Newman,
1:623–626. New York: W. W. Norton.

———. 1987b. *Econometric History.* Basingstoke: Macmillan.

———. 1989. "The Open Fields of England: Rent, Risk, and the Rate of Interest, 1300–1815." In *Markets in History: Economic Studies of the Past,* ed.
David W. Galenson, 5–51. Cambridge: Cambridge University Press.

———. 1990. *If You're So Smart: The Narrative of Economic Expertise.*
Chicago: University of Chicago Press.

———. 1992. *The Prudent Peasant: English Open Fields, 1200–1800.* Princeton: Princeton University Press.

———. 1993. "Some Consequences of Conjective Economics." In *Beyond Economic Man: Feminist Theory and Economics,* ed. Marianne A. Ferber and

Julie A. Nelson, 69–93. Chicago: University of Chicago Press.

McCloskey, Donald N., and John Nash. 1984. "Corn at Interest: The Extent and Cost of Grain Storage in Medieval England." *American Economic Review* 74, no. 1: 174–187.

McCloskey, Donald N., and J. Richard Zecher. 1976. "How the Gold Standard Worked, 1880–1913." In *The Monetary Approach to the Balance of Payments*, ed. J. A. Frenkel and H. G. Johnson, 357–385. Toronto: University of Toronto Press.

McElroy, Marjorie B., and Mary Jean Horney. 1981. "The Household Allocation Problem: Results from a Bargaining Model." Discussion paper, Department of Economics, Duke University, Durham, N.C.

Meadows, Donella H., Dennis L. Meadows, Jørgen Randers, and William W. Behrens III. 1972. *The Limits to Growth: A Report for the Club of Rome's Project on the Predicament of Mankind*. New York: Universe Books.

Meese, Richard, and Kenneth Rogoff. 1983. "Empirical Exchange Rate Models of the Seventies: How Well Do They Fit Out of Sample?" *Journal of International Economics* 14, no. 1: 3–24.

Megill, Allan, and Donald N. McCloskey. 1987. "The Rhetoric of History." In *The Rhetoric of the Human Sciences*, ed. J. S. Nelson, Allan Megill, and Donald N. McCloskey, 221–238. Madison: University of Wisconsin Press.

Meltzer, Alan H. 1976. "Monetary and Other Explanations of the Great Depression." *Journal of Monetary Economics* 2, no. 4: 455–476.

Metzer, Jacob. 1974. "Railroad Development and Market Integration: The Case of Tsarist Russia." *Journal of Economic History* 34, no. 3: 529–550.

Meyer, Stephen, III. 1981. *The Five Dollar Day: Labor Management and Social Control in the Ford Motor Company, 1908–1921*. Albany: State University of New York Press.

Milgrom, Paul, and John Roberts. 1992. *Economics, Organization, and Management*. Englewood Cliffs, N.J.: Prentice Hall.

Mill, John Stuart. 1871. *Principles of Political Economy*. Vol. 1. London: Longmans, Green.

Miller, Preston J., ed. 1994. *The Rational Expectations Revolution: Readings from the Front Line*. Cambridge, Mass.: MIT Press.

Mints, Lloyd W. 1945. *A History of Banking Theory in the United States and the United Kingdom*. Chicago: University of Chicago Press.

Mirowski, Philip. 1988. *Against Mechanism: Protecting Economics from Science*. Totowa, N.J.: Roman and Littlefield.

Miskimin, H. A. 1984. *Money and Power in Fifteenth-Century France*. New Haven: Yale University Press.

Mitchell, B. R. 1982. *International Historical Statistics: Africa and Asia*. New York: New York University Press.

———. 1988. *British Historical Statistics*. Cambridge: Cambridge University Press.

———. 1992. *International Historical Statistics: Europe, 1750–1988*. Rev. ed. Basingstoke: Macmillan.

———. 1993. *International Historical Statistics: The Americas, 1750–1988*. 2d ed. New York: Stockton Press.

Mitchell, Wesley Clair. 1908. *Gold, Prices, and Wages under the Greenback Standard.* Berkeley: University of California Press.

———. 1960 (1903). *A History of the Greenbacks.* Chicago: University of Chicago Press.

Mokyr, Joel. 1977. "Demand vs. Supply in the Industrial Revolution." *Journal of Economic History* 37, no. 4: 981–1008.

Mokyr, Joel, and N. Eugene Savin. 1976. "Stagflation in Historical Perspective: The Napoleonic Wars Revisited." *Research in Economic History* 1: 198–259.

Moore, Sally Falk. 1993. "Changing Perspectives on a Changing Africa: The Work of Anthropology." In *Africa and the Disciplines,* ed. Robert H. Bates, V. Y. Mudimbe, and Jean O'Barr, 3–57. Chicago: University of Chicago Press.

Morgenstern, Oskar. 1960. *On the Accuracy of Economic Observations.* Princeton: Princeton University Press.

Myers, Ramon H. 1980. *The Chinese Economy: Past and Present.* Belmont, Calif.: Wadsworth.

"The Mystery of the New Fashioned Goldsmiths or Bankers." 1974. In *Money and Banking in England: The Development of the Banking System, 1694–1914,* ed. B. L. Anderson and P. L. Cottrell. London: David and Charles.

Nan-k'ai chih shu tzu liao hui pien 1913 nien–1952 nien (Compendium of Nan-k'ai index number materials, 1913–1952). 1958. Peking: T'ung chi chu pan she.

Nelson, Julie A. 1992. "Gender, Metaphor, and the Definition of Economics." *Economics and Philosophy* 8, no. 1: 103–125.

Nelson, Richard R. 1987. *Understanding Technical Change as an Evolutionary Process.* Amsterdam: North Holland.

Neuberger, Hugh M., and Houston H. Stokes. 1974. "German Banks and German Economic Growth, 1883–1913: An Empirical View." *Journal of Economic History* 34, no. 3: 710–731.

———. 1975. "German Banking and Japanese Banking: A Comparative Analysis." *Journal of Economic History* 35, no. 1: 238–252.

Newbery, David M. G. 1977. "Risk Sharing, Sharecropping, and Uncertain Labour Markets." *Review of Economic Studies* 44, no. 3: 585–594.

Newbery, David M. G., and Joseph E. Stiglitz. 1979. "Sharecropping, Risk Sharing, and the Importance of Imperfect Information." In *Risk, Uncertainty, and Agricultural Development,* ed. J. A. Roumasset, J.-M. Boussard, and I. Singh, 311–341. New York: Agricultural Development Council.

Newton, Isaac. 1966. "Representations on the Subject of Money, 1712—1717." In *A Select Collection of Scarce and Valuable Tracts on Money,* ed. John R. McCulloch. 1856. Reprint, New York: Augustus M. Kelley.

Nordhaus, William, and James Tobin. 1972. "Is Growth Obsolete?" In *Economic Growth,* 5:1–80. Fiftieth Anniversary Colloquium. New York: National Bureau of Economic Research.

North, Douglass C. 1968. "Sources of Productivity Change in Ocean Shipping, 1600–1850." *Journal of Political Economy* 76, no. 5: 953–970.

———. 1981. *Structure and Change in Economic History.* New York: W. W. Norton.

————. 1984. "Government and the Cost of Exchange in History." *Journal of Economic History* 44, no. 2: 255–264.

————. 1990. *Institutions, Institutional Change, and Economic Performance.* New York: Cambridge University Press.

North, Douglass C., and Robert Paul Thomas. 1973. *The Rise of the Western World: A New Economic History.* Cambridge: Cambridge University Press.

Nurkse, Ragnar. 1953. *Problems of Capital Formation in Underdeveloped Countries.* New York: Oxford University Press.

O'Brien, P. K., and S. L. Engerman. 1981. "Changes in Income and Its Distribution during the Industrial Revolution." In *The Economic History of Britain since 1700*, ed. Roderick Floud and Donald N. McCloskey, 1:164–181. Cambridge: Cambridge University Press.

Ohkawa, Kazushi, and Henry Rosovsky. 1973. *Japanese Economic Growth: Trend Acceleration in the Twentieth Century.* Stanford: Stanford University Press.

Ohlin, G. 1966. "No Safety in Numbers: Some Pitfalls of Historical Statistics." In *Industrialization in Two Systems*, ed. Henry Rosovsky, 68–96. New York: Wiley.

Olmstead, Alan L. 1975. "The Mechanization of Reaping and Mowing in American Agriculture 1833–1870." *Journal of Economic History* 35, no. 2: 327–352.

Olson, Mancur. 1965. *The Logic of Collective Action: Public Goods and the Theory of Groups.* Cambridge, Mass.: Harvard University Press.

————. 1982. *The Rise and Decline of Nations: Economic Growth, Stagflation, and Social Rigidities.* New Haven: Yale University Press.

Owen, John. 1976. *Working Hours: An Economic Analysis.* Lexington: Lexington Books.

Parker, William N. 1987. "New England's Early Industrialization: A Sketch." In *Quantity and Quiddity: Essays in U.S. Economic History*, ed. Peter Kilby, 17–81. Middletown, Conn.: Wesleyan University Press.

Parkin, Michael. 1992. *Macroeconomics.* 2d ed. Englewood Cliffs, N.J.: Prentice Hall.

Perkins, Dwight H. 1969. *Agricultural Development in China, 1368–1968.* Chicago: Aldine.

————. 1975a. "Growth and Changing Structure of China's Twentieth-Century Economy." In *China's Modern Economy in Historical Perspective*, 115–165. Stanford: Stanford University Press.

———, ed. 1975b. *China's Modern Economy in Historical Perspective.* Stanford: Stanford University Press.

Perkins, Dwight H., and Moshe Syrquin. 1989. "Large Countries: The Influence of Size." In H. B. Chenery and T. N. Srinivasan, eds., *Handbook of Development Economics.* Amsterdam: North Holland.

Perkins, Dwight H., and Shahid Yusuf. 1984. *Rural Development in China.* Baltimore: Johns Hopkins University Press.

Phelps, Edmund S. 1967. "Phillips Curves, Expectations of Inflation, and Optimal Unemployment over Time." *Economica* 34, no. 135: 254–281.

Phelps-Brown, E. H., and Sheila V. Hopkins. 1956. "Seven Centuries of the

Prices of Consumables, Compared with Builders' Wage Rates." *Economica*, n.s., 23, no. 92: 296–314.

———. 1981. *A Perspective on Wages and Prices*. London: Methuen.

Phillips, A. W. 1958. "The Relation between Unemployment and the Rate of Change of Money Wages in the United Kingdom, 1861–1957." *Economica*, n.s., 25, no. 100: 283–299.

Polanyi, Karl. 1944. *The Great Transformation*. Boston: Beacon Press.

Pomeranz, Kenneth. 1992. "Local Interest Story: Political Conflict and Regional Differences in the Shandong Capital Market, 1900–1937." In *Chinese History in Economic Perspective,* ed. Thomas G. Rawski and Lillian M. Li, 295–318. Berkeley: University of California Press.

Poole, William. 1978. *Money and the Economy: A Monetarist View*. Reading, Mass: Addison Wesley.

Popkin, Samuel L. 1979. *The Rational Peasant: The Political Economy of Rural Society in Vietnam*. Berkeley: University of California Press.

Porter, Richard D., and Amanda S. Bayer. 1989. "Monetary Perspective on Underground Economic Activity in the United States." In *The Underground Economies: Tax Evasion and Information Distortion,* ed. Edgar L. Feige, 129–158. New York: Cambridge University Press.

Quiggin, A. Hingston. 1949. *A Survey of Primitive Money: The Beginnings of Currency*. London: Methuen.

Radford, R. A. 1945. "The Economic Organization of a P.O.W. Camp." *Economica*, n.s., 12: 189–201. Reprinted in *Readings in Economics,* ed. Paul A. Samuelson, 6th ed. (New York: McGraw-Hill, 1970).

Raff, Daniel M. G. 1988. "Wage Determination Theory and the Five-Dollar Day at Ford." *Journal of Economic History* 48, no. 2: 387–400.

Raftis, J. Ambrose. 1964. *Tenure and Mobility: Studies in the Social History of the Mediaeval English Village*. Toronto: Pontifical Institute of Mediaeval Studies.

Ranis, Gustav, and John C. H. Fei. 1961. "A Theory of Economic Development." *American Economic Review* 51, no. 4: 533–565.

Ransom, Roger L. 1970. "Social Returns from Public Transport Investment: A Case Study of the Ohio Canal." *Journal of Political Economy* 78, no. 5: 1041–1060.

———. 1989. *Conflict and Compromise: The Political Economy of Slavery, Emancipation, and the American Civil War*. New York: Cambridge University Press.

Ransom, Roger L., and Richard Sutch. 1975. "The Impact of the Civil War and Emancipation on Southern Agriculture." *Explorations in Economic History* 12, no. 1: 1–28.

———. 1977. *One Kind of Freedom: The Economic Consequences of Emancipation*. New York: Cambridge University Press.

Rawski, Thomas G. 1975. "The Growth of Producer Industries." In *China's Modern Economy in Historical Perspective,* ed. Dwight H. Perkins, 115–166. Stanford: Stanford University Press.

———. 1978. "China's Republican Economy: An Introduction." Discussion paper no. 1, Joint Centre on Modern East Asia, Toronto.

————. 1989. *Economic Growth in Prewar China*. Berkeley: University of California Press.

————. 1992. "Ideas About Studying China's Rural Economy: A Comment on the Commentaries." *Republican China* 17, no. 1: 146–159.

Rawski, Thomas G., and Lillian M. Li, eds. 1992. *Chinese History in Economic Perspective*. Berkeley: University of California Press.

Rayack, Elton. 1967. *Professional Power of American Medicine: The Economics of the American Medical Association*. Cleveland: World Publishing.

Rees, Albert. 1961. *Real Wages in Manufacturing, 1890–1914*. Princeton: National Bureau of Economic Research.

————. 1993. "The Salaries of Ph.D.'s in Academe and Elsewhere." *Journal of Economic Perspectives* 7, no. 1: 151–158.

Reid, Joseph D., Jr. 1973. "Sharecropping as an Understandable Market Response: The Postbellum South." *Journal of Economic History* 33, no. 1: 106–130.

————. 1977. "The Theory of Share Tenancy Revisited—Again." *Journal of Political Economy* 85, no. 2: 403–407.

————. 1979. "White Land, Black Labor, and Agricultural Stagnation." *Explorations in Economic History* 16, no. 1: 31–55.

Reynolds, Bruce L. 1974. "Weft, The Technological Sanctuary of Chinese Handspun Yarn." *Ch'ing-shih wen-t'i* 3, no. 2: 1–18.

————. 1975. "The Impact of Trade and Foreign Investment on Industrialization: Chinese Textiles, 1875–1931." Ph.D. diss., University of Michigan.

Richards, Richard Davis. 1929. *The Early History of Banking in England*. London: P. S. King and Son.

Riskin, Carl. 1975. "Surplus and Stagnation in Modern China." In *China's Modern Economy in Historical Perspective*, ed. Dwight H. Perkins, 49–84. Stanford: Stanford University Press.

Rockoff, Hugh. 1974. "The Free Banking Era: A Re-examination." *Journal of Money Credit and Banking* 6, no. 2: 141–167. Reprinted in *The Free Banking Era: A Re-examination* (New York: Arno Press, 1975).

Roediger, David R., and Philip S. Foner. 1989. *Our Own Time: A History of American Labor and the Working Day*. New York: Greenwood Press.

Rolnick, Arthur J., and Warren E. Weber. 1983. "New Evidence on the Free Banking Era." *American Economic Review* 73: 1080–1091.

————. 1984. "The Causes of Free Bank Failures: A Detailed Examination of the Evidence." *Journal of Monetary Economics* 14, no. 3: 267–291.

————. 1986. "Gresham's Law or Gresham's Fallacy?" *Journal of Political Economy* 94, no. 1: 185–199.

Romer, Christina D. 1986a. "Is the Stabilization of the Postwar Economy a Figment of the Data?" *American Economic Review* 76, no. 3: 314–334.

————. 1986b. "Spurious Volatility in Historical Unemployment Data." *Journal of Political Economy* 94, no. 1: 1–37.

————. 1992. "What Ended the Great Depression?" *Journal of Economic History* 52, no. 4: 757–784.

Romer, Christina D., and David Romer. 1989. "Does Monetary Policy Matter? A New Test in the Spirit of Friedman and Schwartz." *NBER Macroeconomics Annual* 44: 121–170.

Root, Hilton L. 1994. *The Fountain of Privilege: Political Foundations of Economic Markets in Old Regime France and England.* Berkeley: University of California Press.

Rosenbloom, Joshua L. 1990. "One Market or Many? Labor Market Integration in the Late-Nineteenth Century United States." *Journal of Economic History* 50, no. 1: 85–108.

Rosenberg, Nathan. 1963. "Technological Change in the Machine Tool Industry." *Journal of Economic History* 23, no. 4: 414–443. Reprinted in *Perspectives on Technology* (New York: Cambridge University Press, 1976), 9–31.

Rosenzweig, Mark R., and T. Paul Schultz. 1982. "Market Opportunities, Genetic Endowments, and Interfamily Resource Distribution: Child Survival in Rural India." *American Economic Review* 72, no. 4: 803–815.

Roth, Alvin. 1990. "New Physicians: A Natural Experiment in Market Organization." *Science*, 14 December, 1524–1528.

Rothenberg, Winifred B. 1981. "The Market and Massachusetts Farmers, 1750–1855." *Journal of Economic History* 41, no. 2: 283–314.

———. 1985. "The Emergence of a Capital Market in Rural Massachusetts." *Journal of Economic History* 45, no. 4: 781–808.

———. 1992. *From Market Places to a Market Economy: The Transformation of Rural Massachusetts, 1750–1850.* Chicago: University of Chicago Press.

Samuelson, Paul A., ed. 1970. *Readings in Economics.* 6th ed. New York: McGraw-Hill.

Samuelson, Paul A., and William D. Nordhaus. 1985. *Economics.* 12th ed. New York: McGraw-Hill.

Sandberg, Lars G., and Donald N. McCloskey. 1971. "From Damnation to Redemption: Judgments on the Late Victorian Entrepreneur." *Explorations in Economic History* 9, no. 1: 89–108.

Sargent, Thomas J. 1982. "The Ends of Four Big Inflations." In *Inflation: Causes and Effects*, ed. Robert E. Hall, 41–98. Chicago: University of Chicago Press.

———. 1986. *Rational Expectations and Inflation.* New York: Harper and Row.

Sargent, Thomas J., and Neil Wallace. 1982. "The Real Bills Doctrine versus the Quantity Theory: A Reconsideration." *Journal of Political Economy* 90, no. 6: 1212–1236.

Sayers, Richard Sidney. 1976. *The Bank of England, 1891–1944*, 3 vols. Cambridge: Cambridge University Press.

Schatz, Ronald W. 1983. *The Electrical Workers: A History of Labor at GE and Westinghouse, 1923–1960.* Urbana: University of Illinois Press.

Scheffrin, Steven M. 1983. *Rational Expectations.* Cambridge: Cambridge University Press.

Schilke, Oscar G., and Raphael Solomon. 1964. *America's Foreign Coins with Legal Tender Status in the United States, 1793–1857.* New York: Coin and Currency Institute.

Schultz, Theodore W. 1964. *Transforming Traditional Agriculture.* New Haven: Yale University Press.

Schwartz, Anna J. 1947. "The Beginning of Competitive Banking in Philadelphia, 1782–1809." *Journal of Political Economy* 55, no. 5: 417–431.

———. 1973. "Secular Price Change in Historical Perspective." *Journal of Money Credit and Banking* 5, no. 1, part 2: 243–269.

———. 1981. "Understanding 1929–1933." In *The Great Depression Revisited,* ed. Karl Brunner, 5–48. Boston: Martinus Nijhoff.

Scott, James C. 1976. *The Moral Economy of the Peasant: Rebellion and Subsistence in Southeast Asia.* New Haven: Yale University Press.

Sellers, James L. 1927. "The Economic Incidence of the Civil War in the South." *Mississippi Valley Historical Review* 14 (September): 179–191.

Sen, Amartya. 1980. "Economic Development: Objectives and Obstacles." In *China's Development Experience in Comparative Perspective,* ed. Robert F. Dernberger, 19–37. Cambridge, Mass.: Harvard University Press.

———. 1981. *Poverty and Famines: An Essay on Entitlement and Deprivation.* Oxford: Clarendon Press.

Shang-hai mai fen shih ch'ang tiao ch'a (Survey of Shanghai's wheat and flour markets). 1935. Shanghai: Institute of Social and Economic Research.

Shapiro, Carl, and Joseph E. Stiglitz. 1984. "Equilibrium Unemployment as a Worker Discipline Device." *American Economic Review* 74, no. 3: 433–444.

Sheridan, James E. "Chinese Warlords: Tigers or Pussycats?" *Republican China* 10, no. 2: 35–41.

Shiells, Martha Ellen. 1990. "Collective Choice of Working Conditions: Hours in British and U.S. Iron and Steel, 1890–1923." *Journal of Economic History* 50, no. 2: 379–392.

Shiells, Martha Ellen, and Gavin Wright. 1983. "Night Work as a Labor Market Phenomenon: Southern Textiles in the Interwar Period." *Explorations in Economic History* 20, no. 4: 331–350.

Shina no kôun (China's shipping). 1944. Tokyo: Tôa Kaiun Kabushiki Gaisha.

Simon, Herbert. 1991. "Organizations and Markets." *Journal of Economic Perspectives* 5, no. 2: 25–44.

Sjöstrand, Sven-Erik. 1992. "On the Rationale Behind 'Irrational' Institutions." *Journal of Economic Issues* 26, no. 4: 1007–1039.

Skinner, G. William. 1964. "Marketing and Social Structure in Rural China." Part 1. *Journal of Asian Studies* 24, no. 1: 3–43.

Slichter, Sumner. 1929. "The Current Labor Policies of American Industries." *Quarterly Journal of Economics* 43, no. 2: 393–435.

Smith, Adam. 1937 (1776). *Inquiry into the Nature and Causes of the Wealth of Nations,* ed. Edwin Cannan. New York: Random House.

Sokoloff, Kenneth L. 1984. "Was the Transition from the Artisanal Shop to the Nonmechanized Factory Associated with Gains in Efficiency?" *Explorations in Economic History* 21, no. 4: 351–382.

Solomou, Solomos. 1988. *Phases of Economic Growth, 1850–1973: Kondatrieff Waves and Kuznets Swings.* Cambridge: Cambridge University Press.

Solow, Barbara Lewis. 1971. *The Land Question and the Irish Economy, 1870–1903.* Cambridge, Mass.: Harvard University Press.

Solow, Robert M. 1990. *The Labor Market as a Social Institution.* Cambridge: Basil Blackwell.

———. 1994. "Perspectives on Growth Theory." *Journal of Economic Perspectives* 8, no. 1: 45–54.

Spufford, P. 1988. *Money and Its Use in Medieval Europe.* Cambridge: Cambridge University Press.

Stigler, George J. 1966. *The Theory of Price.* 3d ed. New York: Macmillan.

———. 1968. *The Organization of Industry.* Homewood, Ill.: Irwin.

Stiglitz, Joseph E. 1986. "The New Development Economics." *World Development* 14, no. 2: 257–265.

———. 1987. "The Causes and Consequences of the Dependence of Quality on Price." *Journal of Economic Literature* 25, no. 1: 1–48.

———. 1991. "Symposium on Organizations and Economics." *Journal of Economic Perspectives* 5, no. 2: 15–24.

———. 1993. *Economics.* New York: W. W. Norton.

Strassmann, Dianna. 1993. "Not a Free Market: The Rhetoric of Disciplinary Authority in Economics." In *Beyond Economic Man: Feminist Theory and Economics,* ed. Marianne A. Ferber and Julie A. Nelson, 54–68. Chicago: University of Chicago Press.

Summers, Lawrence H. 1991. "The Scientific Illusion in Empirical Macroeconomics." *Scandinavian Journal of Economics* 93, no. 2: 129–148.

Summers, Robert, and Alan Heston. 1988. "A New Set of International Comparisons of Real Product and Price Levels: Estimates for 180 Countries, 1950–1985." *Review of Income and Wealth,* s. 34, no. 1: 1–25.

Sundstrom, William A. 1990. "Was There a Golden Age of Flexible Wages? Evidence from Ohio Manufacturing." *Journal of Economic History* 50, no. 2: 309–320.

———. 1992. "Rigid Wages or Small Equilibrium Adjustments? Evidence from the Contraction of 1893." *Explorations in Economic History* 29, no. 3: 430–455.

"Survey Report on Routes and Quantities of Raw Material Shipments in Central China." 1941. *Chôsa geppô* 2, no. 6: 113–256.

Sutch, Richard. 1991. "All Things Reconsidered: The Life-Cycle Perspective and the Third Task of Economic History." *Journal of Economic History* 51, no. 2: 271–289.

Swedberg, Richard. *Economics and Sociology: Redefining Their Boundaries: Conversations with Economists and Sociologists.* Princeton: Princeton University Press.

Swen, W. Y. 1928. "Types of Farming, Costs of Production, and Annual Labor Distribution in Weihsien County, Shantung, China." *Chinese Economic Journal* 3, no. 2: 642–680.

"Symposium on 'New Growth Theory'." 1994. *Journal of Economic Perspectives* 8, no. 1: 3–72.

Taylor, Arthur J., ed. 1975. *The Standard of Living in Britain in the Industrial Revolution.* London: Methuen.

Temin, Peter. 1976. *Did Monetary Forces Cause the Great Depression?* New York: W. W. Norton.

Tentler, Leslie Woodcock. 1979. *Wage-Earning Women.* New York: Oxford University Press.

Thiesenhusen, William C., ed. 1989. *Searching for Agrarian Reform in Latin America.* Boston: Unwin and Hyman.

Thomas, Brinley. 1954. *Migration and Economic Growth*. Cambridge: Cambridge University Press.

Thomas, Robert Paul, and Richard Nelson Bean. 1974. "The Fishers of Men: The Profits of the Slave Trade." *Journal of Economic History* 34, no. 4: 885–914.

Thompson, E. P. 1964. *The Making of the English Working Class*. New York: Pantheon.

Thorp, Rosemary, and Geoffrey Betram. 1978. *Peru 1890–1977: Growth and Policy in an Open Economy*. New York: Columbia University Press.

Timberlake, Richard. 1978. *The Origins of Central Banking in the United States*. Cambridge, Mass.: Harvard University Press.

Timmer, C. Peter, Walter P. Falcon, and Scott R. Pearson. 1983. *Food Policy Analysis*. Baltimore: Johns Hopkins University Press.

Tufte, Edward R. 1983. *The Visual Display of Quantitative Information*. Cheshire, Conn.: Graphics Press.

Tyers, Rodney, and Kym Anderson. 1992. *Disarray in World Food Markets*. Cambridge: Cambridge University Press.

U.S. Bureau of the Census. 1975. *Historical Statistics of the United States, Colonial Times to 1970*. Bicentennial ed. Washington, D.C.: Government Printing Office.

Wade, Robert. 1990. *Governing the Market: Economic Theory and the Role of Government in East Asian Industrialization*. Princeton: Princeton University Press.

Walsh, Mary Roth. 1977. *Doctors Wanted: No Women Need Apply*. New Haven: Yale University Press.

Weitzman, Martin L. 1984. *The Share Economy: Conquering Stagflation*. Cambridge, Mass.: Harvard University Press.

Whaples, Robert. 1990. "Winning the Eight-Hour Day, 1909–1919." *Journal of Economic History* 50, no. 2: 393–406.

White, Eugene Nelson. 1983. *The Regulation and Reform of the American Banking System, 1900–1929*. Princeton: Princeton University Press.

White, Lawrence J. 1984. *Free Banking in Britain: Theory, Experience, and Debate, 1800–1845*. New York: Cambridge University Press.

Wicker, Elmus R. 1965. "Federal Reserve Monetary Policy, 1929–1933: A Reinterpretation." *Journal of Political Economy* 73, no. 4: 325–343.

———. 1986. "Terminating Hyperinflation in the Dismembered Habsburg Monarchy." *American Economic Review* 76, no. 3: 350–364.

Will, Pierre-Etienne, and R. Bin Wong. 1991. *Nourish the People: The State Civilian Granary System in China, 1650–1850*. Ann Arbor: University of Michigan Center for Chinese Studies.

Williamson, Jeffrey G. 1974. *Late Nineteenth-Century American Development: A General Equilibrium History*. Cambridge: Cambridge University Press.

Williamson, Oliver E. 1975. *Markets and Hierarchies*. New York: Free Press.

———. 1985. *The Economic Institutions of Capitalism*. New York: Free Press.

Williamson, Oliver E., and Sidney G. Winter, eds. 1993. *The Nature of the Firm: Origins, Evolution, and Development*. New York: Oxford University Press.

Winch, Donald. 1973. "The Emergence of Economics as a Science, 1750–1870." In *The Fontana Economic History of Europe*, ed. Carlo M. Cippola. Vol. 3, *The Industrial Revolution*, 507–573. London: Collins/Fontana Books.

Wolfe, Lillian. 1922. "How and Why I Chose My First Job." *The Bryn Mawr Daisy*, 8 July 1922. Hilda Smith papers. Mimeographed.

World Bank. 1982. *World Development Report 1982*. Washington, D.C.: World Bank.

———. 1986. *World Development Report 1986*. Washington, D.C.: World Bank.

———. 1993. *The East Asian Miracle: Economic Growth and Public Policy*. New York: Oxford University Press.

Wright, Carroll D. 1893. "Cheaper Living and the Rise of Wages." *Forum* 16 (September): 221–228.

Wright, Gavin. 1978. *Political Economy of the Cotton South: Households, Markets, and Wealth in the Nineteenth Century*. New York: W. W. Norton.

———. 1979. "Freedom and the Southern Economy." *Explorations in Economic History* 16, no. 1: 90–108.

———. 1986. *Old South, New South: Revolutions in the Southern Economy Since the Civil War*. New York: Basic Books.

———. 1987. "Labor History and Labor Economics." In *The Future of Economic History*, ed. Alexander J. Field, 313–347. Boston: Kluwer-Nijhoff.

———. 1990. "The Origins of American Industrial Success, 1879–1940." *American Economic Review* 80, no. 4: 651–668.

———. 1991. Review of *Understanding the Gender Gap*, by Claudia Goldin. *Journal of Economic Literature* 29, no. 3: 1153–1163.

Wright, Gavin, and Howard Kunreuther. 1975. "Cotton, Corn, and Risk in the Nineteenth Century." *Journal of Economic History* 353: 526–551.

Wright, Stanley F. 1980 (1920). *Kiangsi Native Trade and Its Taxation*. Reprint, New York: Garland.

Wright, Tim. 1981. "Growth of the Modern Chinese Coal Industry: An Analysis of Supply and Demand." *Modern China* 7, no. 3: 317–350.

Yamamura, Kozo. 1973. "Toward an Examination of the Economic History of Tokugawa Japan." *Journal of Economic History* 33, no. 3: 509–546.

Yasuba, Yasukichi. 1961. "The Profitability and Viability of Plantation Slavery in the United States." *Economic Studies Quarterly* 12, no. 1: 60–67. Reprinted in *The Reinterpretation of American Economic History*, ed. Robert W. Fogel and Stanley L. Engerman (New York: Harper and Row, 1971), 362–368.

———. 1978. "Freight Rates and Productivity in Ocean Transportation for Japan, 1875–1943." *Explorations in Economic History* 15, no. 1: 11–39.

Yeh, K. C. 1979. "China's National Income, 1931–36." In *Modern Chinese Economic History*, ed. Chi-ming Hou and Tzong-shian Yu, 95–132. Taipei: Institute of Economics, Academica Sinica.

Zevin, Robert Brooke. 1971. "The Growth of Cotton Textile Production after 1815." In *The Reinterpretation of American Economic History*, ed. Robert W. Fogel and Stanley L. Engerman, 122–147. New York: Harper and Row.

Index